MW00717482

General Music Workbook: Level 1A

By Rob & Sam Young

Published by: Young Music, LLC

ISBN: 978-1-7320173-7-5

Copyright © 2020

Young Music, LLC
2358 Dutch Neck Road
Smyrna, DE 19977

www.prodigies.com

Prodigies Playground

THIS BOOK BELONGS TO:

_____

Table of Contents

General Music Level 1A Workbook

INTRODUCTION

Dear families & teachers,

Welcome to the new and improved Prodigies General Music Workbook: Level IA. We've made some big changes to the program layout and the corresponding materials and we are so excited to share them with you. Equally as important, we've listened to your feedback and concerns and have done our best to integrate those suggestions into this new publication.

Prodigies 5.0

2020 saw many big changes for Prodigies. We launched the Prodigies Academy and we upgraded our content delivery systems to streamline the way teachers and students use the program. Our aim was to bring a more cohesive feel to Prodigies Play, Prodigies Academy and the Prodigies workbooks.

Customer Feedback

Teaching and learning are all about communication. You spoke and we listened. These books will help you make the most of the program and help to understand the new layout and the new progressions. Our content team worked diligently on updating the overall aesthetic of these books with new art and sheet music. We've revised instructions, eliminated preschool labels and revamped some of the older activities. The new titles no longer implement a decimal system so that you can choose to a linear or tangential path to our curriculum.

Thanks to many customer suggestions, we revised the cube design to make it easier to assemble and more structurally sound. Lastly, thanks to the help of our loyal customers, we've identified errors and squashed them to give you the best version possible.

We've worked really hard on this project and we hope you enjoy the results!

Happy Musicing,

Mr. Rob and the Prodigies Team

Beats and Measures

The Measure

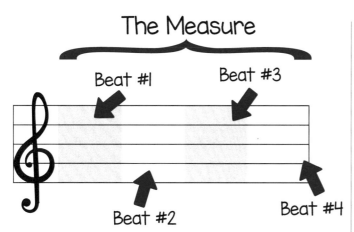

Music lives inside a space called a measure. Each measure is filled with different beats. Usually, we have 4 beats in one measure. Do you see them above?

Quarter Note = 1 Beat

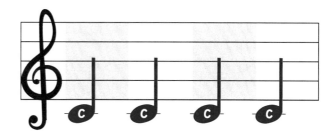

A musical sound is called a note. Above, you can see four notes! These are our most popular kind of note, and they are called QUARTER NOTES.

Half Note = 2 Beats

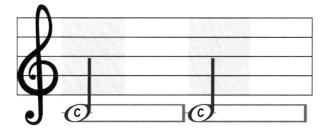

Some notes take up 2 BEATS. We call those HALF NOTES, because they take up one-half of our measure. How many half notes does it take to fill our measure?

Whole Note = 4 Beats

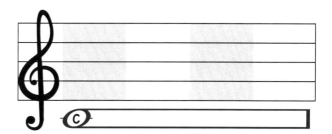

Some notes take up all 4 BEATS. We call those WHOLE NOTES, because they take up our whole measure.

Play The Rests

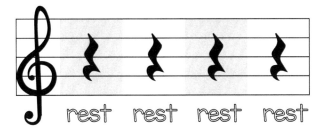

rest   rest   rest   rest

When you see a 𝄽 you don't play any notes!

This is what we call a REST.

Don't ignore the rests – instead, try to play them. You can say the word "rest", or the sound "shh", or you can just make no noise at all for that beat!

Whichever you choose, it's important that you give that rest as much time as a regular beat!

Singing the Lyrics

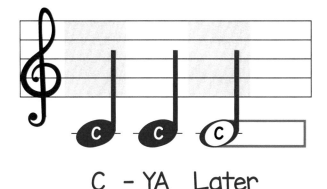

C – YA   Later

The LYRICS are the words of the song. They are written underneath the musical notes! You can see, that they are color-coded to match!

Before you practice singing the LYRICS, make sure you've tried singing with the colors and the letter names!

When you start singing the lyrics, take it slow. Play the note on your instrument, and then use your ears and your voice to match your singing to the musical note. Try to use a clear and steady voice!

We call a set of lyrics a VERSE or a CHORUS, depending on where it is in the song.

Some songs have two VERSES. This means you'll play the whole song singing the lyrics for the first verse, and then you'll play it again while singing the words for second the verse.

The last verse of the songs of this book are sung in Solfège. You can even hand-sign along with the Solfège verses!

Learn more about the Solfège verses on the next page!

The Solfège Hand-Signs

You can also hand-sign along with the songs in this book!

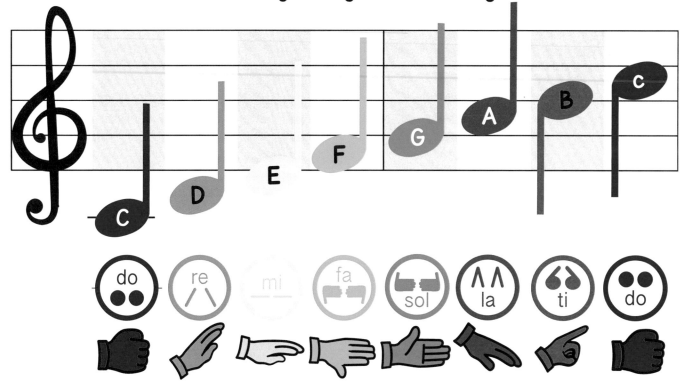

Each musical note (C, D, E etc.) has a Solfège name as well.

The Solfège names are
Do, Re, Mi, Fa, Sol, La and Ti.

The Solfège syllables are a fun and easy way to talk about musical notes.
Plus, each syllable comes with a different hand-sign!

Hand-signing while you sing helps you memorize and recall the sound of
the musical notes.

In this book, we use the simple circles above to represent the
hand-signs. To get familiar with the hand-signs and the symbols we use in
this book, visit:

Prodigies.com

and check out PsP Melodies for lots of hand-sign practice.

The Workbook Pages

In each section, you will use bells, crayons and sometimes scissors and tape or glue.

Before each section, there is a lesson guide with helpful information about each section's activities. For additional guidance, check out our lesson planson the Resources page in the Playground.

The first activity of each section begins with introductory sheet music that reinforces the concepts featured in that section's video. Each section contains both musical and cross-curricular activities for students to complete. The aim of these activities varies, giving students opportunites to practice colors, numbers, letters, hand-writing, math, patterns, differences, creativity, confidence, cutting, folding and gluing, all while practicing music!

To ensure that each child gets the opportunity for meaningful exposure to pitch, ecourage the child to play the bells before or after he or she completes each activity.

Hello Bells

Meet all of the bells! Using the appropriate colors, trace the letters, numbers and Solfège name that belongs to each note!

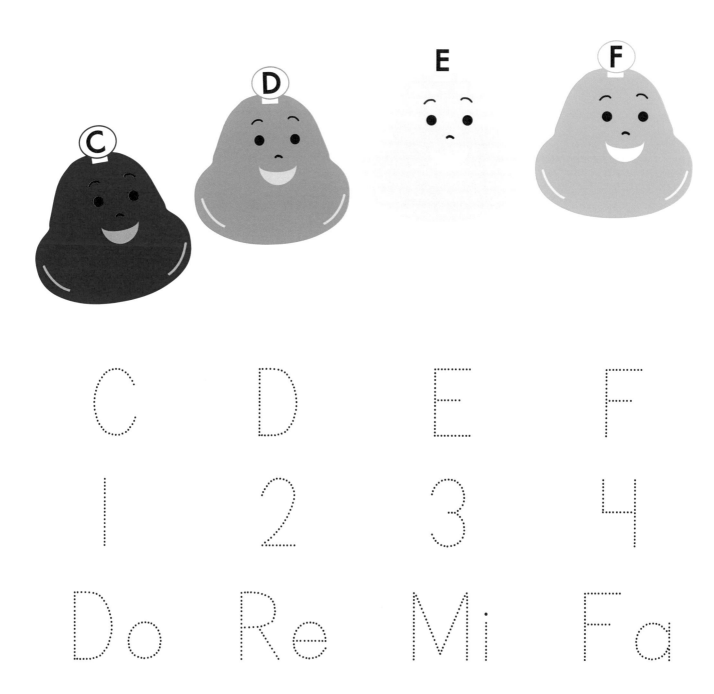

C D E F

1 2 3 4

Do Re Mi Fa

General Music Level 1A Workbook

CHAPTER ONE

Dear families & teachers,

Welcome to Prodigies Music Lessons! Let the fun begin :-)

This workbook moves step-by-step with the videos inside Chapter 1. For the most part, one section equals one song, and depending on your child's age and level, we generally recommend that you...

1. Start by watching the video (1-3 times depending on how fast your child engages)
2. Follow up by reading the sheet music for each section. Do this without the video and go as slow as you need. Try to play in time, and use a metronome to keep a steady beat when you're ready.
3. After playing through the sheet music, complete the pencil-and-paper activities that follow. Keep your bells nearby and some crayons to match the colors.
4. Continue to practice with the video and the sheet music until your child is singing and playing the song with confidence and accuracy. Repetition is important.

The pacing of the program will depend on each unique child and how much time you have to commit each week. For children 3-5, it's important to spend AT LEAST one month on each chapter. Spending time with each bell, chord, rhythm, etc. will help develop your child's sense of memorized pitch and their sense of mastery over the concepts.

Especially with preschool children, aim to create memorable, meaningful and enjoyable musical moments. Focus on the individual notes, on simple call-and-response songs, and keep it as fun as possible.

You want to create a musical practice that is regular, fun and positive. The process of playing and exploring the musical notes is the most important part!

Along similar lines, try to end your sessions on a positive note, even if it means cutting the lesson a few minutes short! You want to leave a good, lasting impression at the end, so kids leave with a positive memory.

Happy Musicing!

- Rob & the Prodigies Team

Year 1, Week 1

Chapter 1 - Hello C

LEQ: How can Prodigies help me learn music?

Week 1 Checklist

	Watched Video	Sang/Played Along	Played Sheet Music 1-3 times	Completed Workbook Activities	Repeat video 2-5 tiunes or as needed for mastery
Activator: Beet & Cherry	*		N/A	N/A	
Core Lesson: Hello C	*	*	*	*	
Performance: Hello C	*	*		N/A	
Extension: Campfire Song			N/A		

⋆ Suggested Priority Activity

I. Overview: The first week is all about introductions! In this lesson, students meet Mr. Rob, the note C, Beet & Cherry, practice the call and response format, sing a silly song with Do, Re, Mi and even learn a few hand-signs.

II. Objective: By the end of this lesson, students should be able to connect the note C to the color red and the Solfege name Do. Students should also understand that Mr. Rob is the host of Prodigies Music lessons—where they will learn rhythms and the Solfege scale.

III. Activator: To introduce the program, Mr. Rob and the concept of rhythm, students begin by watching "Beet & Cherry". Students should tap and clap along using the call and response format with Mr. Rob.

Before beginning, the teacher should review call and response, and explain to students that they should clap or tap along with Beet and Cherry after Mr. Rob demonstrates.

After watching the video, the teacher should ask students what their favorite part of the video was and how that part might help them learn something about music.

IV. Core Lesson: The teacher should explain to students that they will meet the C note today. Before playing along with "Hello C", students begin by singing and hand-signing.

Students may need to watch the video a few times before feeling comfortable enough to play along. Once they are ready, students take out their C bell and play along with the video.

After the video, the class should play through the sheet music for "Hello C" as a group (or in smaller stations if that works better for the group). The teacher should lead the students by conducting a slow and steady tempo, or using a metronome at 60-90 BPM to help keep the beat.

Year 1, Week 1

Chapter 1 - Hello C

LEQ: How can Prodigies help me learn music?

After playing through the sheet music, students should complete the "Hello C" worksheet activities that all reinforce the connections between the note C, the Solfege name Do, the color red and the number 1.

 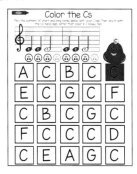  

V. Performance: As a group (or as assigned homework), students play along with "Hello C", which features scrolling sheet music in the treble clef, as well as a handful of parts for other instruments (percussion, lyrics, hand-signs, chord arrangements, etc).

VI. Summarizer: If students played the performance together, the teacher should instruct students to share one thing they liked about the performance with the person next to them (or with the whole group).

Before moving onto the extension lesson, the teacher should review today's lesson by asking students some or all of the following questions: *which color is the C note?; what is the Solfege name for C?; what is the name of the Prodigies Music Lessons host?; what were the names of the fruit and vegetable we used to identify a quarter note and an eighth note?.*

VII. Extension: As a final activity (or as homework), students watch "Campfire Song" featuring Do, Re & Mi. This is a fun sing along that gives students a chance to sing, sign and/or play a few more notes.

After watching the video, the teacher should ask students how the notes D and E compare with C.

If there is time, students can write an additional verse using their own name or classmates' names. The teacher should share an example of this using his or her own name.

In addition to this discussion and song writing activity, there are optional worksheets for "Campfire Song". These worksheets are simpler than the core lesson activities because they are a part of the Playtime series.

Hello, C

☆☆☆☆☆

Play and sing each line 2 times, then move onto the next line.
Then repeat the song with the Solfège hand-signs!

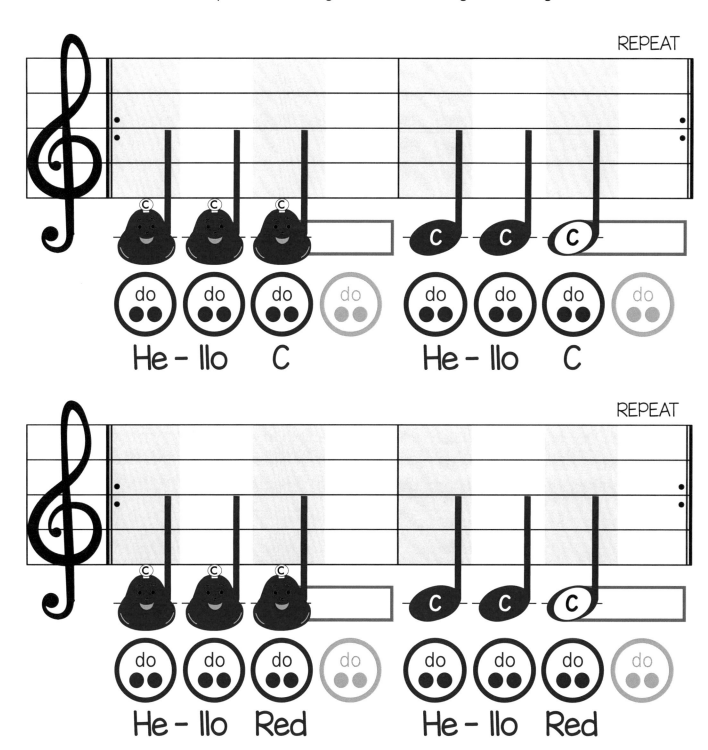

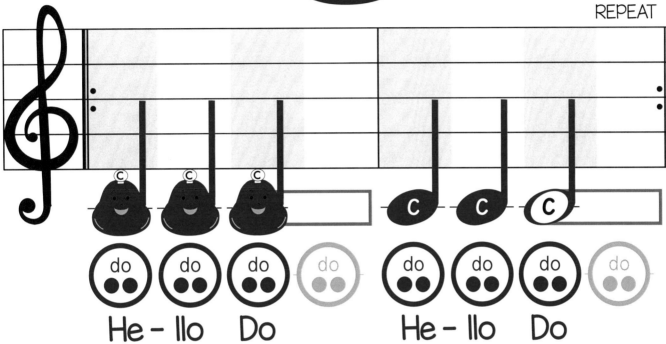

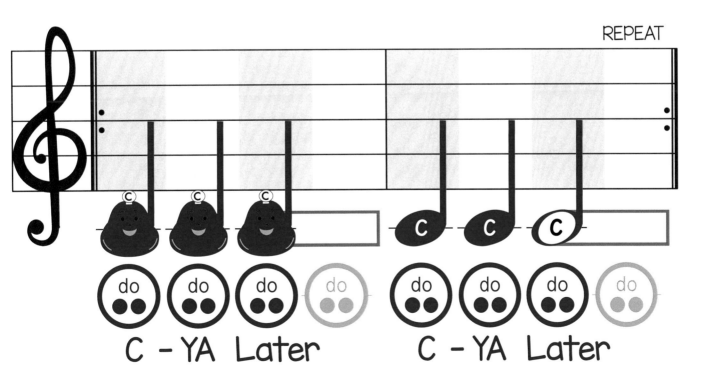

c c c c c c c c c c

l l l l l l l one one one

red red red red red

do do do do do do do

C C C C C C C C C

l l l l l l ONE ONE ONE

RED RED RED RED

DO DO DO DO DO DO

Color the Cs

Play the pattern of short and long notes below with your C bell. Then sing it with the Do hand-sign. After that, color in C boxes red.

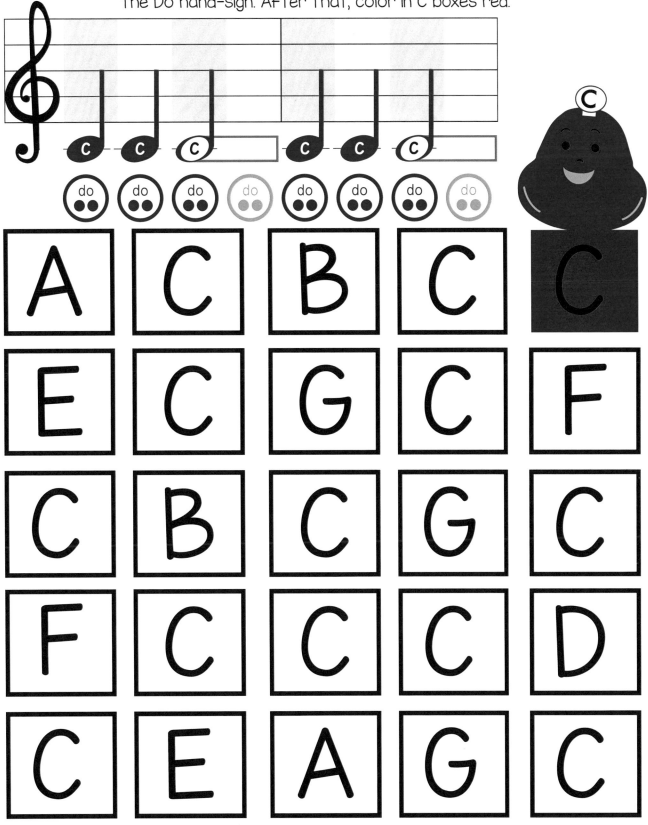

Circle the Cs

Practice writing the words below. Then circle the pictures
that begin with C.

apple   cat   trees

dog   bird   cake

cherry   crab   fish

Circle the Cs

Practice writing the words below. Then circle the pictures that begin with C.

bunny

cow

pear

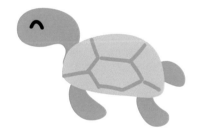

clock

turtle

duck

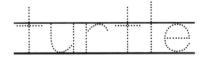

bear

chair

lemon

Hello C
One Note Studies

Color the Campsite

Color & Trace

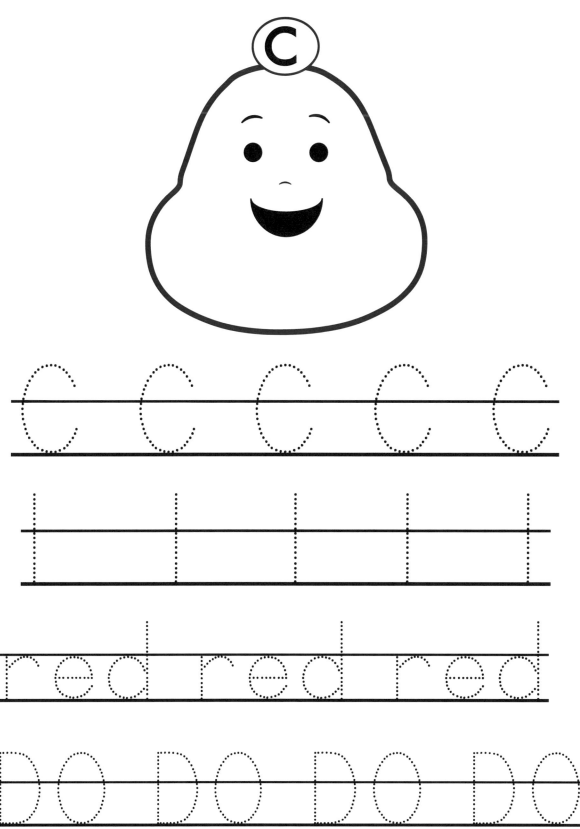

C C C C C

I I I I I

red red red

DO DO DO DO DO

Orange

Color & Trace

D D D D D

2 2 2 2 2

orange orange

RE RE RE RE

Color & Trace

E

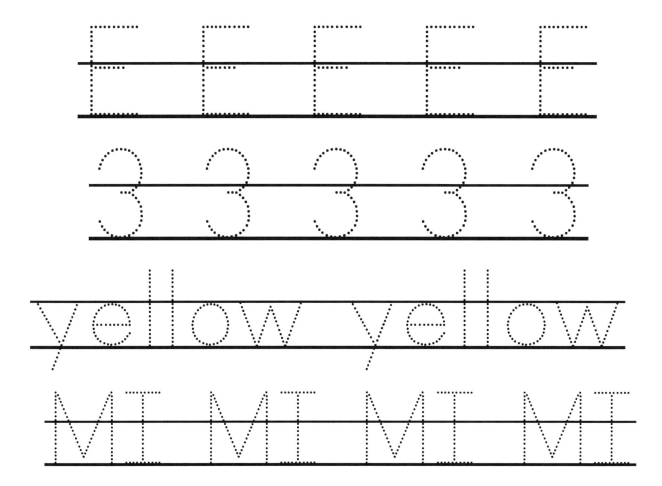

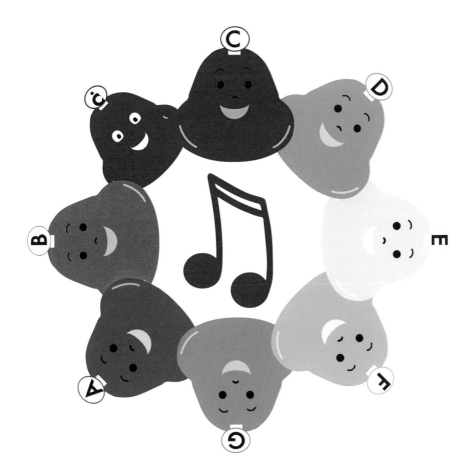

Hand Sign Cut Outs

Teacher cuts out hand-signs
Students arrange short patterns to sign

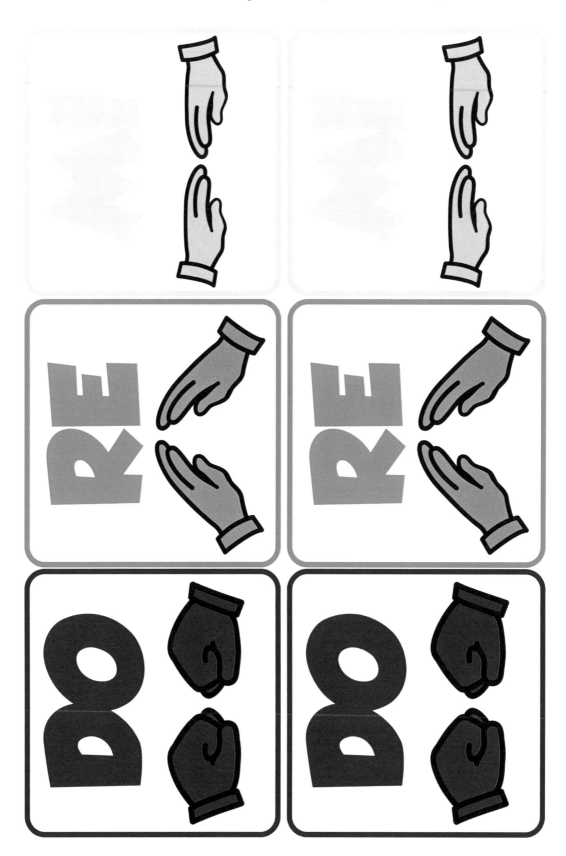

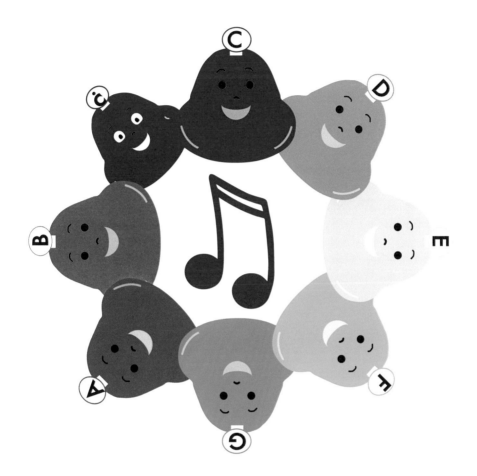

More Hand Sign Cut Outs
Teacher cuts out hand-signs
Students arrange short patterns to sign

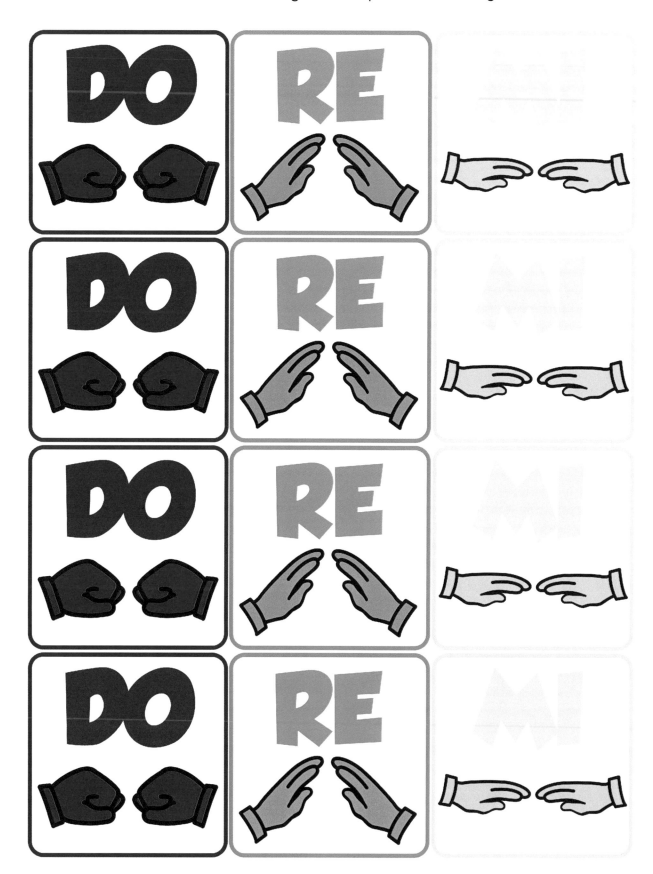

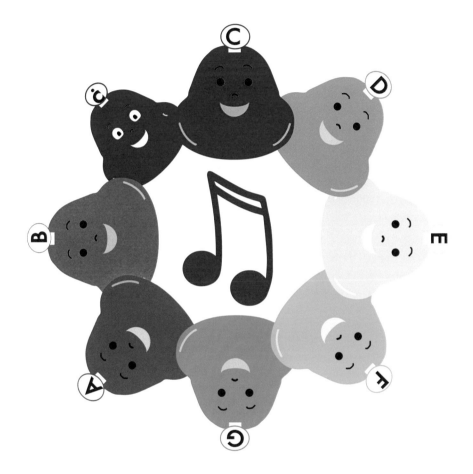

Year 1, Week 2

Chapter 1 - Short and Long Stars

LEQ: How can a student vary playing a note?

Week 2 Checklist

	Watched Video	Sang/Played Along	Played Sheet Music 1-3 times	Completed Workbook Activities	Repeat video 2-5 tiunes or as needed for mastery
Activator: Beet & Melon	*		N/A	N/A	
Core Lesson: Short and Long Stars	*	*	*	*	
Performance: Doo Wop D	*	*		N/A	
Review: Hello C				N/A	

* Suggested Priority Activity

I. Overview: In this lesson, students will work with the simplest rhythm concepts: short and long. After the core lesson, students meet the note D in "Doo Wop D".

II. Objective: By the end of this lesson, students should be able to play the C bell using both long and short notes. In the Performance section of this lesson, students will meet the note D and should be able to connect it to the color orange, the Solfege name Re, and the number 2.

III. Activator: At the beginning of class, the teacher should explain to students that today's lesson is all about rhythm. If students are unfamiliar with this term, the teacher should explain to students that they used rhythm to sing and clap along with "Sweet Beets" in the previous lesson.

If no student can explain what rhythm means, the teacher should explain that the definition of rhythm is a strong, regular, repeated pattern of movement or sound. Today's lesson will be about rhythm, but first, students will sing and clap along with a new version of "Sweet Beets" today--"Beet & Melon".

In this version of "Sweet Beets", instead of clapping eighth and quarter notes, students will clap half and quarter notes.

IV. Core Lesson: The teacher should explain to students that they will continue their practice with rhythm using short and long stars. Students should take out only their C bell and play along with the "Short and Long Stars" video.

After the video, the class should play through the song sheets for "Short and Long Stars" as a group (or in smaller stations if that works better for the group). The teacher should lead the students by conducting a slow and steady tempo, or use a metronome at 60-90 BPM to help

Year 1, Week 2

Chapter 1 - Short and Long Stars

LEQ: How can a student vary playing a note?

After playing through the sheet music, students should complete the "Short and Long Stars" worksheet activities that all reinforce rhythm, patterns, and counting.

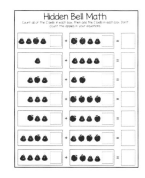
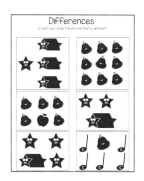

V. Performance: As a group (or as assigned homework), students take out their D bell and play along with "Doo Wop D", which features scrolling sheet music in the treble clef, as well as a handful of parts for other instruments (percussion, lyrics, hand-signs, chord arrangements, etc).

VI. Summarizer: If students played the performance together, the teacher should instruct students to share one thing they liked about the performance with the person next to them (or with the whole group).

Before moving onto the review, the teacher should review today's lesson by asking students some or all of the following questions: *What are the two lengths that we played today?; What is an example of a musical pattern?; How many short sounds make up a long sound?*

VII. Review: As a final activity (or as homework), students review "Hello C", the performance they played in the previous lesson.

Students play the performance portion of last week's lesson only. Then, after playing the performance, students should share with one classmate or the whole group what they liked about the performance, and what was different about it from the previous lesson's performance.

Short and Long Stars

☆☆☆☆☆

Play and sing each line 2 times, then move onto the next line.
Repeat the song with the Solfège hand-signs!

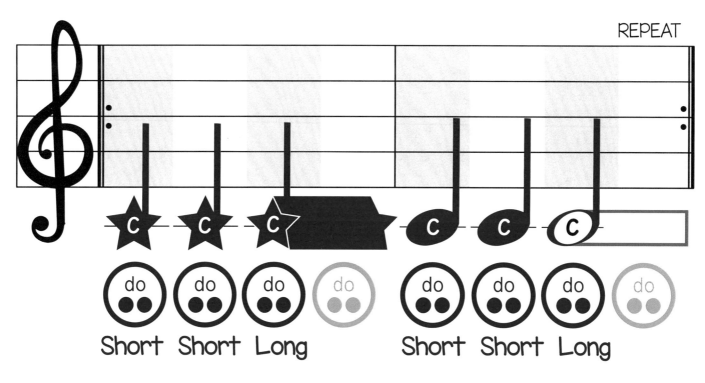

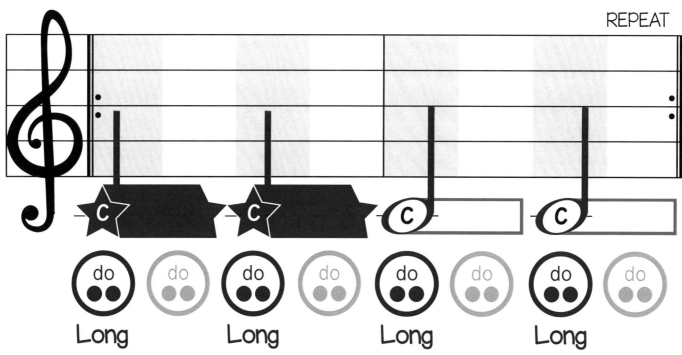

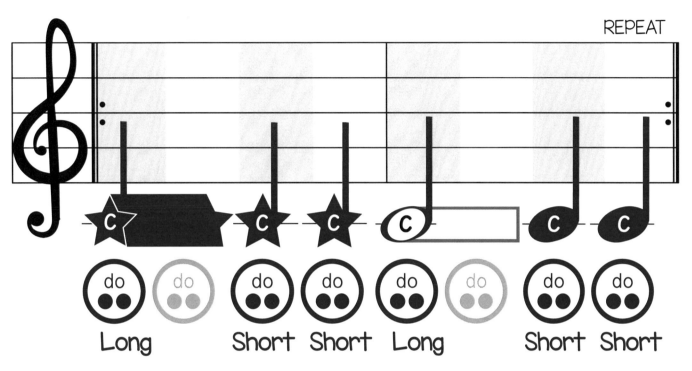

Patterns

Complete the pattern by circling either short or long.

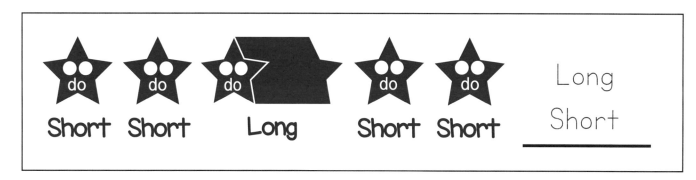

Short   Short   Long   Short   Short   Long
                                                      Short
                                                      _____

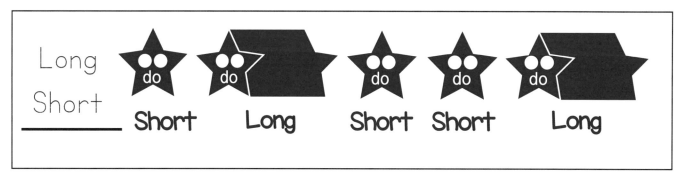

Long   Short   Long   Short   Short   Long
Short
_____

Long   Short   Long   Short   Long   Short
                      Short
                      _____

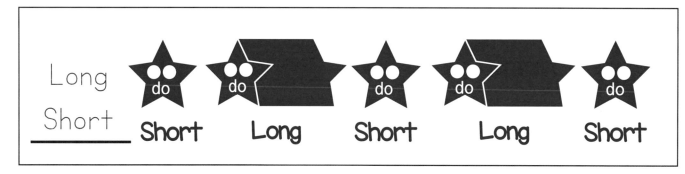

Long   Short   Long   Short   Long   Short
Short
_____

Cut & Paste Pt. 1

Cut each star along the dotted line and paste it to the next page.

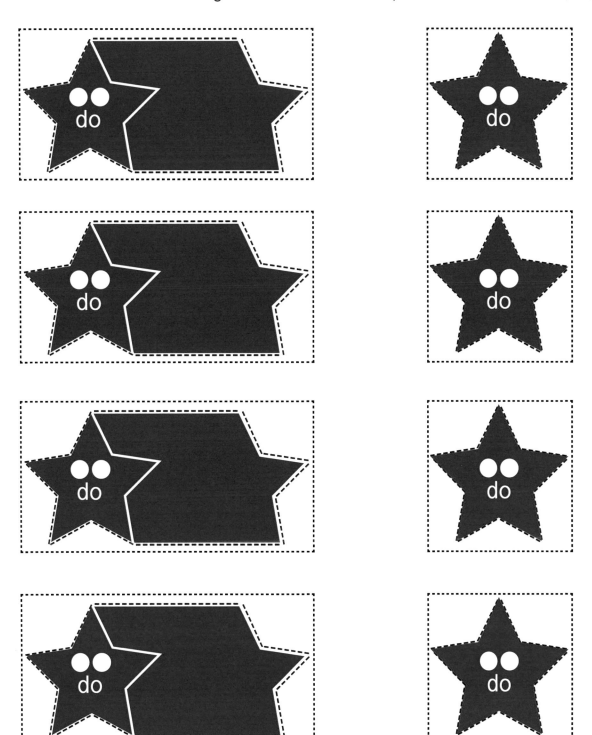

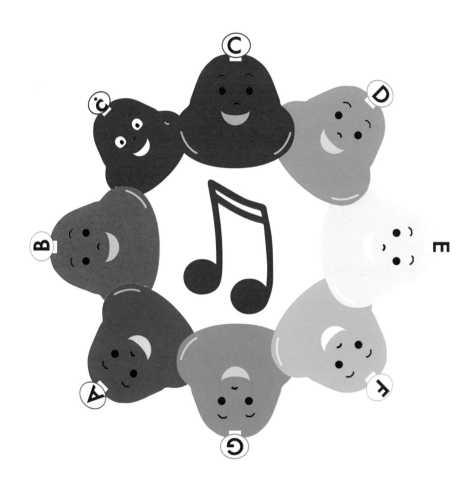

Cut & Paste Pt. 2

Paste each star from the previous page in the appropriate space.

Long   Short   Short

Short   Short   Long

Long   Long

Hidden Bell Math

Count all of the C bells in each box, then add the C bells in each box. Don't count the apples in your equations.

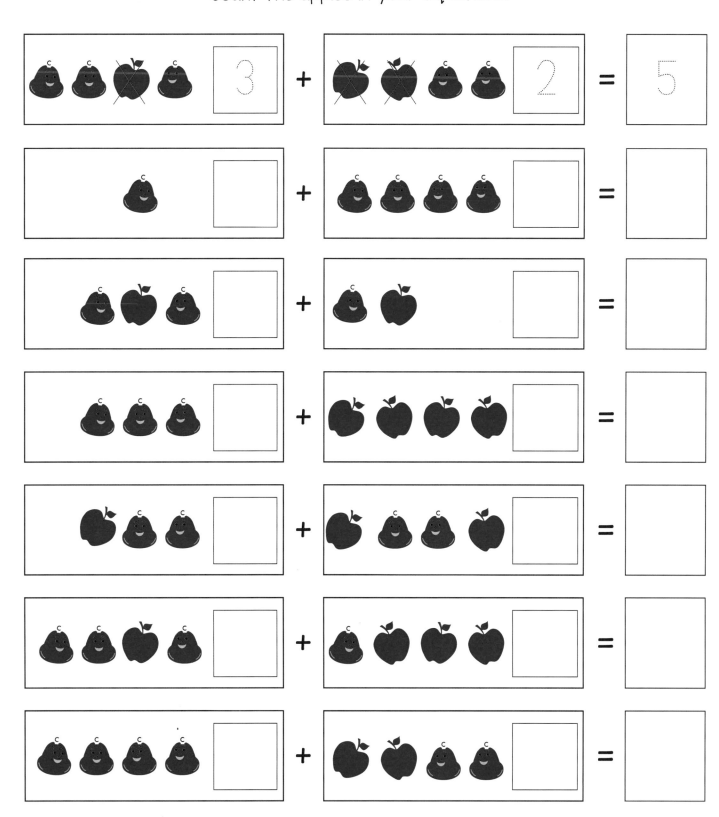

Differences

In each box, circle the picture that is different.

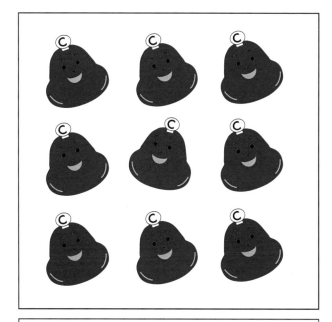

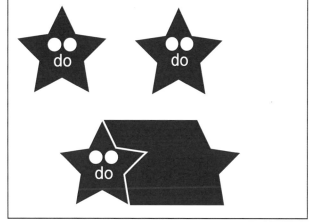

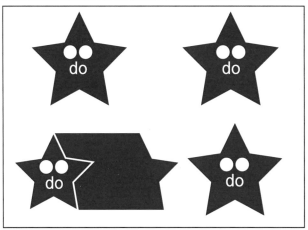

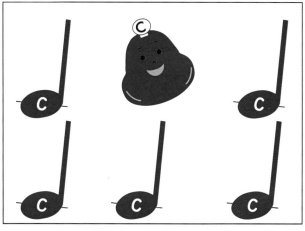

Doo Wop D
One Note Studies

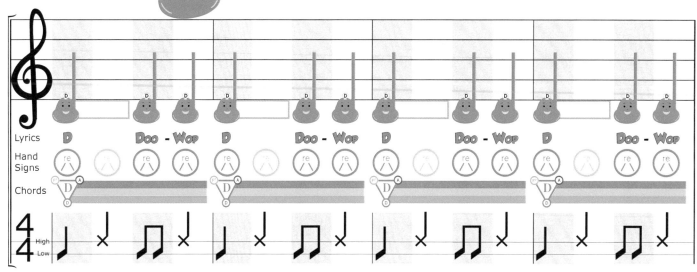

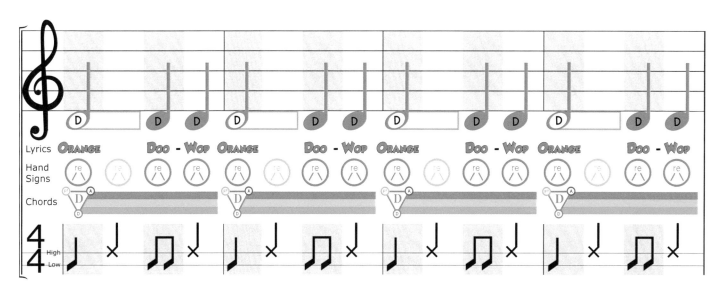

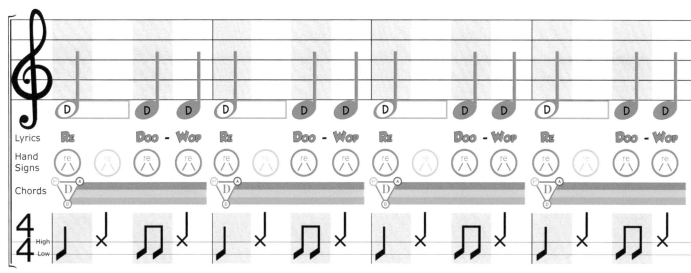

Hello C
One Note Studies

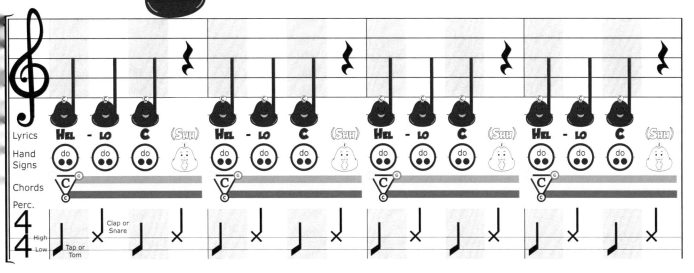

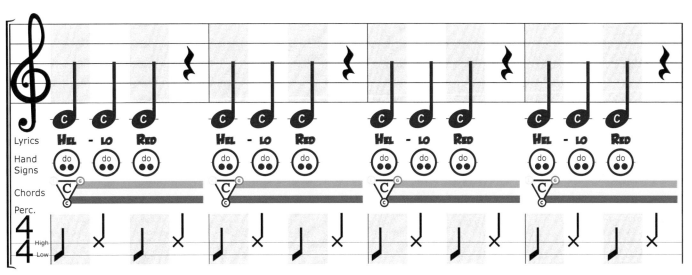

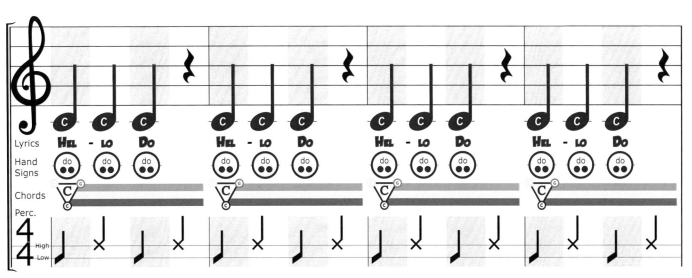

Year 1, Week 3

Chapter 1 - C and Shh

LEQ: How can a student use rests in music?

Week 3 Checklist

	Watched Video	Sang/Played Along	Played Sheet Music 1-3 times	Completed Workbook Activities	Repeat video 2-5 tiunes or as needed for mastery
Activator: Beet & Shh	*		N/A	N/A	
Core Lesson: C & Shh	*	*	*	*	
Performance: Hola E	*	*		N/A	
Extension: Vivaldi's Spring			N/A	N/A	

⋆ Suggested Priority Activity

I. Overview: In this lesson, students will work with the concept of rests. After the core lesson, students play along with "Hola E" and meet the note E.

II. Objective: By the end of this lesson, students should be able to play the C bell and incorporate rests. In the Performance section of this lesson, students will meet the note E and should be able to connect it to the color yellow, the Solfege name Mi, and the number 3.

III. Activator: At the beginning of class, the teacher should explain that students will continue to practice rhythm. Students will practice resting in between playing, which is a very important aspect of every great piece of music.

Students will sing and clap along with a new version of Sweet Beets today--"Beet & Shh". In this version of "Sweet Beets", students will practice resting with the "shh" sound and learn the Kodaly vocabulary for a quarter note: "ta".

IV. Core Lesson: The teacher should explain to students that they will continue their practice with rhythm using rests. Students should take out only their C bell and play along with "C and Shh".

After the video, the class should play through the sheet music for "C and Shh" as a group (or in smaller stations if that works better for the group). The teacher should lead the students by conducting a slow and steady tempo, or use a metronome at 60-90 BPM to help keep the beat.

Year 1, Week 3

Chapter 1 - C and Shh

LEQ: How can a student use rests in music?

After playing through the sheet music, students should complete the "C and Shh" worksheet activities that all reinforce rhythm, patterns, and identifying differences.

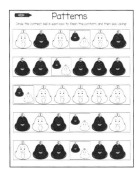   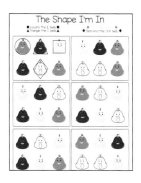

V. Performance: As a group (or as assigned homework), students take out their E bell and play along with "Hola E", which features scrolling sheet music in the treble clef, as well as a handful of parts for other instruments (percussion, lyrics, hand-signs, chord arrangements, etc).

VI. Summarizer: If students played the performance together, the teacher should instruct students to share one thing they liked about the performance with the person next to them (or with the whole group).

Before moving onto the extension lesson, the teacher should review today's lesson by asking students some or all of the following questions: *How does a rest change music?; What is the hand-sign for a rest?(finger to lips); What is another way to describe a rest? (pause or shh).*

VII. Extension: As a final activity (or as homework), students play "Vivaldi's Spring".

This classical song is simplified so that it is only played with one note: E. The teacher should guide the students so that they are playing their bell only when the animation hits the circle on the screen. It may take them a few tries to get the timing right, so this is a great time to reinforce what they learned today about rests and pauses.

C & Shh

☆☆☆☆☆

Play and sing each line 2 times, then move onto the next line.
Then repeat the song with the Solfège hand-signs!

A **metronome** is a small machine that helps keep the beat!
These days, you can find all kinds of metronomes on the Internet!

Find a metronome website or app, and try to play this song
with a metronome! Start slow with 60 BPM.

As your metronome beeps, you play the notes!
Try to play right on the beat.

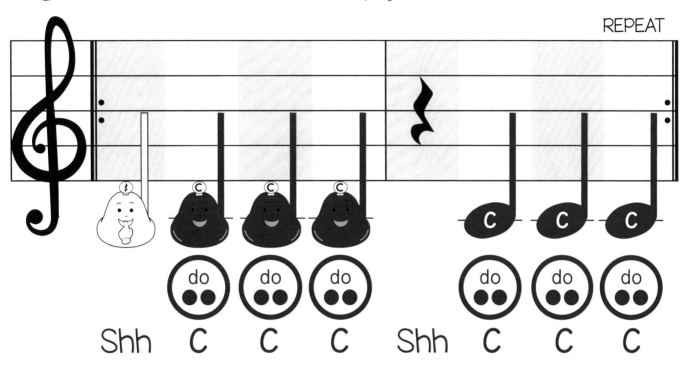

Shh   C   C   C   Shh   C   C   C

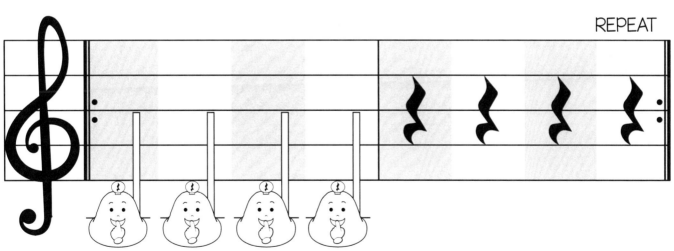

Shh   Shh   Shh   Shh   Shh   Shh   Shh   Shh

Patterns

Circle the correct bell in each box to finish the pattern, and then play along!

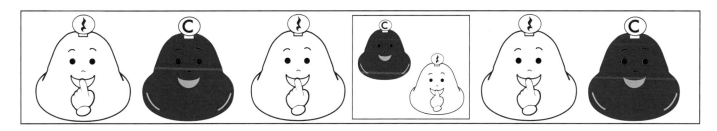

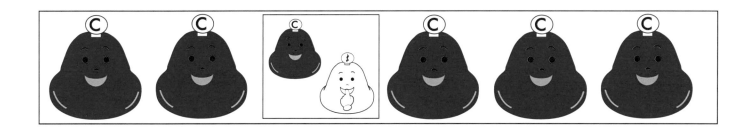

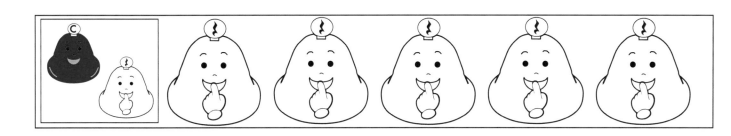

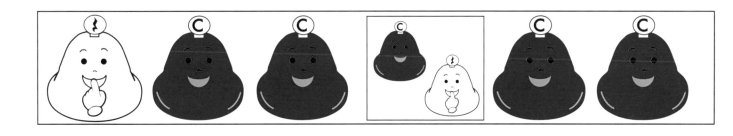

Write a Song

Write your own song, by writing "C" or "Shh" in each bell.

_____   _____
Song Title   Song Composer

Coloring Page

The Shape I'm In

■Square the E bells■
▲Triangle the C bells▲

● Circle the G bells ●
◆ Diamond the Shh bells ◆

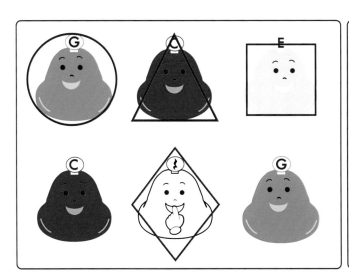

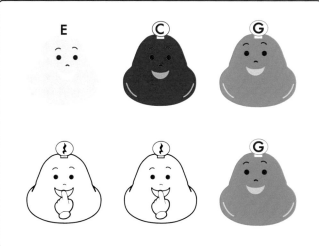

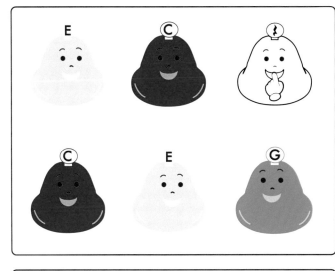

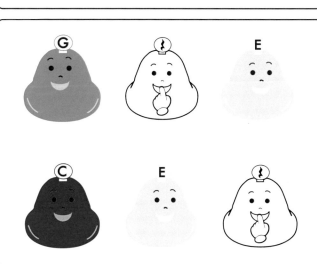

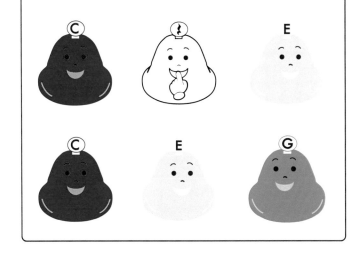

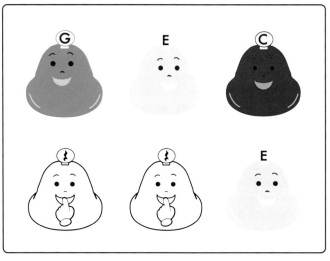

51

Hola E
One Note Studies

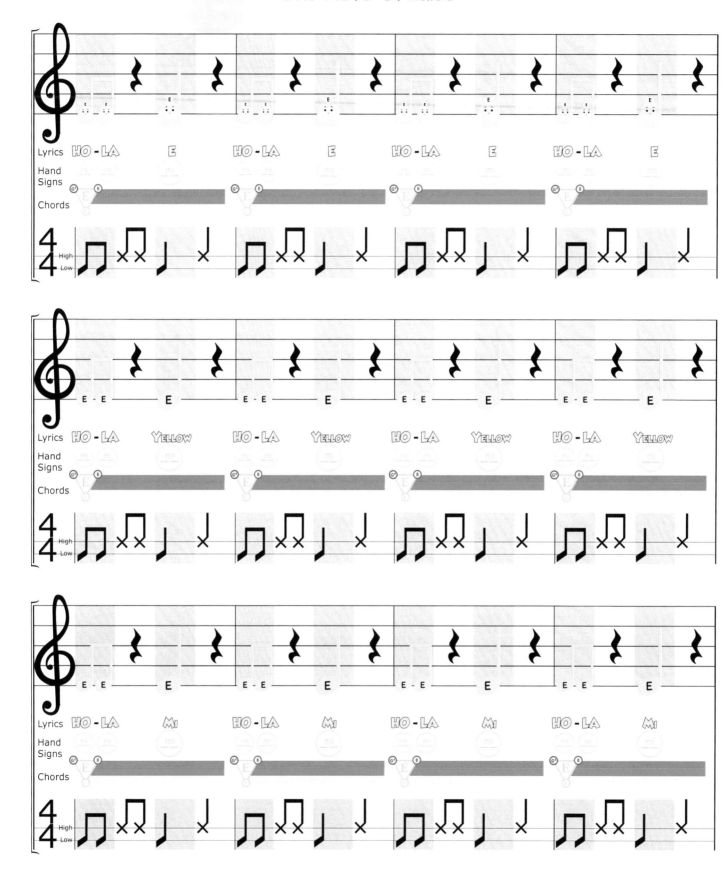

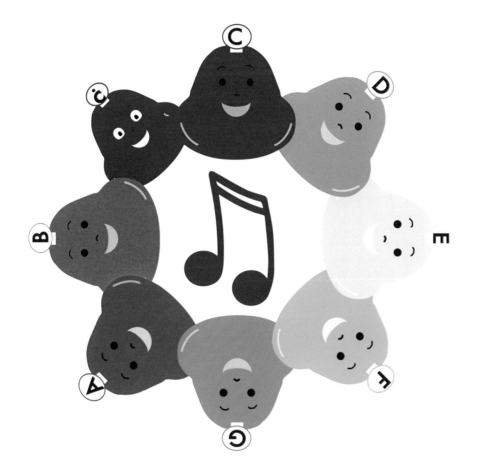

Year 1, Week 4

Chapter 1 - Beet and Shh

LEQ: How can rests affect rhythm?

Week 4 Checklist

	Watched Video	Sang/Played Along	Played Sheet Music 1-3 times	Completed Workbook Activities	Repeat video 2-5 tiunes or as needed for mastery
Activator: I'm a Nut	*		N/A	N/A	
Core Lesson: Beet & Shh	*	*	*	*	
Performance: Fabulous F	*	*		N/A	
Extension: Beet & Cherry			N/A	N/A	

*Suggested Priority Activity

I. Overview: In this lesson, students practice the concept of rests and the simple quarter note rhythm represented by the word "beet". After the core lesson, students meet the note F as they play along with "Fabulous F".

II. Objective: By the end of this lesson, students should know that a quarter note is represented by the words "ta" and "beet" and the number 1. They should also be able to replicate a rhythm pattern using a rest. In the Performance section of this lesson, students will meet the note F and should be able to connect it to the color green, the Solfege name Fa and the number 4.

III. Activator: To begin, students watch "I'm a Nut", a silly clapping song. This sing-a-long is a great way to get students engaged and ready for a lesson full of rhythm. Before singing along, the teacher should review the format for call and response with students.

IV. Core Lesson: The teacher should explain to students that they will spend today's lesson combining what they've learned in previous lessons: "Sweet Beets" and "C & Shh". Before playing along with "Beet & Shh", students begin by singing and hand-signing.

Students may need to watch the video a few times before feeling comfortable enough to clap along.

After the video, the class should play through the song sheets for "Beet & Shh" as a group (or in smaller stations if that works better for the group). The teacher should lead the students by conducting a slow and steady tempo, or use a metronome at 60-90 BPM to help keep the beat.

Year 1, Week 4

Chapter 1 - Sweet Beets and Shh

LEQ: How can rests affect rhythm?

After playing through the song sheets, students should complete the "Beet & Shh" worksheet activities that all reinforce counting, patterns and addition.

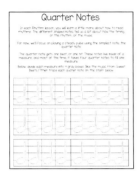

V. Performance: As a group (or as assigned homework), students play along with "Fabulous F", which features scrolling sheet music in the treble clef, as well as a handful of parts for other instruments (percussion, lyrics, chord arrangements, etc).

VI. Summarizer: If students played the performance together, the teacher should instruct students to share one thing they liked about the performance with the person next to them (or with the whole group).

Before moving onto the extension lesson, the teacher should review today's lesson by asking students some or all of the following questions: *how can we refer to quarter notes? how can we refer to rests? how can call and response help us learn music and rhythm? who's got some sweet beets?*.

VII. Extension: As a final activity (or as homework), students watch "Beet & Cherry", the very first "Sweet Beets" video they watched.

After watching the video, and singing and clapping along, the teacher should ask students to identify the differences between these two versions of "Sweet Beets". Students should reference eighth notes, quarter notes and rests in their responses; if not, the teacher should lead student responses there.

Beet & Shh

☆☆☆☆☆

Sing the chorus to Sweet Beets while tapping a steady beat. Then in the verses, tap, clap or stomp with Beet and Cherry.

CHORUS 1

Sweet Beets, we've got some!

If you **want some** Sweet Beets, we've got 'em.

If you want Sweet Beets, we've got some,

If you **want some** Sweet Beets, we've got 'em.

VERSE 1

BEET BEET SHH **BEET** SHH SHH **BEET BEET**

SHH **BEET** SHH **BEET BEET BEET BEET** SHH

CHORUS 2

Sweet Beets, we've got some!
If you want some Sweet Beets, we've got 'em.
If you want Sweet Beets, we've got some,
If you want some Sweet Beets, we've got 'em.

VERSE 2

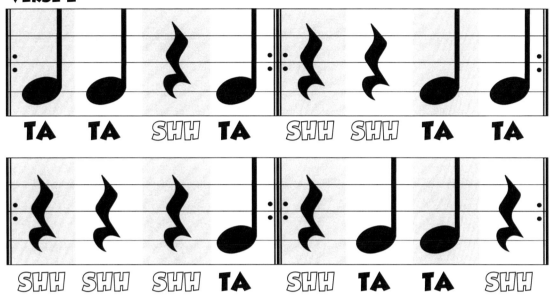

CHORUS 3

Sweet Beets, we've got some!
If you want some Sweet Beets, we've got 'em.
If you want Sweet Beets, we've got some,
If you want some Sweet Beets, we've got 'em.

VERSE 3

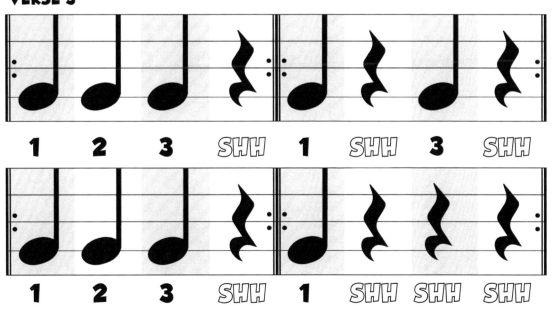

CHORUS 4: REPEAT CHORUS 3

Quarter Notes

In each Rhythm lesson, you will learn a little more about how to read rhythms. The different shaped notes tell us a lot about how the timing, or the rhythm, of the music.

For now, we'll focus on playing a steady pulse using the simplest note, the quarter note.

The quarter note gets one beat, or one hit. These notes live inside of a measure, and most of the time, it takes four quarter notes to fill one measure.

Below, divide each measure into 4 gray boxes (like the music from Sweet Beets).Tthen trace each quater note on the staff below.

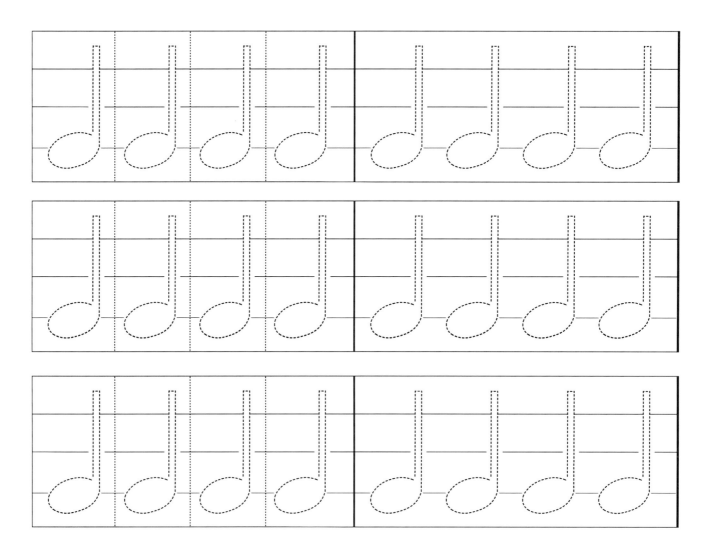

Count the Beats

In each box, count the number of quarter notes, then write the
total of each box in the square to the right.

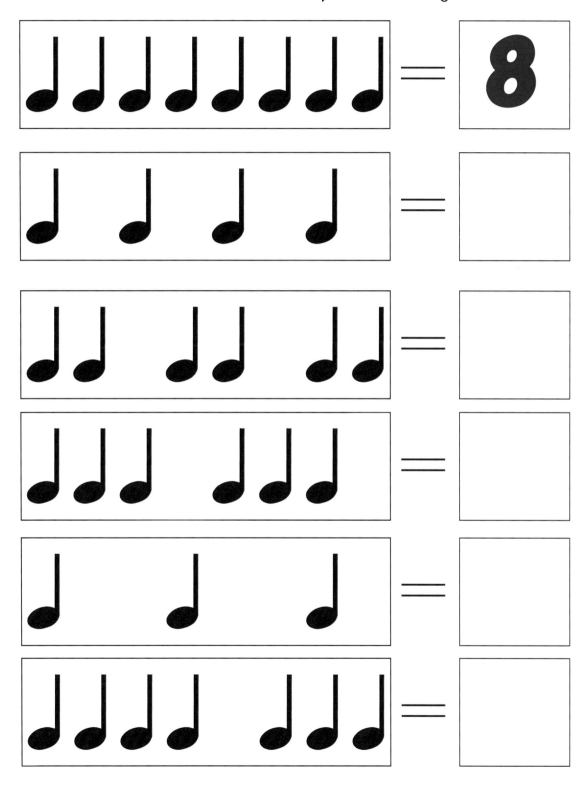

Beat Math

In each row, count the number of quarter notes, then write the total next to each equal sign. Hint: the rests still take up 1 beat!

♩ = **1**

♩ + ♩ =

♩ + ♩ + ♩ =

𝄽 + 𝄽 =

♩ + ♩ =

♩ + 𝄽 =

𝄽 = **1**

𝄽 + 𝄽 + 𝄽 =

𝄽 + 𝄽 =

♩ + ♩ + ♩ + ♩ =

𝄽 + ♩ =

𝄽 + ♩ + 𝄽 =

Write Your Own Rhythm

Below are some blank measures! Use Beet, Shh, quarter notes, or TA to write your own rhythms. Then clap your rhythm once you've recorded it.

Note Bank **BEET** *SHH* **TA** ♩ 𝄽

Rhythm #1

Rhythm #2

Rhythm #3

Rhythm #4

Fabulous F
One Note Studies

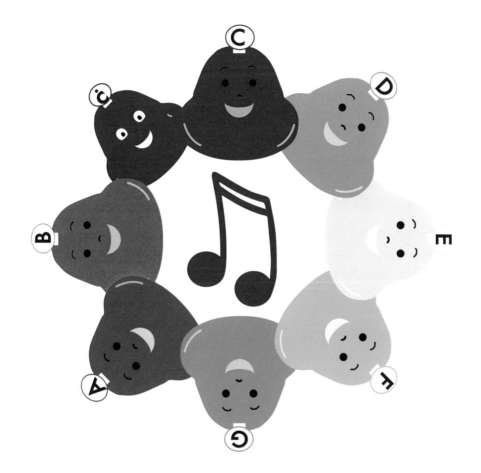

Year 1, Week 5

Chapter 1 - Do Mi Sol Slide

LEQ: How can a student identify a C major chord?

Week 5 Checklist

	Watched Video	Sang/Played Along	Played Sheet Music 1-3 times	Completed Workbook Activities	Repeat video 2-5 tiunes or as needed for mastery
Activator: Beethoven's Fifth	*		N/A	N/A	
Core Lesson: Do Mi Sol Slide	*	*	*	*	
Performance: G Oh Gee	*	*		N/A	
Extension: Row Your Boat				N/A	

* Suggested Priority Activity

I. Overview: In this lesson, students learn the concept of chords. Chords are musical sounds made up of multiple notes. Students study the C Major Chord, made up of the notes: C, E and G. After the core lesson, students play along with "G Oh Gee".

II. Objective: By the end of this lesson, students should be able to connect the notes C, E and G to the C Major Chord. In the Performance section of this lesson, students will also meet the note G and should be able to connect it to the color teal, the Solfege name Sol and the number 5.

III. Activator: At the beginning of class, the teacher should explain to students that today's lesson is all about groups of notes, specifically, the notes C, E and G, which are the notes of the C major chord. The teacher should clarify that a chord is simply a group of notes that sound nice together.

To begin, students sing and hand-sign along with "Beethoven's Fifth", using just the hand-signs for Do and Sol. A student volunteer should demonstrate each hand-sign, and then the students should watch and sign along with "Beethoven's Fifth".

IV. Core Lesson: The teacher should explain to students that they will play three bells today: C, G and E. Students should practice a few times as a class playing all three bells at the same time. Once everyone is ready, students sing and play along with "Do Mi Sol Slide".

After the video, the class should play through the song sheets for "Do Mi Sol Slide" as a group (or in smaller stations if that works better for the group). The teacher should lead the students by conducting a slow and steady tempo, or use a metronome at 60-90 BPM to help keep the beat.

Year 1, Week 5

Chapter 1 - Do Mi Sol Slide

LEQ: How can a student identify a C major chord?

After playing through the sheet music, students should complete the "Do Mi Sol Slide" worksheet activities that all connect the notes G and E with colors teal and yellow.

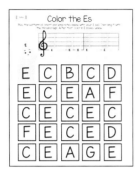 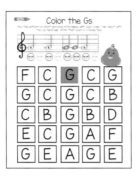  

V. Performance: As a group (or as assigned homework), students take out their G bell and play along with "G Oh Gee", which features scrolling sheet music in the treble clef, as well as a handful of parts for other instruments (percussion, lyrics, hand-signs, chord arrangements, etc.).

VI. Summarizer: If students played the performance together, the teacher should instruct students to share one thing they liked about the performance with the person next to them (or with the whole group).

Before moving onto the extension lesson, the teacher should review today's lesson by asking students some or all of the following questions: *What letter is associated with the color teal?; What letter is associated with the color yellow?; Which notes make up the C Major Chord?*

VII. Extension: As a final activity (or as homework), students watch "Row Your Boat", a performance in Chapter 3: Do and Sol.

Students play along with the performance using their red and teal bells. Then, either in small groups or as a class, students share what the class did well in their performance.

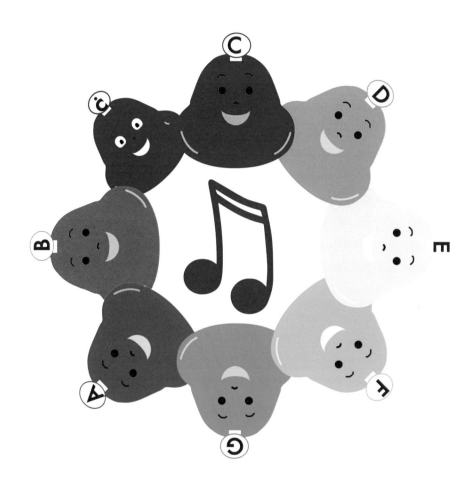

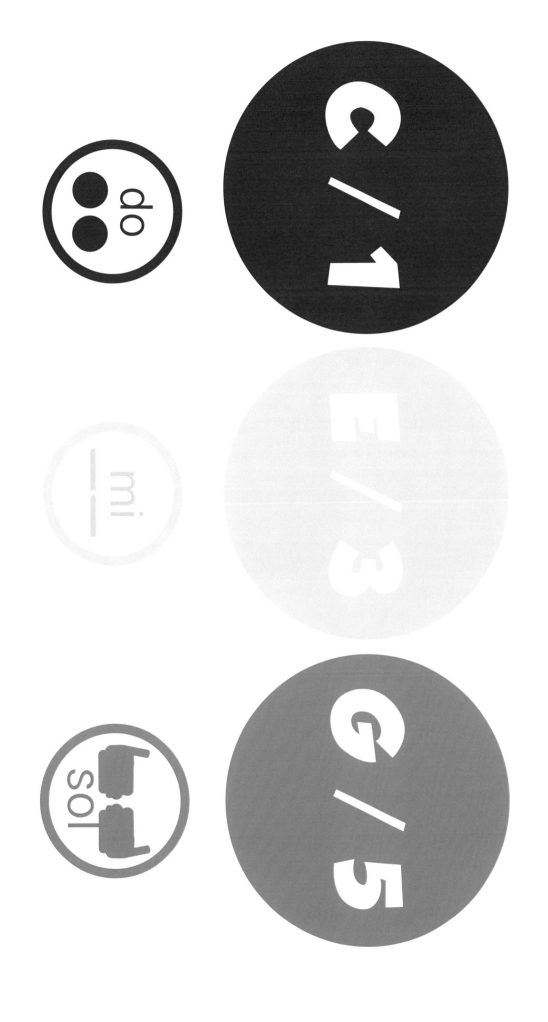

Do Mi Sol Bell Mat

Use this bell mat when practicing Do, Mi and Sol, and when playing along with the rest of this chapter.

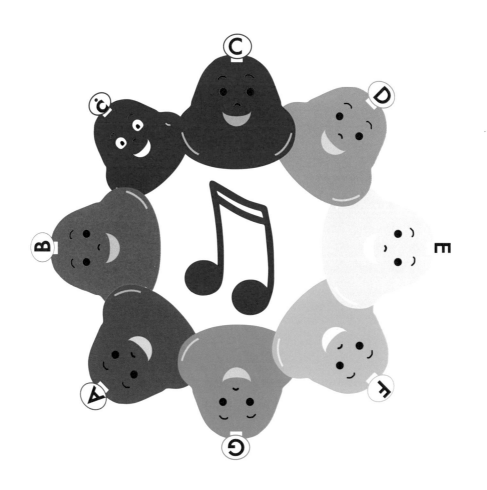

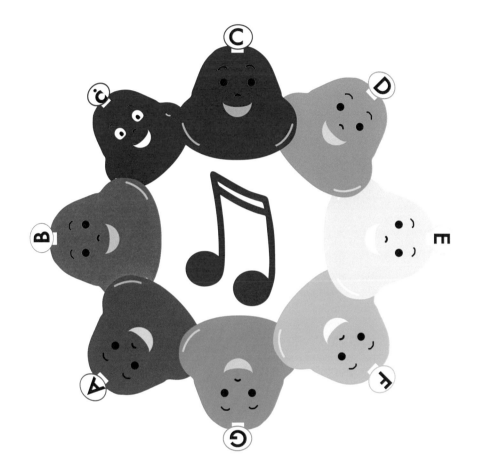

Do Mi Sol Slide

Play and sing with three notes, C E & G. When you reach the end, repeat the whole song one more time and then try it with the hand-signs!

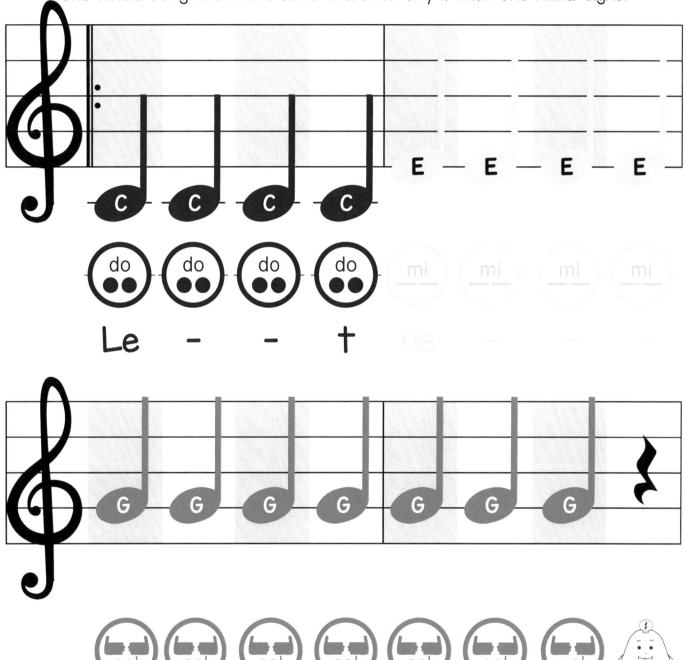

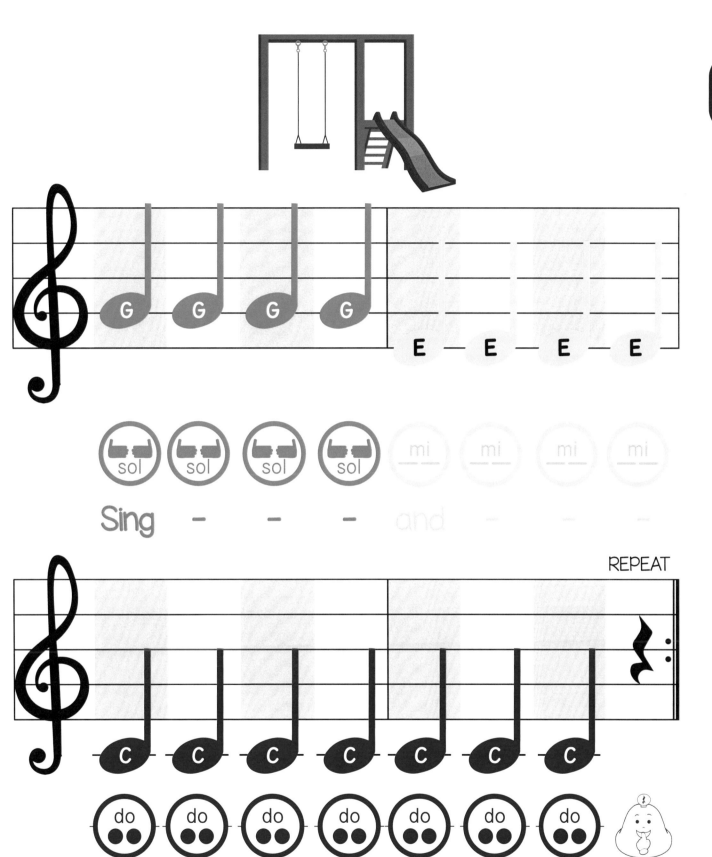

Color the Es

Play the pattern of short and long notes below with your E bell. Then sing it with the Mi hand-sign. After that, color in E boxes yellow.

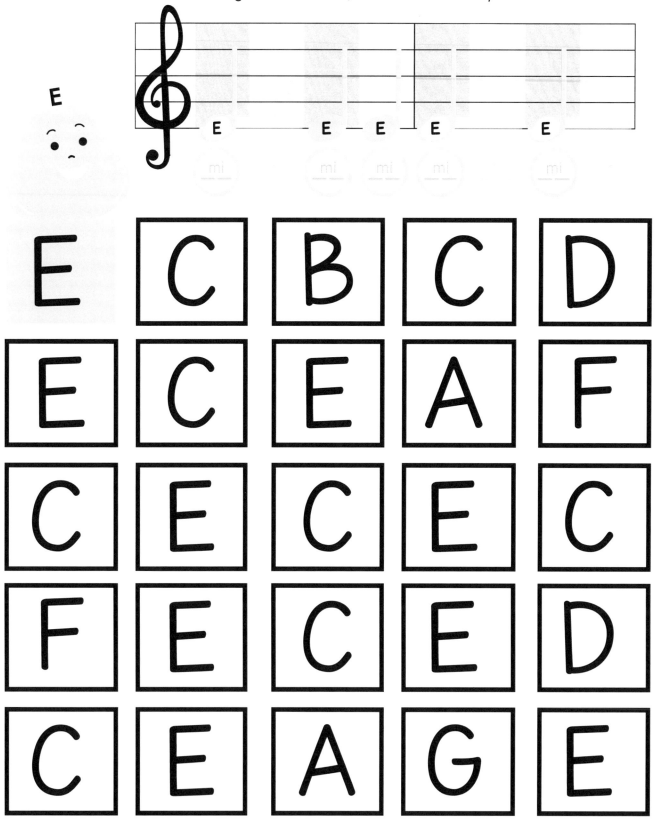

Color the Gs

Play the pattern of short and long notes below with your G bell. Then sing it with the Sol hand-sign. After that, color in G boxes teal.

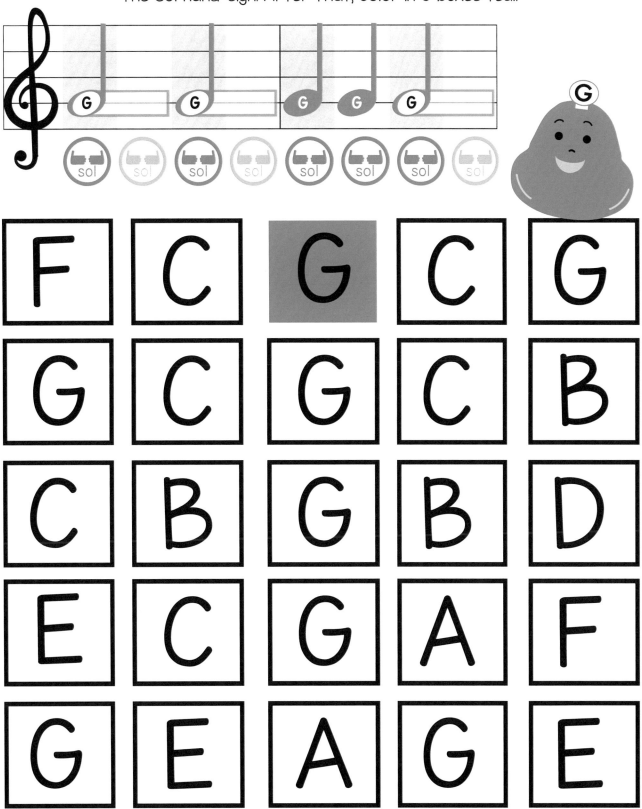

Circle the Es

Practice writing the words below. Then circle the pictures that begin with E.

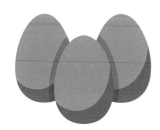

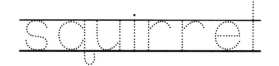

squirrel

egg

house

fox

pig

eyes

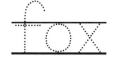

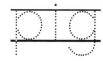

bug

earth

whale

74

 Teal

Circle the Gs
Practice writing the words below. Then circle the pictures
that begin with G.

1

guitar   car   lion

grapes   truck   orange

frog   goat   horse

Gee-Oh-G
One Note Studies

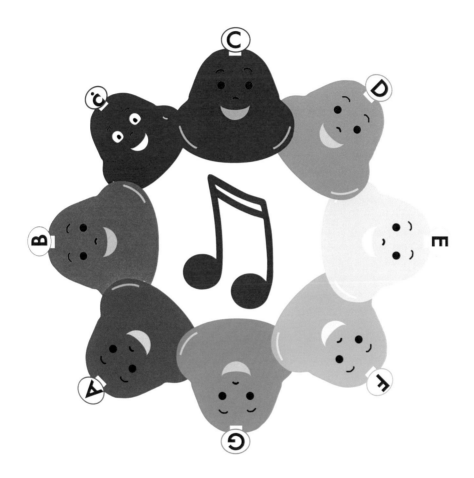

Year 1, Week 6

Chapter 1 - Chord Watching

LEQ: How can a student distinguish G & E from C?

Week 6 Checklist

	Watched Video	Sang/Played Along	Played Sheet Music 1-3 times	Completed Workbook Activities	Repeat video 2-5 tiunes or as needed for mastery
Activator: Do Mi Sol Slide	*		N/A	N/A	
Core Lesson: Chord Watching	*	*	*	*	
Performance: Hola E, G Oh Gee, Hello C	*	*		N/A	
Extension: What Note Is It? #1			N/A		

* Suggested Priority Activity

I. Overview: In this lesson, students continue practice with the C Major Chord. By playing both individual notes and notes together as a chord, learners will begin to distinguish the G bell and E bell from the C bell.

II. Objective: By the end of this lesson, students should be able distinguish the G bell and E bell from the C bell.

III. Activator: At the beginning of class, the teacher should explain that students will continue to practice the C Major chord. To begin, students will watch and play along with last week's core lesson: "Do Mi Sol Slide".

The teacher should explain to students that in today's lesson they will need to listen and identify each note, so they should listen and play carefully once more before moving on.

IV. Core Lesson: The teacher should explain to students that they will continue their practice with C major by listening and trying to identify each note. Students won't need their bells for this lesson, unless the teacher would like them to identify the note they hear that way.

The teacher should explain to students that they should listen and not play during this video. As students listen, they should indicate their guess for each question by writing it down, coloring with a matching crayon, or pushing that bell(s) forward.

After the video, the class should play through the sheet music for "Chord Watching" as a group (or in smaller stations if that works better for the group). The teacher should lead the students by conducting a slow and steady tempo, or use a metronome at 60-90 BPM to help keep the beat.

Year 1, Week 6

Chapter 1 - Chord Watching

LEQ: How can a student distinguish G & E from C?

After playing through the sheet music, students should complete the "Chord Watching" worksheet activities that all connect the notes G and E with colors teal and yellow.

   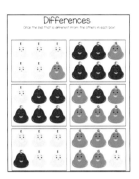

V. Performance: In this lesson, the teacher should choose to review the performance for the note that students seem to have the most trouble identifying first, then the others. If there is time, review each performance track: "Hola E", "G oh Gee", and "Hello C", or simply play through the sheet music as a class.

VI. Summarizer: If students played the performances together, the teacher should instruct students to share one thing they liked about the performance with the person next to them (or with the whole group).

Before moving onto the extension lesson, the teacher should review today's lesson by asking students some or all of the following questions: *What number is associated with the color teal?; What number is associated with the color yellow? ; What is the Solfege name for G?; What is the Solfege name for E?.*

VII. Extension: As a final activity (or as homework), students watch "What Note Is It #1", to assess their understanding of the notes in this lesson.

Chord Watching

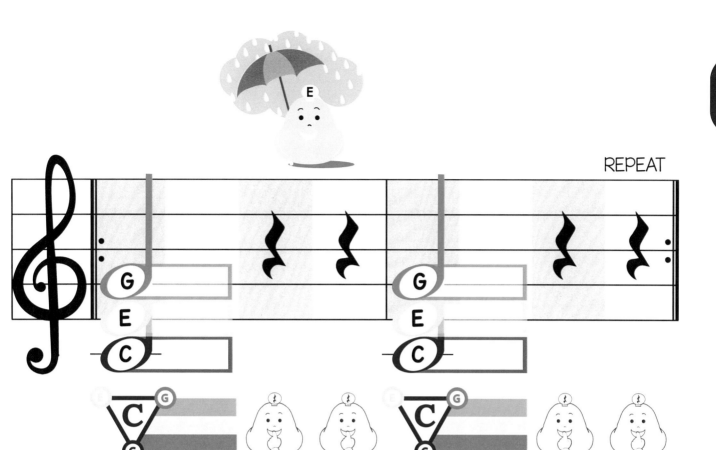

REPEAT

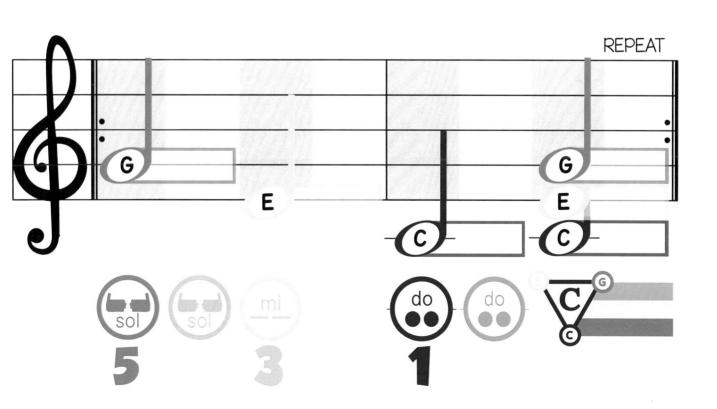

REPEAT

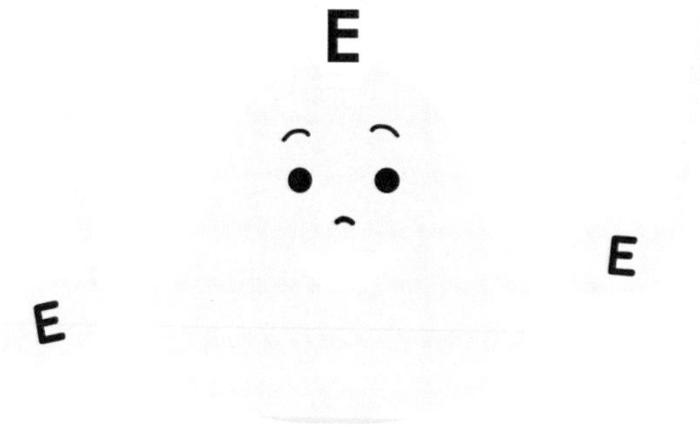

E

E

E

e e e e e e e e e e

3 3 3 3 three three

yellow yellow yellow

mi mi mi mi mi mi mi mi

E E E E E E E E E E

3 3 3 THREE THREE

YELLOW YELLOW

MI MI MI MI MI MI

Teal

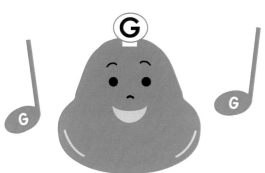

g g g g g g g g g g g

5 5 5 5 five five five

teal teal teal teal

sol sol sol sol sol sol

G G G G G G G G G G

5 5 5 5 TEAL TEAL

TEAL TEAL TEAL

SOL SOL SOL SOL

Find the Bells

Circle the E bells.

Circle the G bells.

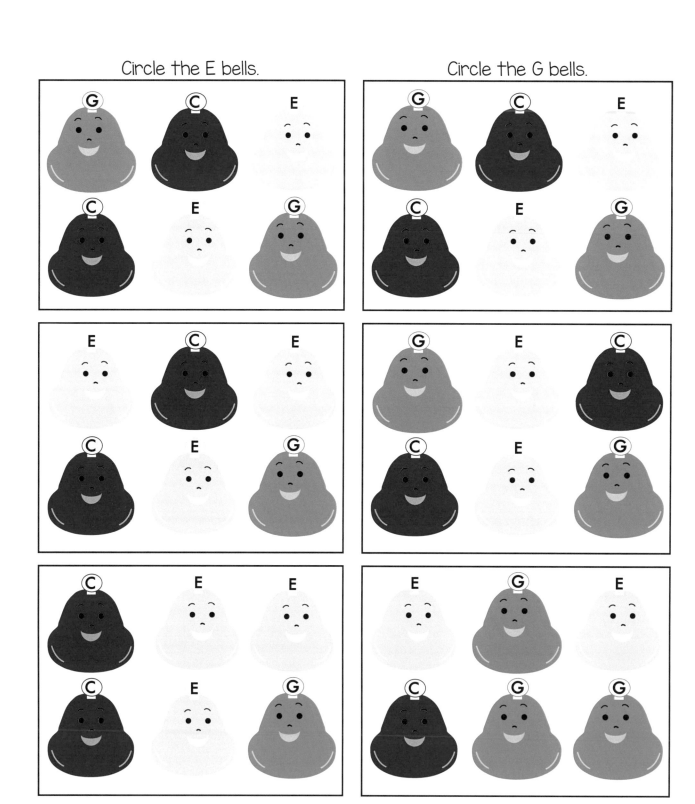

84

Differences

Circle the bell that is different from the others in each box!

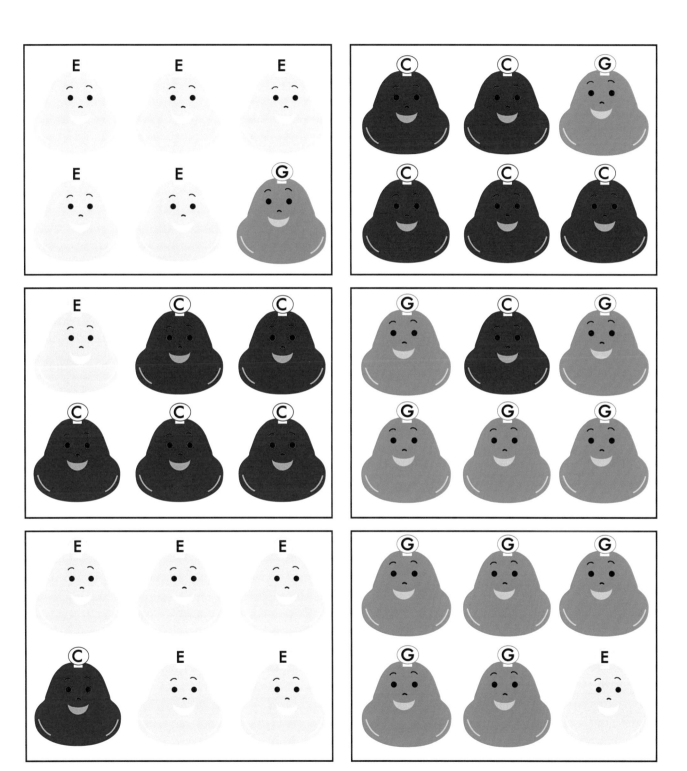

Hello C
One Note Studies

Hola E
One Note Studies

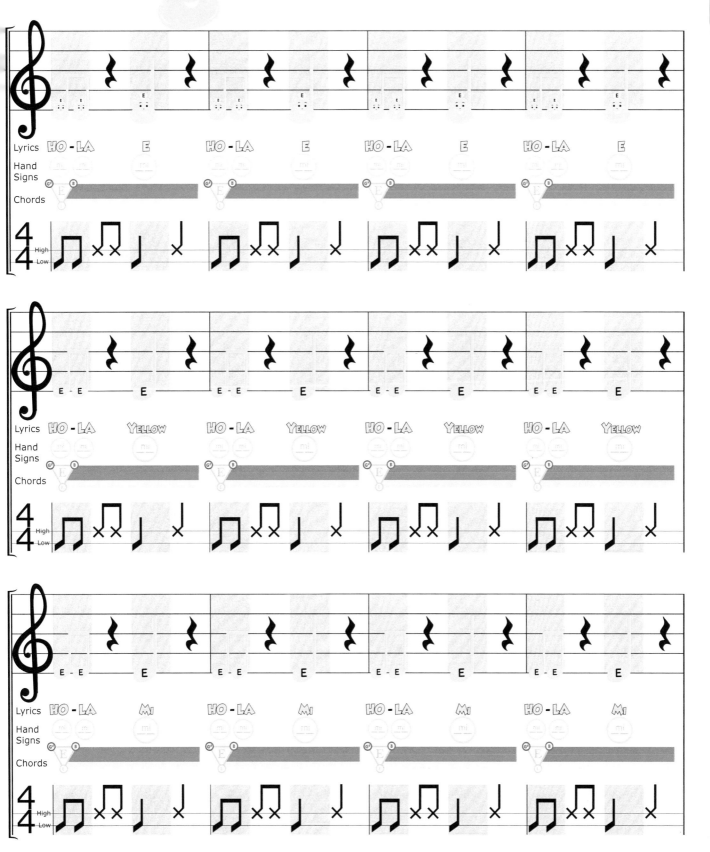

Gee-Oh-G
One Note Studies

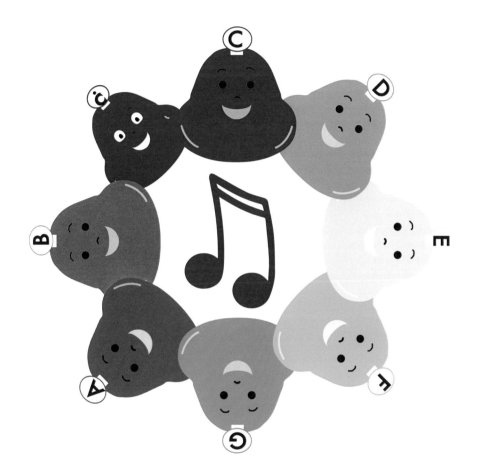

Year 1, Week 7

Chapter 1 - Solfege Slide
LEQ: How can a student identify the notes in the C major scale?

Week 7 Checklist

	Watched Video	Sang/Played Along	Played Sheet Music 1-3 times	Completed Workbook Activities	Repeat video 2-5 tiunes or as needed for mastery
Activator: Let Us Play	*		N/A	N/A	
Core Lesson: Solfege Slide in C Major	*	*	*	*	
Performance: Aloha A and Bonjour B	*	*		N/A	
Extension: Melodies 1 & 2					

★ Suggested Priority Activity

I. Overview: In this lesson, students get to play all 8 bells for the first time. Students will learn that every note has a Solfège name, a number, a color, a note name and a different sound. After the core lesson, students play along with "Aloha A" and "Bonjour B" to meet A & D.

II. Objective: By the end of this lesson, students should know that there are 8 bells, and each has its own number and color.

III. Activator: To begin today's lesson, students will play along with "Let Us Play". This short, call and response song begins about 30 seconds into the video, so teachers should instruct students to wait to play until they hear Mr. Rob call out each bell name and hold out his hand.

This is a short, fun introduction to each note, so students can play it several times before moving onto the main lesson for today.

IV. Core Lesson: The teacher should explain to students that they will learn about all 8 notes on the C major scale today.

As they watch the video, Mr. Rob will introduce each note in comparison with C. This will help students identify each note's placement on the scale and relationship with the note C.

After, the class should play through the sheet music for "Solfege Slide in C Major" as a group (or in smaller stations if that works better for the group). The teacher should lead the students by conducting a slow and steady tempo, or use a metronome at 60-90 BPM to help keep the beat.

Year 1, Week 7

Chapter 1 - Solfege Slide

LEQ: How can a student identify the notes in the C major scale?

After playing through the sheet music, students should complete the "Solfege Slide in C Major" worksheet activities that incorporate all eight notes from the C major scale.

   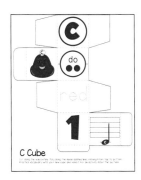

V. Performance: As a group (or as assigned homework), students play along with "Aloha A" and "Bonjour B", which feature scrolling sheet music in the treble clef, as well as a handful of parts for other instruments (percussion, lyrics, hand-signs, chord arrangements, etc).

VI. Summarizer: If students played the performances together, the teacher should instruct students to share one thing they liked about the performance with the person next to them (or with the whole group).

Before moving onto the extension lesson, the teacher should review today's lesson by asking students some or all of the following questions: *How many notes are in the C Major Scale?; Which seven colors match the bells?; What are the Solfege names of each note on the scale?; What are the musical note names on the C major scale?*

VII. Extension: As a final activity (or as homework), students watch "Melodies 1 & 2". These videos from our hand-signing series and will reinforce the notes, colors, Solfege names, and numbers learned in today's lesson. The Melodies series requires no instrument, so this is the perfect activity for students to complete at home, or in small groups around the classroom.

Solfège Slide in C Major

It's time to play with all 8 of our bells. Make sure to repeat each line one time before moving onto the next line. Then at the end, do the whole song again with the hand-signs.

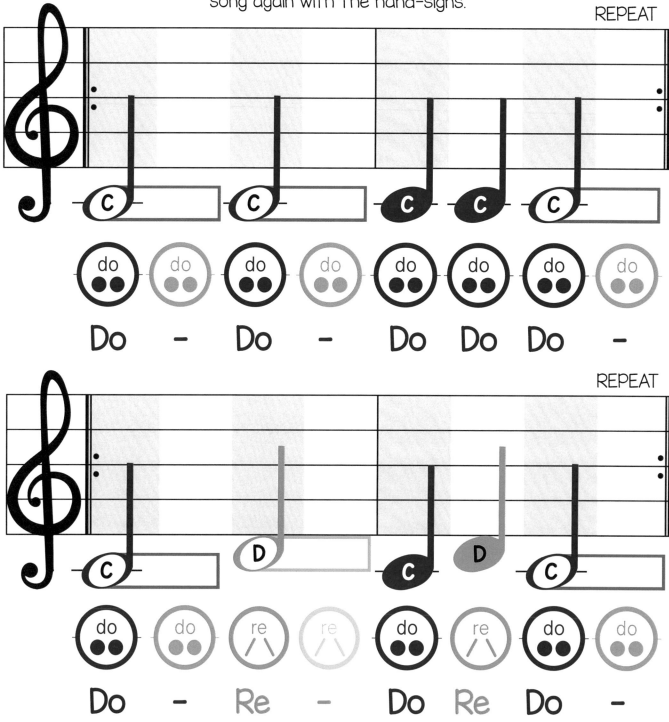

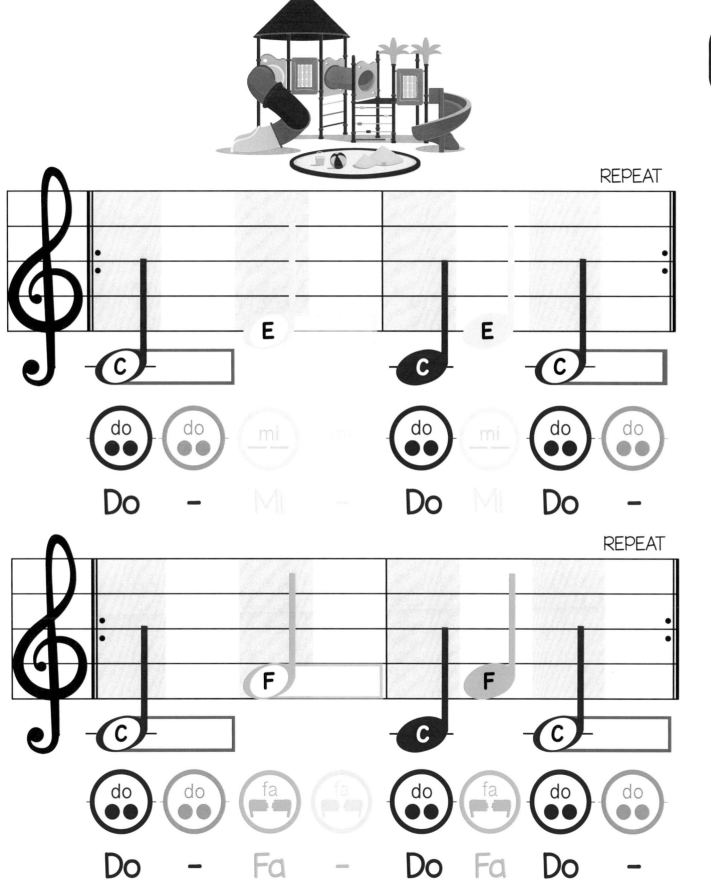

93

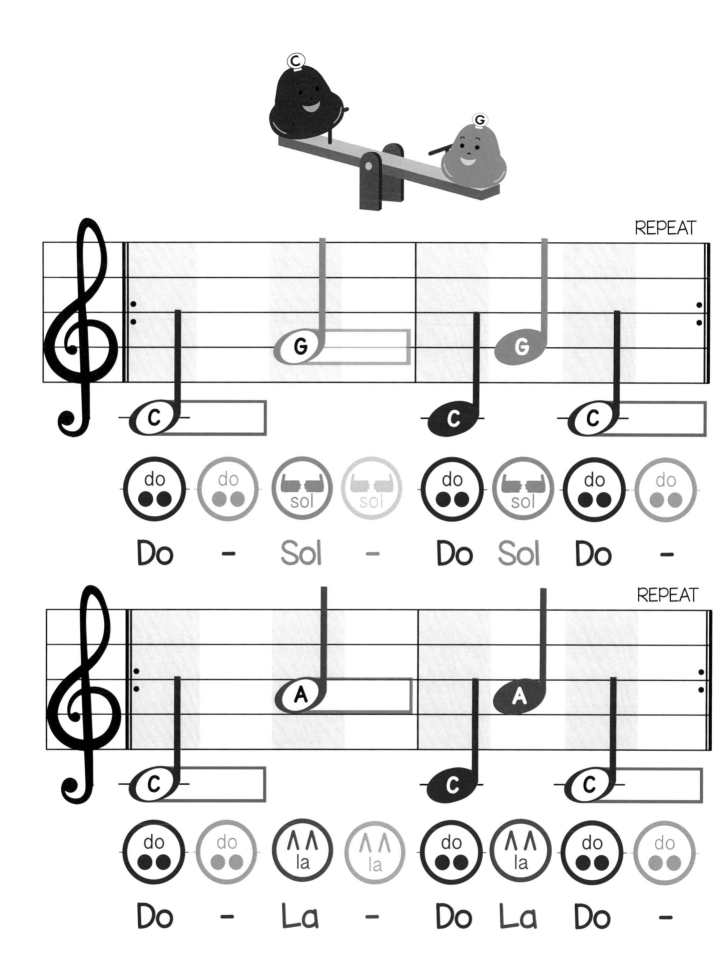

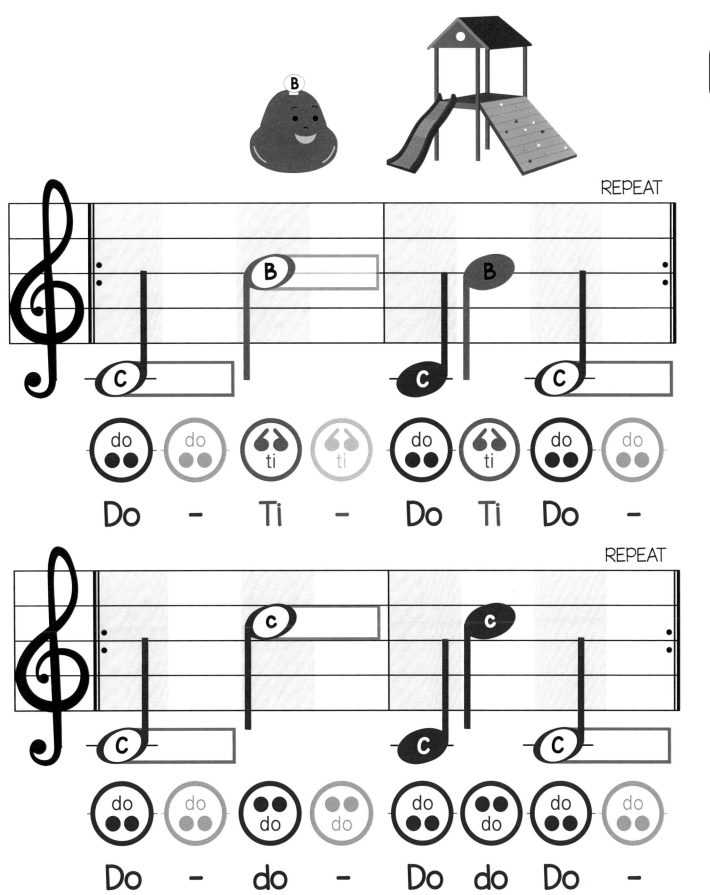

Cut and Paste

Cut out the bells on the following page and paste each one
next to the correct number below.

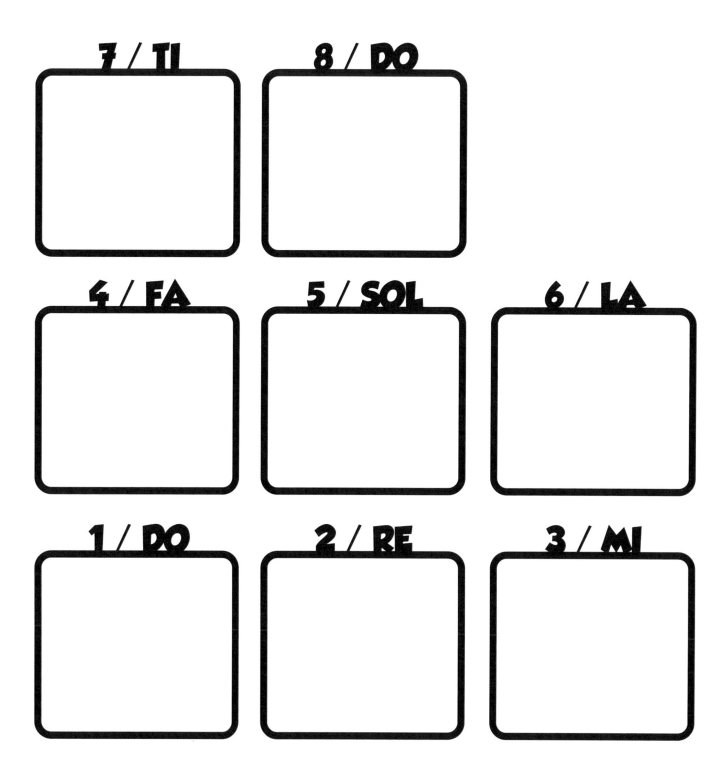

Cut and Paste

Cut out each bell and match it with its number and Solfège on the previous page.

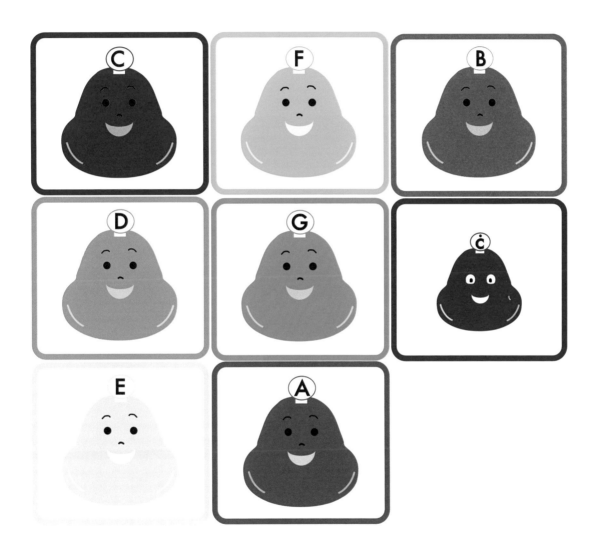

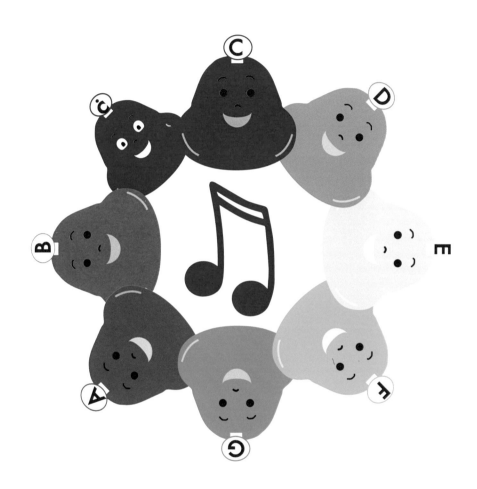

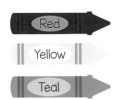

Write a Song

Using the C, E & G bells, write your own song.

Title   Composer

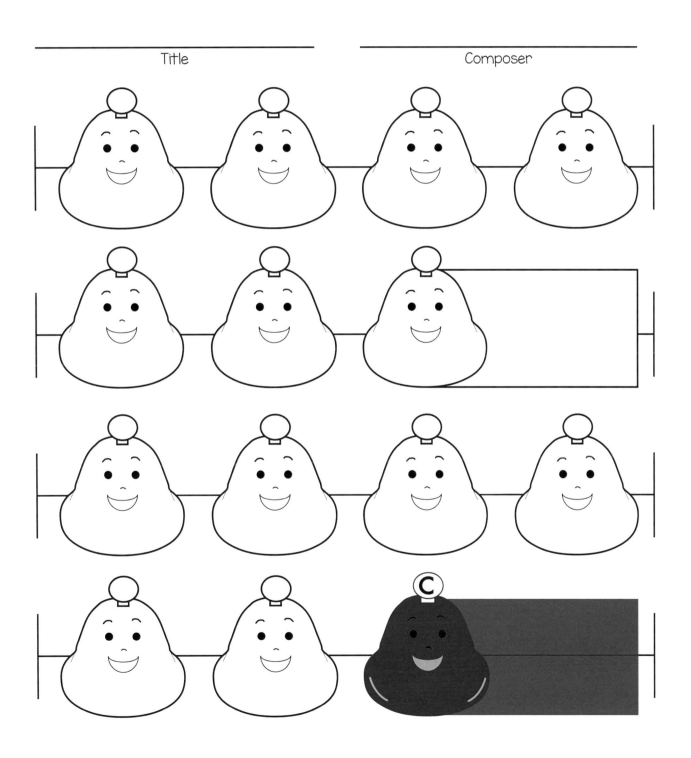

Color by Bell

Color the rainbow & hearts to match the bells below.

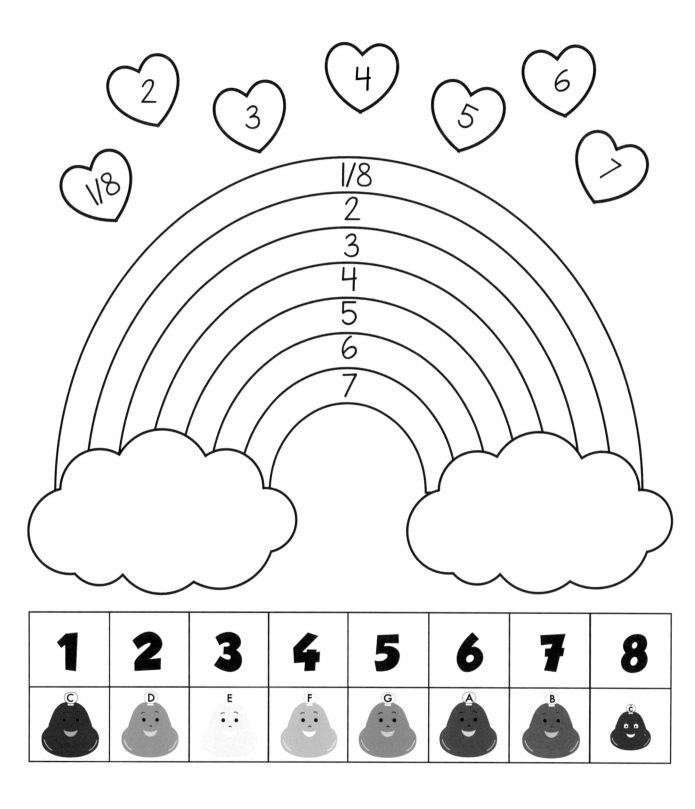

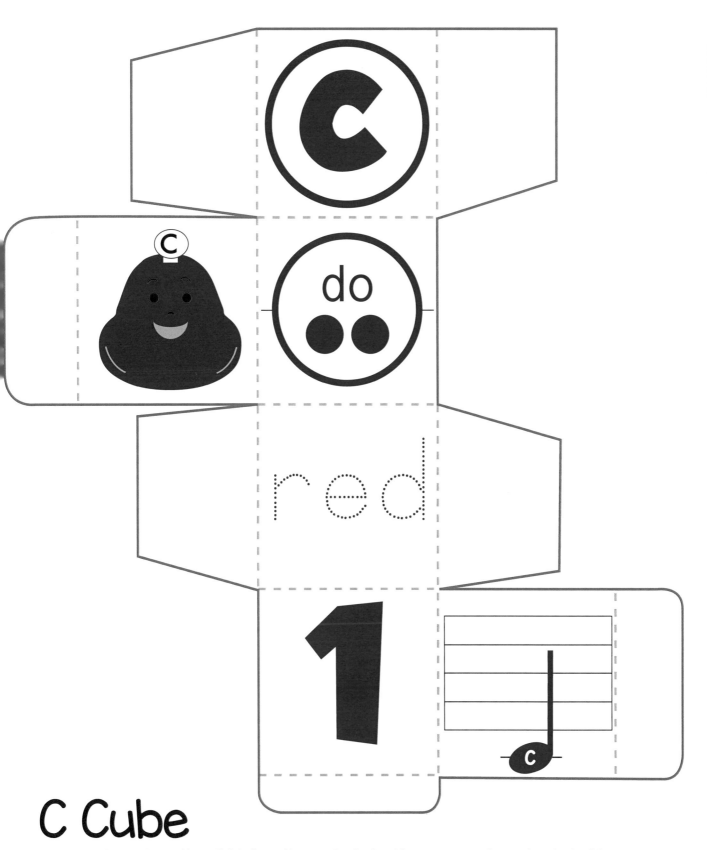

C Cube

Cut along the solid outline. Fold along the inside dashed lines, moving from top to bottom.
Practice vocabulary with your new cube and save it for an activity later this section!

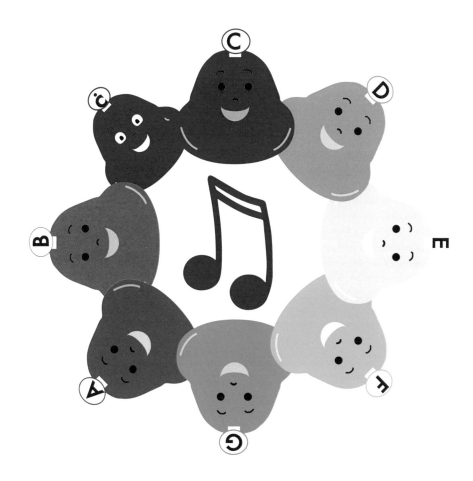

Aloha A
One Note Studies

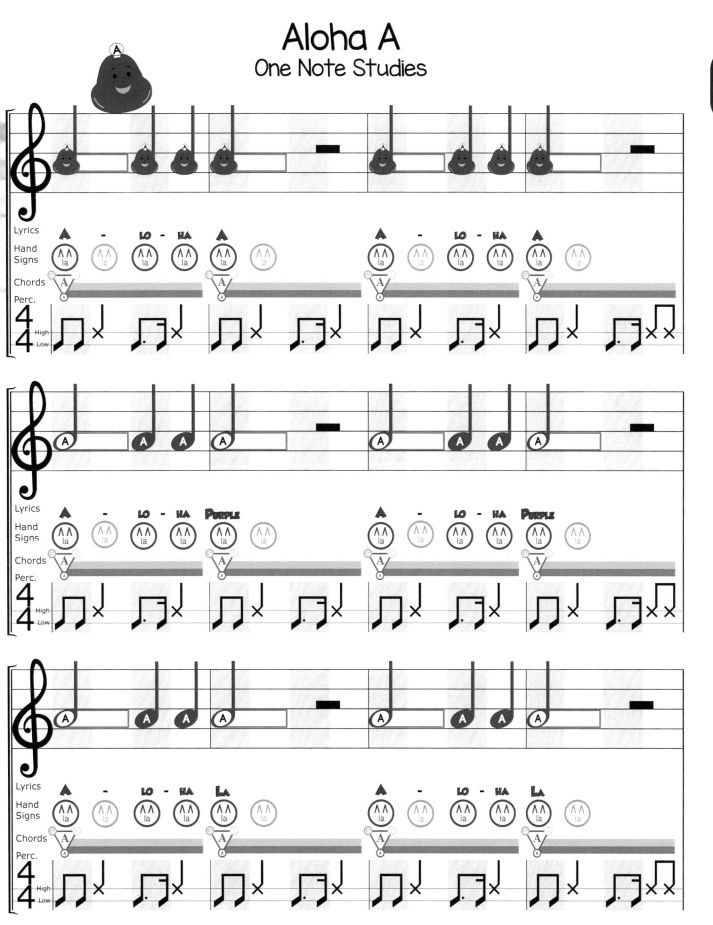

Bonjour B
One Note Studies

MELODY #1:
Do Re Mi Fa Sol La Ti Do

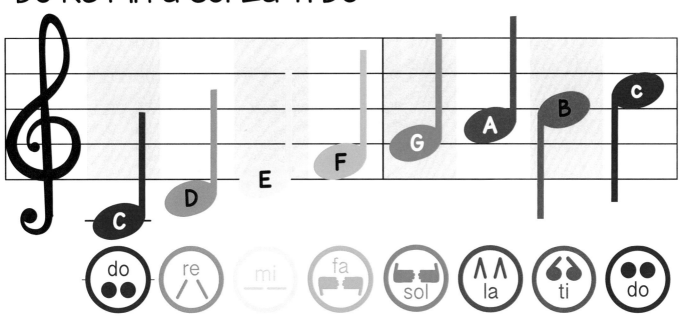

MELODY #2:
Do Ti La Sol Fa Mi Re Do

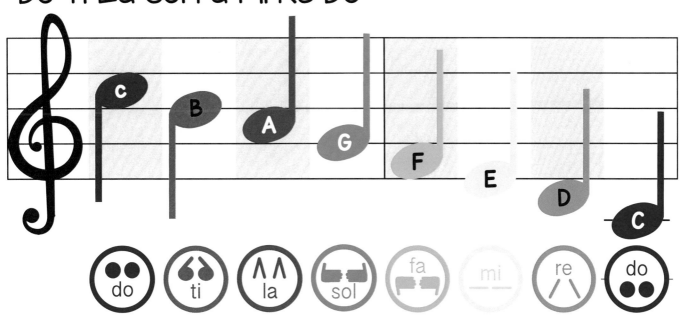

Quiz #1:

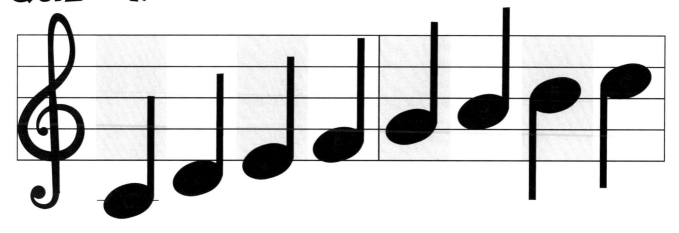

Part I : WHICH NOTE?
Write the notes on
the blank lines!

_____ _____ _____ _____ _____ _____ _____ _____

Part 2 : MIXED UP!
Match the Solfege
Hand Signs to the
notes above!

Quiz #2:

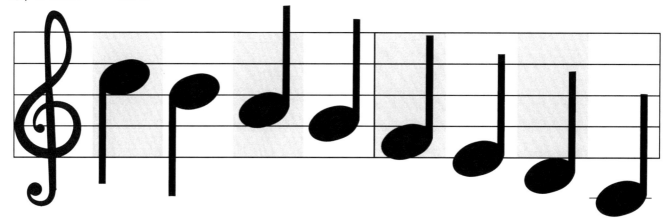

Part I : WHICH NOTE?
Write the notes on
the blank lines!

_____ _____ _____ _____ _____ _____ _____ _____

Part 2 : MIXED UP!
Match the Solfege
Hand Signs to the
notes above!

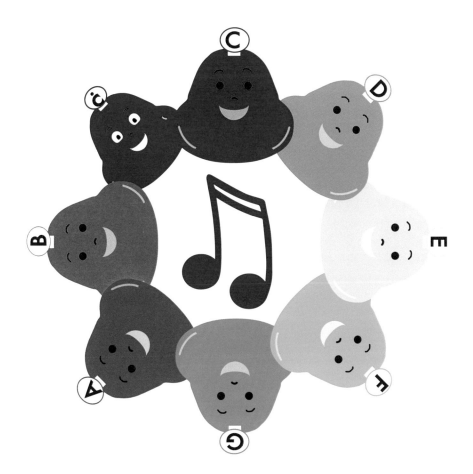

Year 1, Week 8

Chapter 1 - Perform and Assess
LEQ: How can a student perform and identify the notes in the C major scale?
Week 8 Checklist

	Watched Video	Sang/Played Along	Played Sheet Music 1-3 times	Completed Workbook Activities	Repeat video 2-5 tiunes or as needed for mastery
Activator: Hi High C Performance	*	*	N/A	N/A	
Core Lesson: Performance Prodigies Playlist	*	*	N/A	N/A	
Performance: What Note Is It #1 & Name that Note #1	*	*	N/A		
Extension: Interactive Quiz			N/A	N/A	

* Suggested Priority Activity

I. Overview: In this lesson, students take turns performing various performances for the class. Then, students attempt to identify notes just by listening.

II. Objective: By the end of this lesson, students should be familiar with all 8 notes in the C major scale and feel comfortable identifying notes that they hear.

III. Activator: To begin today's lesson, students will play along with "Hi High C". This performance is the last one in Performance Chapter 1 and will get students warmed up for a lesson full of performances.

The teacher should decide how to play this performance--either as a whole class or in small groups. Students can play along as a whole class and then share constructive feedback for the whole group at the end, or students can play in small groups and share more specific feedback with their partners.

IV. Core Lesson: The teacher should explain to students that they will each play a different performance today in front of the class. Students can play individually, or if it makes more sense, in small groups. Students can play the same part or different parts (hand-signing, percussion, etc.)

There is a playlist of all the performance on this week's lesson page, so the teacher can scroll through and assign students a performance track, or (if it's possible with this group of students) students can choose the performance they'd like to perform.

As each student performs, the teacher should play a metronome at 60-90 BPM to keep the beat. The performs can play along with either the video or just the sheet music if they prefer.

Year 1, Week 8

Chapter 1 - Perform and Assess

LEQ: How can a student perform and identify the notes in the C major scale?

V. Performance: Instead of a performance today, students will watch two listening games: "What Note Is It?"and "Name that Note".

The teacher should give each student a copy of the "What Note Is It" handout and explain that as students listen, they should not call out their guess, but circle the matching bell on their paper.

The teacher may decide to model the first guess for students if they are unclear about what to do. The host of the listening game will reveal the answer after each question, so students should mark each of their answers right or wrong.

At the end of the video, the teacher should debrief with students: *which note was easiest to identify?; which note was most difficult to identify?; were there any notes that students consistently got wrong?; were there any notes that students consistently got right?.*

Next, students will attempt to identify all 8 notes. For this activity, the teacher should pause the video after each note, and allow students to guess as a class. Since students have had less practice with all 8 notes compared to the notes in the C major chord, students may struggle to hear each note correctly and that's okay.

If students become frustrated, the teacher should explain that they have 7 more chapters of content to learn before they will really develop their ear, and that they should keep practicing!

VI. Summarizer: The teacher should begin by summarizing the performance part of this week's lesson. The teacher should ask: *what was students' favorite part of the performance?; what were they most impressed by?; what was one thing they were surprised by?; what is one thing that they could do better (personally) next time?*

Since this is the last lesson in Chapter one, the teacher should ask students to reflect on the chapter. Which lesson was their favorite and if there's time, review the essential questions from each lesson: *how can Prodigies help me learn music?; how can a student vary playing a note?; how can a student use rests in music?; how can rests affect rhythm?; how can a student identify a C major chord?; how can a student distinguish G & E from C?; how can a student identify the notes in the C major scale?*

VII. Extension: As a final activity (or as homework), students complete the first interactive quiz directly on the Prodigies site on this week's lesson page.

What Note Is It?

Draw a circle around the bell you hear!

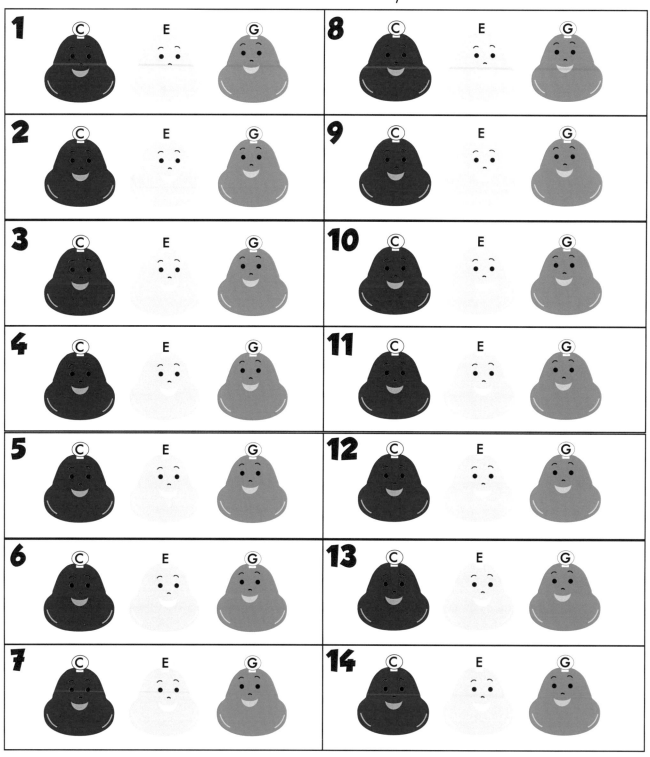

Bonus: What chord is it? _____

Hello C
One Note Studies

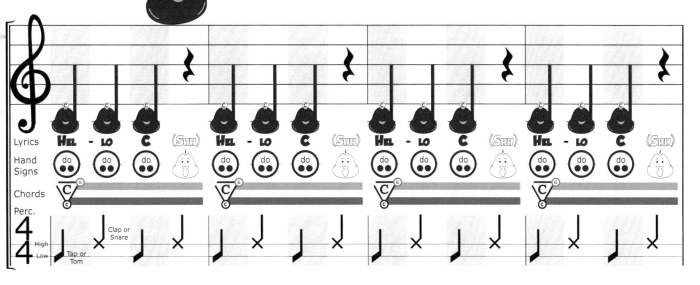

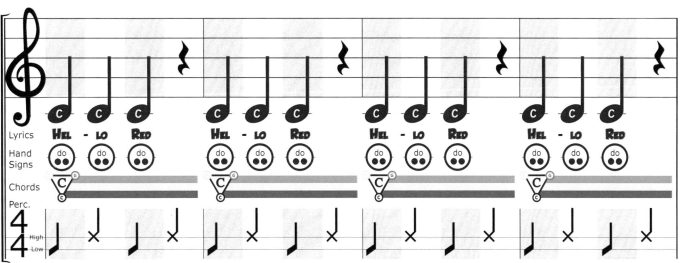

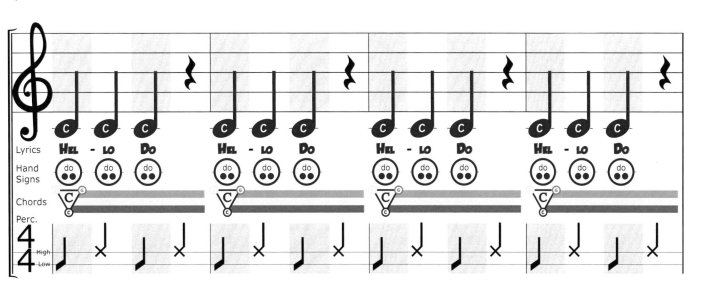

Doo Wop D
One Note Studies

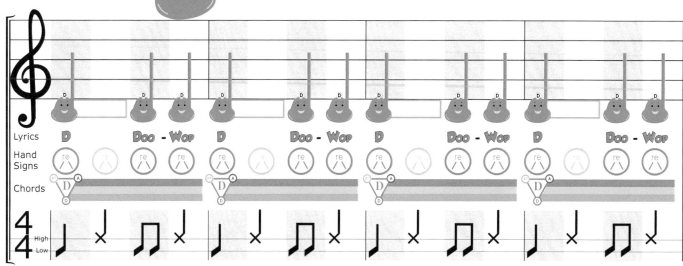

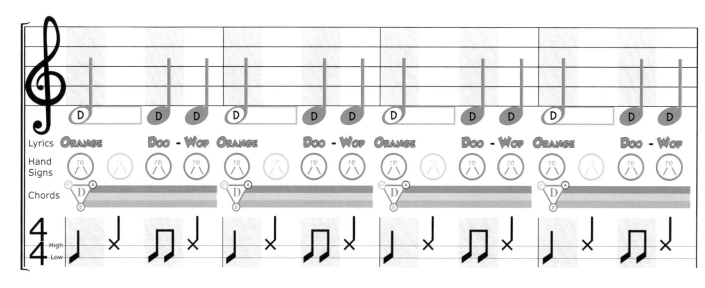

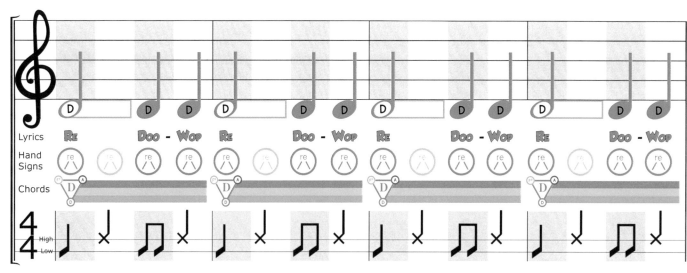

Hola E
One Note Studies

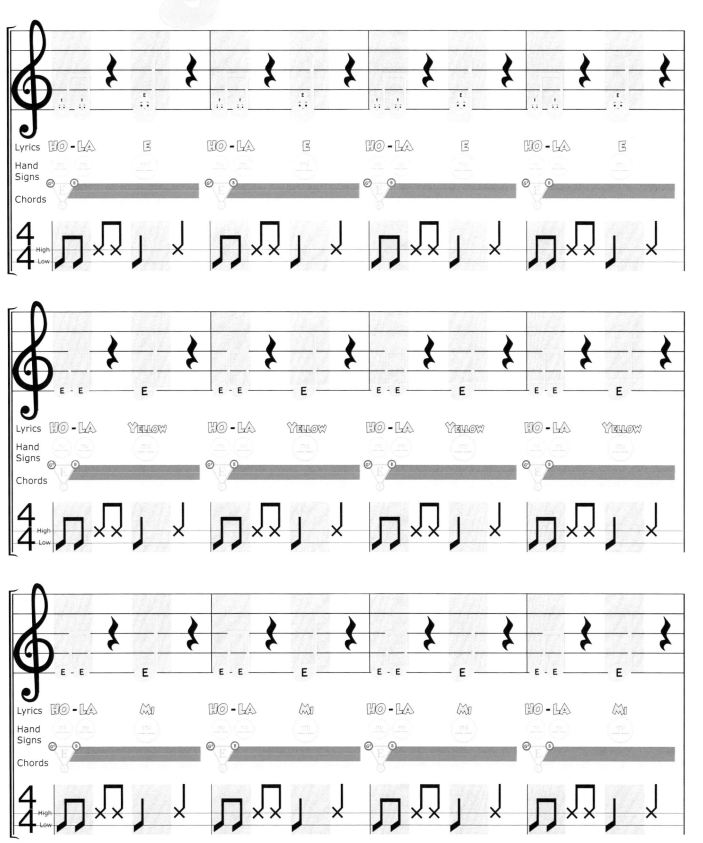

Fabulous F
One Note Studies

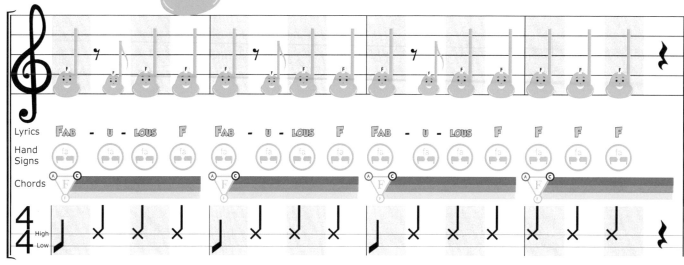

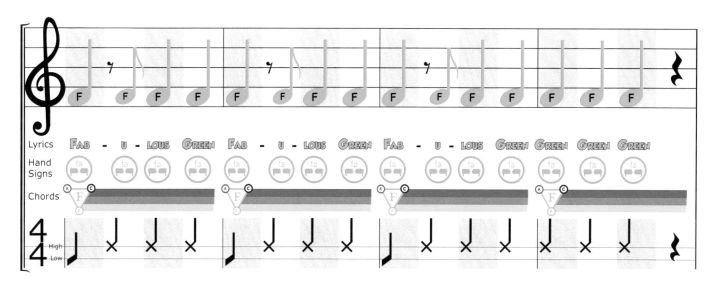

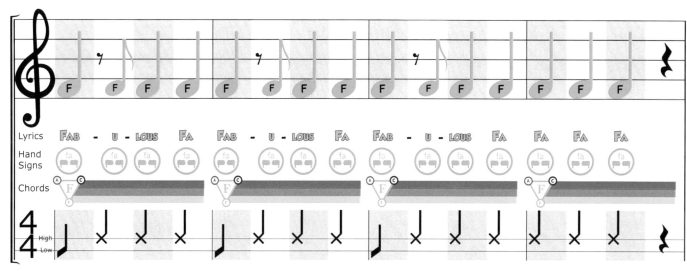

Gee-Oh-G
One Note Studies

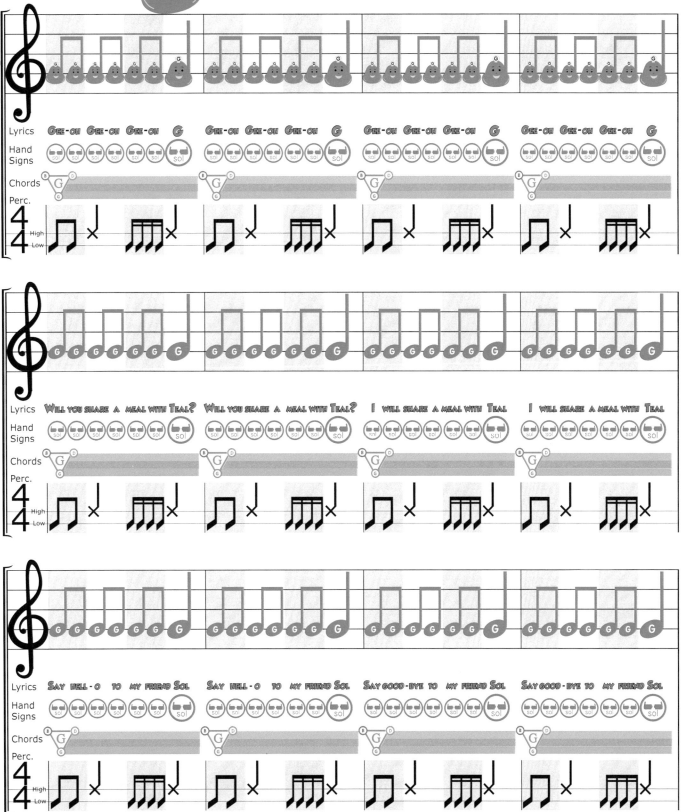

Aloha A
One Note Studies

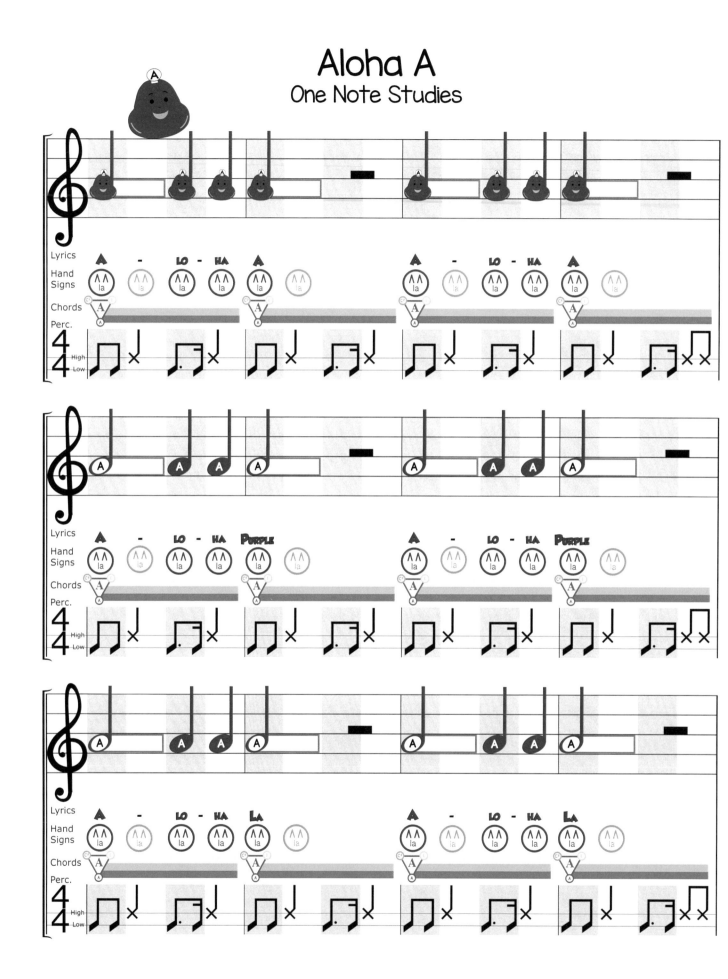

Bonjour B
One Note Studies

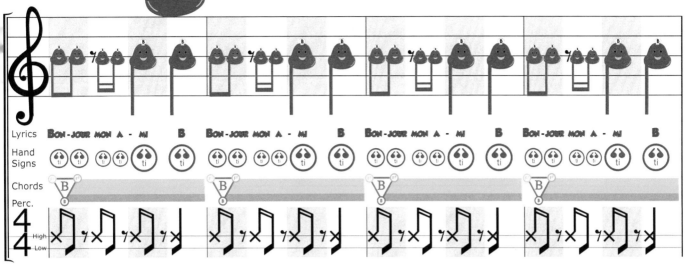

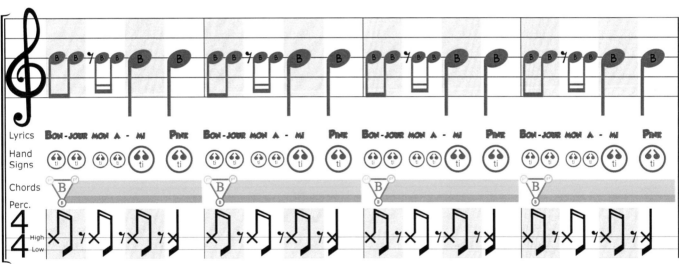

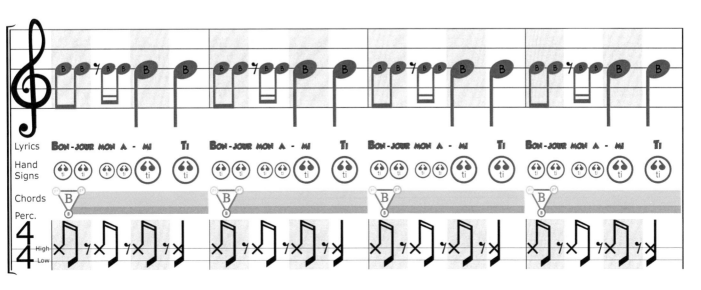

Hi High c
One Note Studies

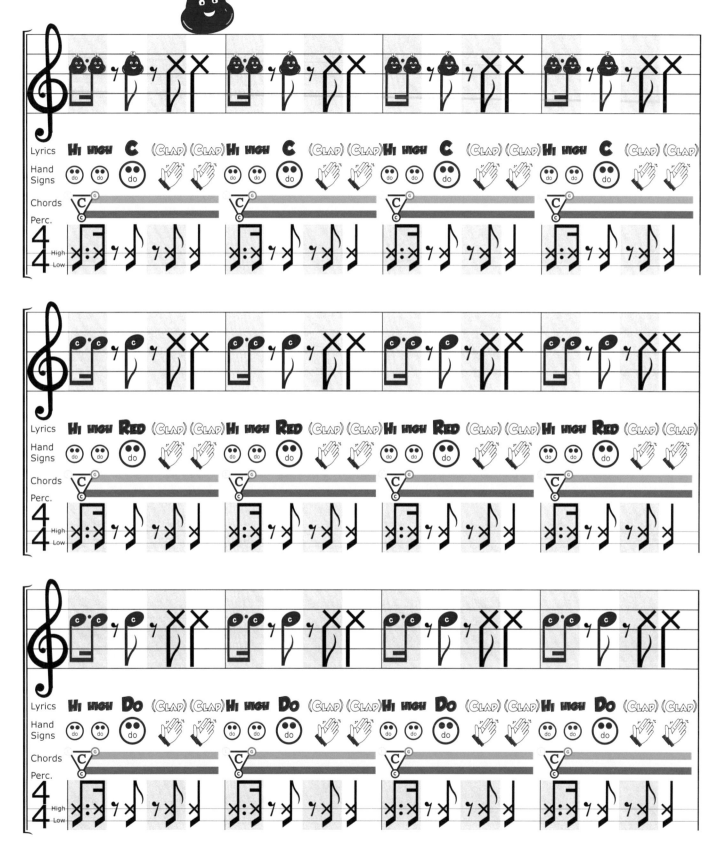

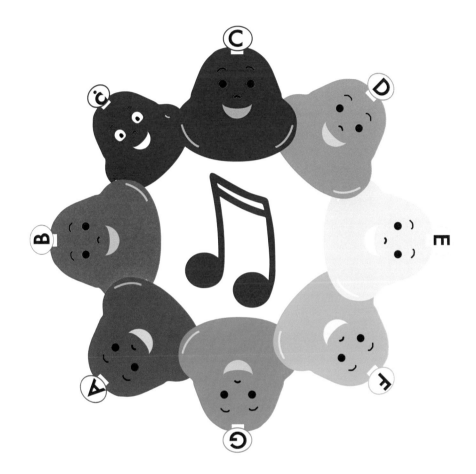

General Music Level 1A Workbook

CHAPTER TWO

2

Dear families & teachers,

Welcome back to the Prodigies Music Lessons Workbooks! It's time for more musical fun with Chapter Two.

In Chapter Two, we'll focus more on the concepts of low and high by introducing the High c bell. We'll also talk about left and right, and we'll continue to develop our understanding of C (Do) as our homebase note. Don't forget that we want to facilitate meaningful and memorable play with the different musical pitches so that your learner can develop a better understanding of pitch.

Like Chapter One, it is very important that you provide your learner with consistent, positive & fun opportunities to practice music. Your kids will benefit from a comfortable and encouraging practicing enviornment, and you are the perfect person to facilitate that for them!

Don't forget that the Playground videos that guide you through the book should be watched before AND after completing the workbook activities. Each section should be approached by watching the video, playing the sheet music, then completing the activities, and then circling back to watch or practice the sheet music again. It's important play the sheet music and the videos multiple times to provide lots of meaningful play with the notes, while also working on the physical skills needed for mastery of the song.

You'll also want to have your bells out while working through the books, that way you can play the sheet music and even play along with the activities as you play through the book.

As always, if you have any questions about the books or video content, we'd love to hear from you at Hello@.prodigies.com.

Happy Musicing!

– Mr. Rob & The Prodigies Team

Year 1, Week 9

Chapter 2 - Low C, High C
LEQ: How can a student distinguish between high and low sounds?

Week 9 Checklist

	Watched Video	Sang/Played Along	Played Sheet Music 1-3 times	Completed Workbook Activities	Repeat video 2-5 tiunes or as needed for mastery
Activator: What Note Is It #2	*		N/A	N/A	
Core Lesson: Low C, High c	*	*	*	*	
Performance: Low and High	*	*		N/A	
Review: Birds Fly				N/A	

* Suggested Priority Activity

I. Overview: In this lesson, students distinguish between high and low sounds in both music and their daily environments. Students play high and low C throughout this lesson.

II. Objective: By the end of this lesson, students should be able to distinguish between high and low C.

III. Activator: Students begin this lesson with the challenge of identifying high c and low C in "What Note Is It? #2".

Before beginning, the teacher should explain to students that they will work with high and low C in this lesson. Students will start by informally attempting to identify each. Students watch the video and call out their guesses. If students are unsure, that is okay; they will have many opportunities to practice in this lesson.

IV. Core Lesson: Students take out their low and high C bells to play along with "Low C, High C", students begin by singing and hand-signing.

Students should tap each bell along with Mr. Rob as the low and high C bells come across the screen!

After the video, the class should play through the sheet music for "Low C, High c" as a group (or in smaller stations if that works better for the group). The teacher should lead the students by conducting a slow and steady tempo, or using a metronome at 60-90 BPM to help keep the beat.

Year 1, Week 9

Chapter 2 - Low C, High c

LEQ: How can a student distinguish between high and low sounds?

After playing through the sheet music, students should complete the "Low C, High c" worksheet activities that review high and low sounds, review patterns and include a song-writing activity.

  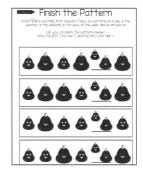 

V. Performance: As a group (or as assigned homework), students play along with "Low & High c", which features scrolling sheet music in the treble clef, as well as a handful of parts for other instruments (percussion, lyrics, hand-signs, chord arrangements, etc).

VI. Summarizer: If students played the performance together, the teacher should instruct students to share one thing they liked about the performance with the person next to them (or with the whole group).

Before moving onto the review lesson, the teacher should review today's lesson by asking students some or all of the following questions: *what is an example of a high sound?; what is an example of a low sound?; where does high C live on the staff?; where does low C live on the staff?*

VII. Review: As a final activity (or as homework), students watch "Birds Fly" featuring high and low Do. This is a fun sing along that gives students a chance to sing along with a song played with only high and low Do.

The teacher should explain to students that they will just play along with the scrolling sheet music the first time through until they learn the lyrics. Then after playing one time through, students sing the lyrics as well.

Low C, High c

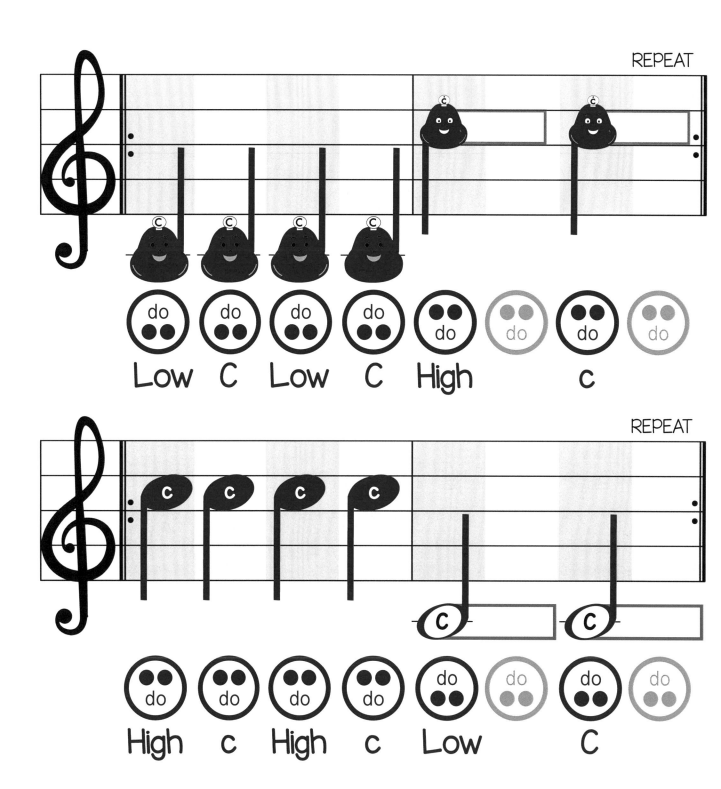

In this song, we're practicing with 2 red bells, Low C and High c.
Don't forget to **sing and play at the same time**! This helps build your musical ear. Also, don't forget to play each line TWO TIMES before moving onto the next line! That's why we have the repeat sign 𝄆 𝄇

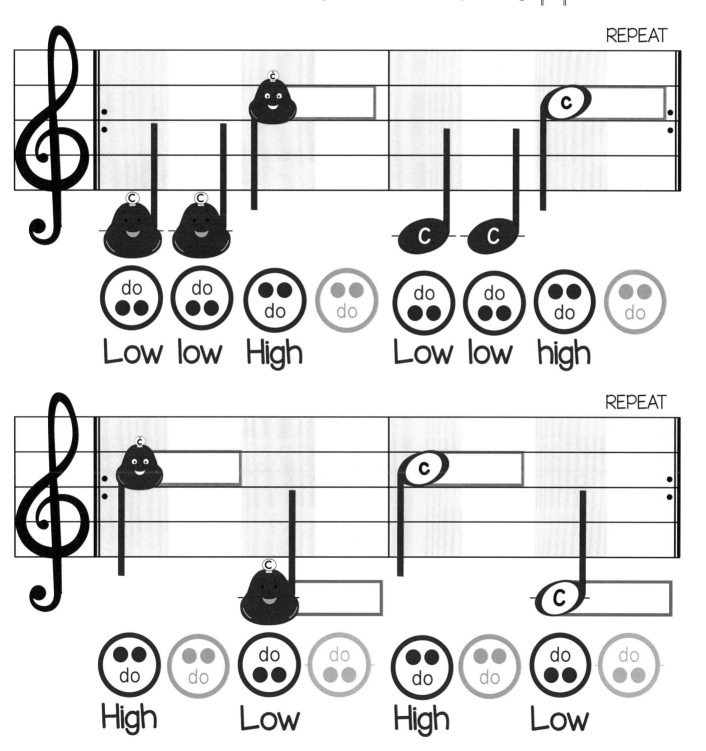

Red

High or Low?

Trace each name of each image below. Does it make a high sound or a low sound? Circle the answer!

lion

high or (low)

dolphin

high or low

dino

high or low

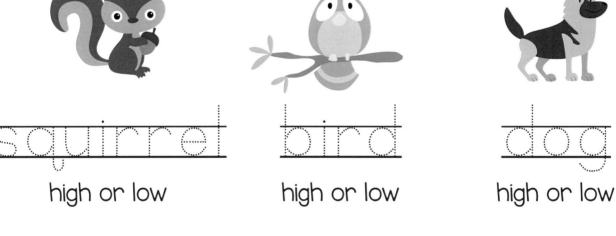

squirrel

high or low

bird

high or low

dog

high or low

truck

high or low

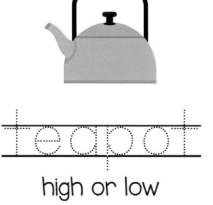

teapot

high or low

bear

high or low

High or Low?

Trace each name of each image below. Does it make a high sound or a low sound? Circle the answer!

boat

high or low

horn

high or low

whistle

high or low

triangle

high or low

drum

high or low

cat

high or low

grandma

high or low

cow

high or low

pirate

high or low

Finish the Pattern

A PATTERN is anything that repeats! There are patterns in music, in the weather, in the seasons, in the days of the week and all around us!

Can you complete the patterns below?
Cirlce the BIG C for low C, and the tiny c for high c.

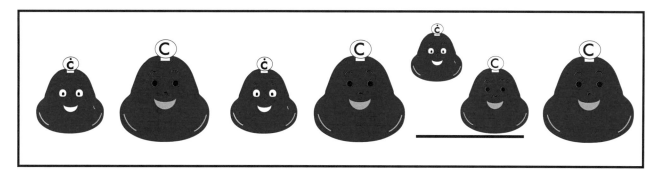

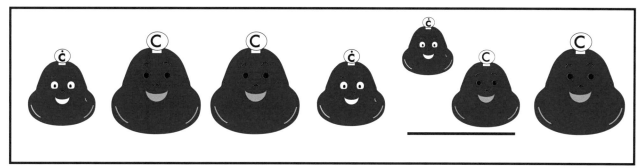

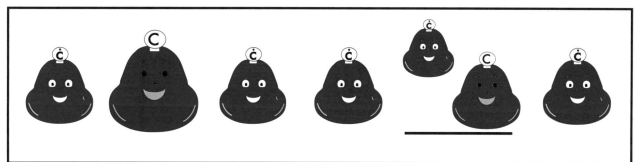

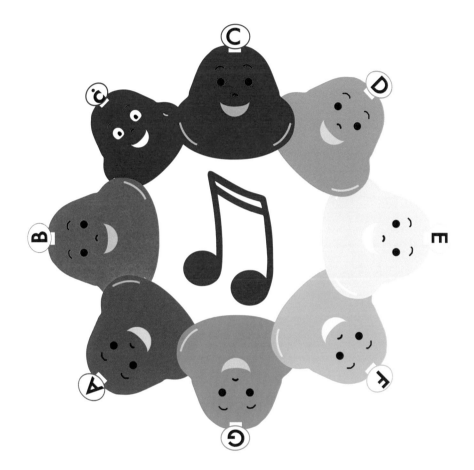

Write a Song

Trace the sound each bell makes, then cut out each square.
Next, paste the squares in the boxes to make a song. Play
your song with high and low C once it's pasted.

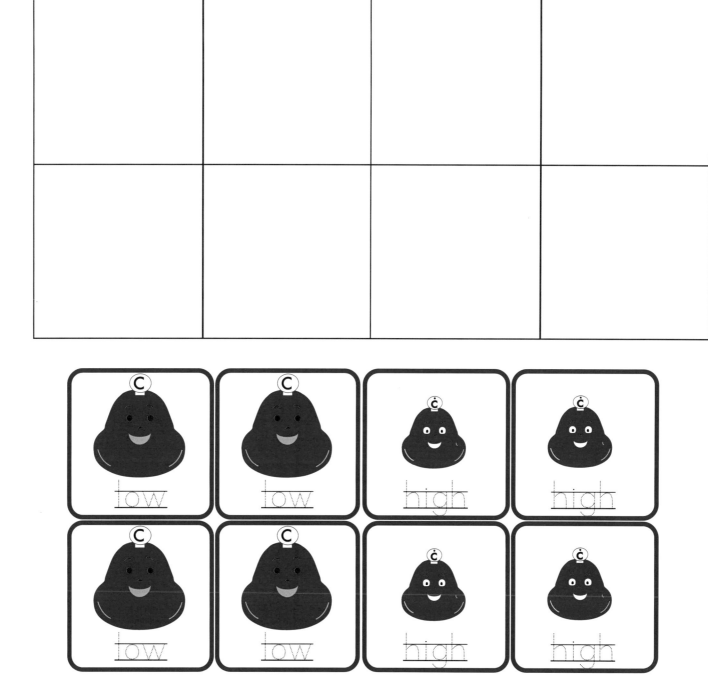

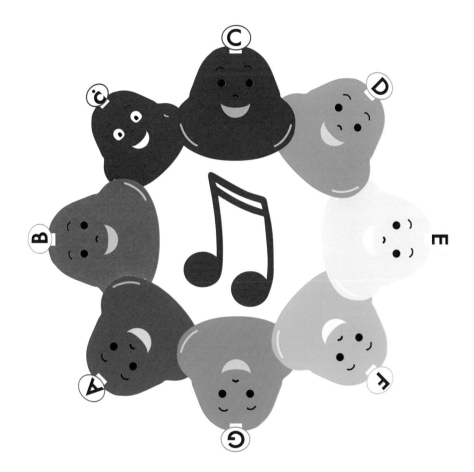

Low High
Low & High Studies

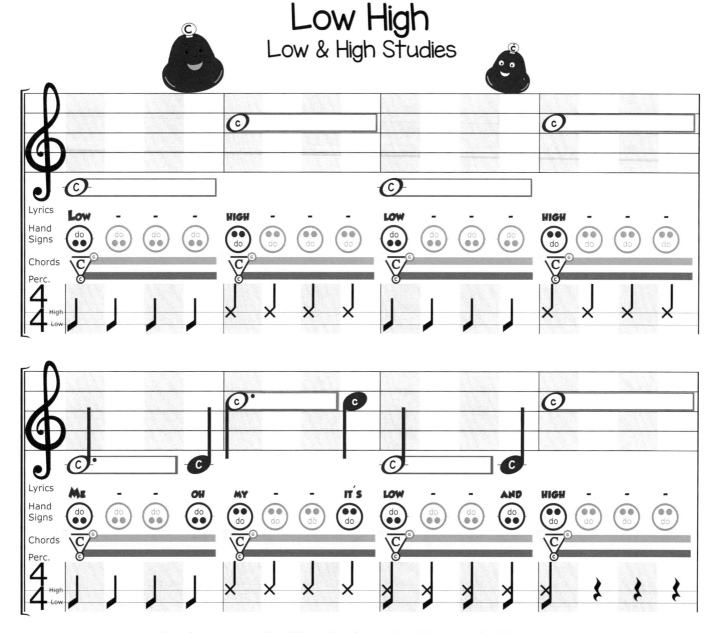

Performance Tip: Play the Low C with your LEFT Hand
& the High c with your RIGHT HAND

Birds Fly
Low & High Studies

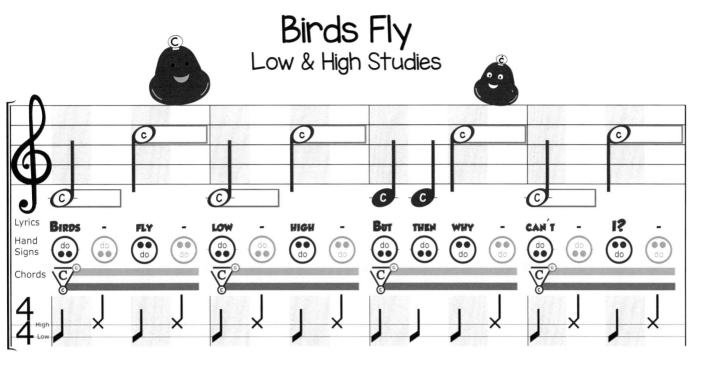

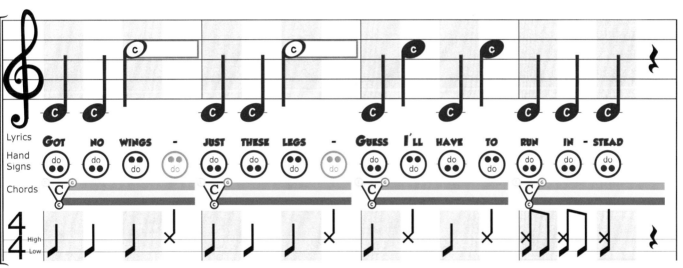

Year 1, Week 10

Chapter 2 - Left C, Right c

LEQ: How can a student distinguish between left and right?

Week 10 Checklist

	Watched Video	Sang/Played Along	Played Sheet Music 1-3 times	Completed Workbook Activities	Repeat video 2-5 tiunes or as needed for mastery
Activator: Beet & Watermelon	*		N/A	N/A	
Core Lesson: Left C, Right c	*	*	*	*	
Performance: Single Stroke Roll	*	*		N/A	
Review: One, Eight! They're Great!				N/A	

* Suggested Priority Activity

I. Overview: In this lesson, students will learn about left and right by playing the Low C/1 bell with the left hand, and the High c/8 bell with the right hand.

II. Objective: By the end of this lesson, students should be able to identify the C/1 bell on the left and the c/8 bell on the right.

III. Activator: Students begin this lesson with the next installment of Sweet Beets: "Beet & Watermelon". Students use "beet", "melon" and "watermelon" to represent the quarter, half and whole notes.

For the whole note, "watermelon", students roll their left and right hands very fast. Mr. Rob models this in the beginning of the video. For clarity, the teacher should model this along with the class and call attention to his or her left and right hands as s/he rolls the whole note.

IV. Core Lesson: Students take out their low and high C bells to play along with "Left C, Right c".

Students learn left and right at different paces--some students may already know the concept, and others will need to practice. If this video is challenging for students, the should play it again.

After the video, the class should play through the sheet music for "Left C, Right c" as a group (or in smaller stations if that works better for the group). The teacher should lead the students by conducting a slow and steady tempo, or using a metronome at 60-90 BPM to help keep the beat.

Year 1, Week 10

Chapter 2 - Left C, Right c

LEQ: How can a student distinguish between
left and right?

After playing through the sheet music, students should complete the "Left C, Right c"
worksheet activities that review left and right.

V. Performance: As a group (or as assigned homework), students play along with "Single Stroke
Roll", which features scrolling sheet music in the treble clef, as well as a handful of parts for
other instruments (percussion, lyrics, hand-signs, chord arrangements, etc).

VI. Summarizer: If students played the performance together, the teacher should
instruct students to share one thing they liked about the performance with the person next to
them (or with the whole group).

Before moving onto the review lesson, the teacher should review today's lesson by asking
students some or all of the following questions: *is the low C on the left side or the right side
of high C?; which hand is your left?; which hand is your right?; why is it helpful to know your
left from your right?*

VII. Review: As a final activity (or as homework), students play along with "One, Eight! They're
Great!" featuring high and low Do. This is a fun sing along that gives students a chance to
sing along with a song played with only high and low Do.

The teacher should explain to students that they should just play along with the scrolling
sheet music the first time through until they learn the lyrics. Then after playing one time
through, students sing the lyrics as well. The teacher should reinforce left and right by calling
out the hand that should be playing along with the sheet music.

Left C & Right c

REPEAT

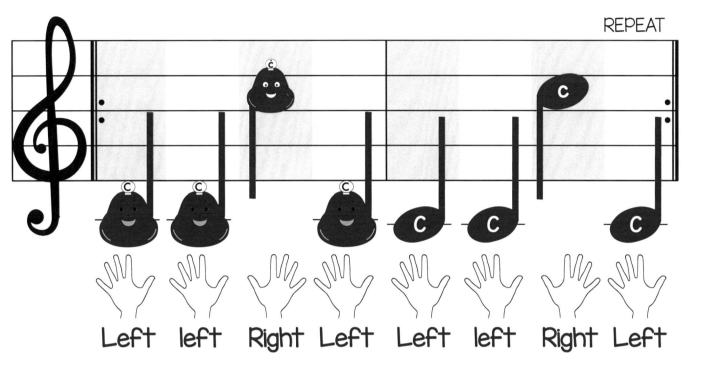

Left   left   Right   Left   Left   left   Right   Left

REPEAT

Right   Right   Left   Right   Right   Right   Left   Right

Left & Right

Trace the words "Left" and "Right". Draw a BIG C on the left hand. Draw a little c bell on the right hand. If you can, write an L or the word left on the left hand. If you can, right an R or the word right on the right hand.

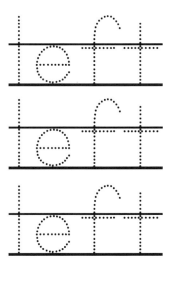

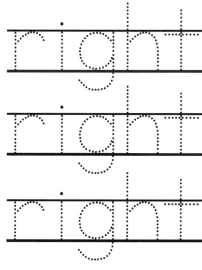

Left or Right?

Trace the words "left" and right", then follow the directions
in each box to circle one of each pair.

 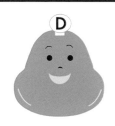

Circle the bell on the left.

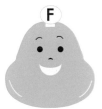 

Circle the bell on the right.

 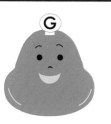

Circle the bell on the left.

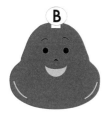 

Circle the bell on the right.

 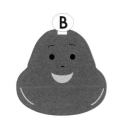

Circle the bell on the left.

Circle the bell on the right.

Circle the bell on the left.

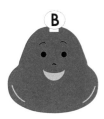 

Circle the bell on the right.

Direction

Some bells are looking left, others are looking right!

Circle the bells that are looking **left**!

Trace each word below:

Circle the bells that are looking **right**!

Trace each word below:

Red

Maze

Let the C bell guide you through the maze below!

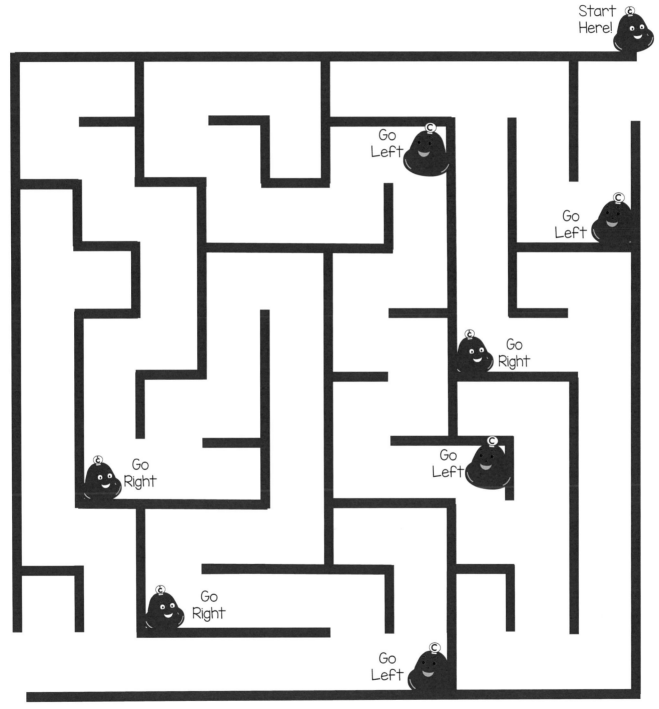

Start Here!

Go Left

Go Left

Go Right

Go Right

Go Left

Go Right

Go Left

You Made It!!!

2

3 Key Rudiments with Right (R) & Left (L)

1 Single Stroke Roll
Start slow with A (R L R L), repeating R L over and over. Speed up gradually until you can't go any faster. Then, repeat with B (L R L R).

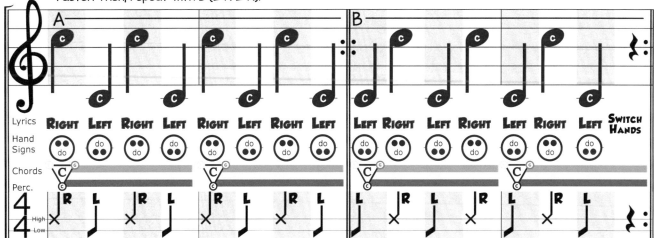

2 Double Stroke Roll
Start slow and speed up as you repeat

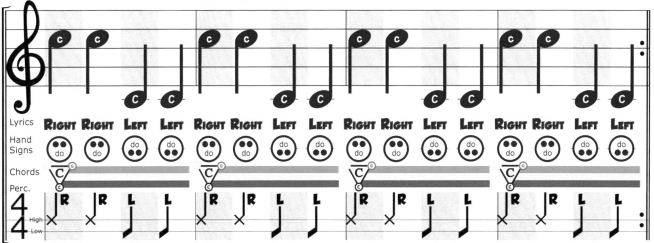

3 Paradiddle
Start slow and speed up as you repeat the paradiddle over and over.

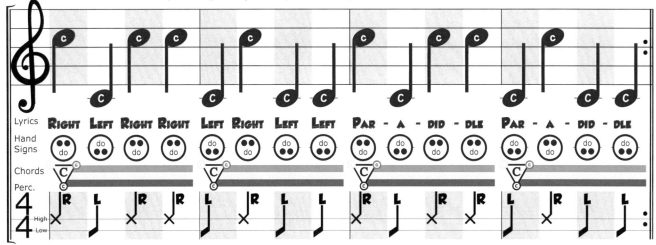

18 They're Great
Low & High Studies

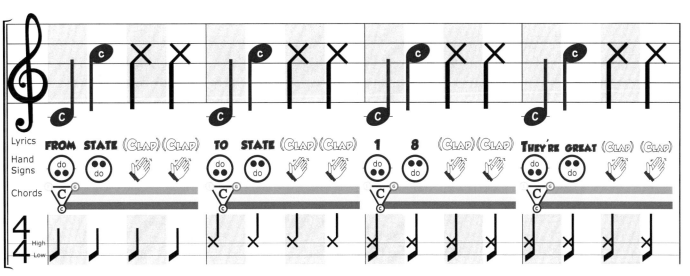

Year 1, Week 11

Chapter 2 - Low C or High c
LEQ: How can a student distinguish between low C and high C?

Week 11 Checklist

	Watched Video	Sang/Played Along	Played Sheet Music 1-3 times	Completed Workbook Activities	Repeat video 2-5 tiunes or as needed for mastery
Activator: Melodies #1	*		N/A	N/A	
Core Lesson: Low C or High c	*	*	*	*	
Performance: Paradiddle	*	*		N/A	
Review: Honu, Go Slow				N/A	

* Suggested Priority Activity

I. Overview: In this lesson, students will play a listening game that challenges them to differentiate between low and high C.

II. Objective: By the end of this lesson, students should be able to differentiate between low C and high C.

III. Activator: Students begin this lesson with the very first Melodies video. Melodies is the Prodigies singing and hand-signing series. The teacher should explain to students that before jumping into their main lesson today, they will review all of the hand-signs with Mr. Rob.

Students should hand-sign and sing the Solfege names as they scroll across the screen.

IV. Core Lesson: The teacher should explain to students that they won't need their bells for the core lesson today because "Low C or High c is a listening game! Students should listen carefully as each bell comes out of the pipe, and call out their guess before Mr. Rob identifies it.

The teacher can decide to varying the guesses a little bit: students could simply call out the answers, or they could work in pairs and share their guess with just their partner.

After the video, the class should play through the sheet music for "Low C or High c" as a group (or in smaller stations if that works better for the group). The teacher should lead the students by conducting a slow and steady tempo, or using a metronome at 60-90 BPM to help keep the beat.

Year 1, Week 11

Chapter 2 - Low C or High C?
LEQ: How can a student distinguish between
low C and high c?

After playing through the sheet music, students should complete the "Low C or High c" worksheet activities that review left and right and low and high sounds.

V. Performance: As a group (or as assigned homework), students play along with "Paradiddle", which features scrolling sheet music in the treble clef, as well as a handful of parts for other instruments (percussion, lyrics, hand-signs, chord arrangements, etc).

VI. Summarizer: If students played the performance together, the teacher should instruct students to share one thing they liked about the performance with the person next to them (or with the whole group).

Before moving onto the review lesson, the teacher should review today's lesson by asking students some or all of the following questions: *which number represents the low C?; which number represents the high c?; is the high c on the left side or the right side of low C?; what is an example of a high sound?; what is an example of a low sound?*

VII. Review: As a final activity (or as homework), students play along with "Honu, Go Slow" featuring high and low Do. This is a fun sing along that gives students a chance to sing along with a song played with only high and low Do.

The teacher should explain to students that they should just play along with the scrolling sheet music the first time through until they learn the lyrics. Then after playing one time through, students sing the lyrics as well. The teacher should reinforce left and right by calling out the hand that should be playing along with the sheet music.

Low C or High c?

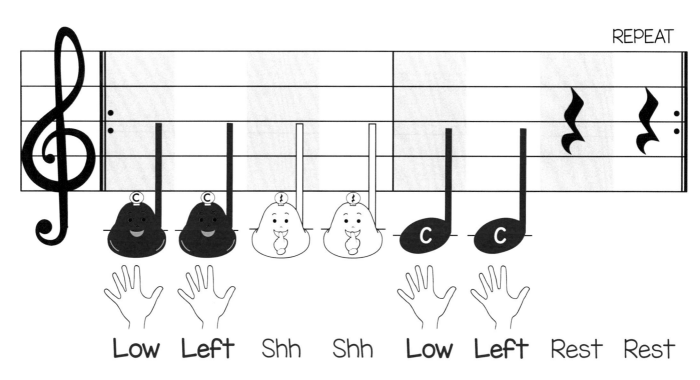

Low   Left   Shh   Shh   Low   Left   Rest   Rest

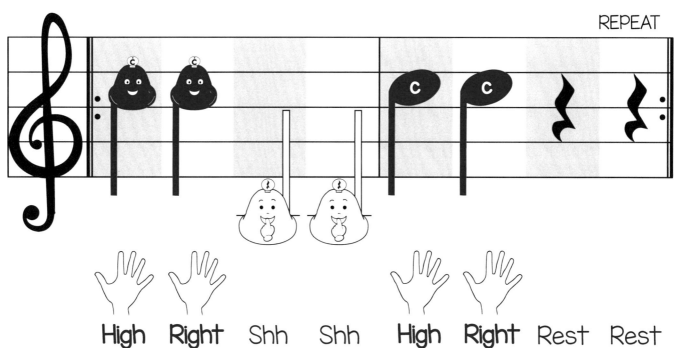

High   Right   Shh   Shh   High   Right   Rest   Rest

Patterns with Left & Right

Let's try some more patterns with Left (Low C) and Right (High c).
The patterns start out okay, but then we have some blank spaces!
Fill in the missing blocks with L or R to complete the pattern!
Then try playing the patterns on your bells.

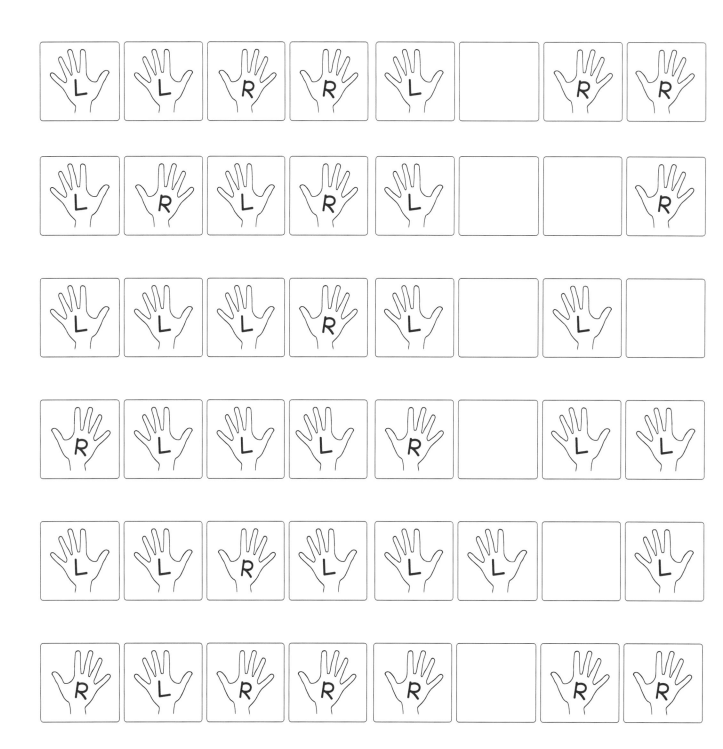

Lions and Birds

Let's play a listening game. You will need two people!
Player 1 has both red bells. Player 2 closes her eyes.
Player 1 plays 1 of the red bells, and then waits.
Player 2 listens, and tries to guess which bell they heard!
If you hear a low sound, circle the lion.
If you hear a high sound, circle the bird.
Play 8 rounds, then switch!

Listening Game Cards

Cut out the rectangles below. Then fold along the middle line and tape/glue a popsicle stick on the inside.
Now you can continue to play listening games like we did in the video and in Lions and Birds. Use your cards to answer and see who has the fastest ears!

Matching

Match Low C to the low sounds and match High c to the high sounds!

3 Key Rudiments with Right (R) & Left (L)

1 Single Stroke Roll
Start slow with A (R L R L), repeating R L over and over. Speed up gradually until you can't go any faster. Then, repeat with B (L R L R).

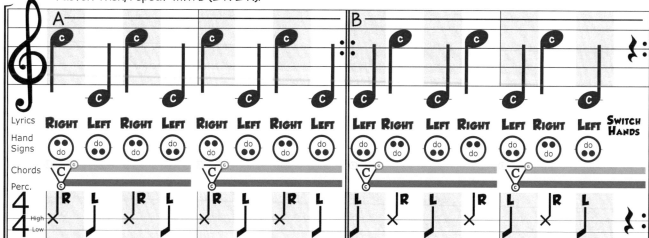

2 Double Stroke Roll
Start slow and speed up as you repeat

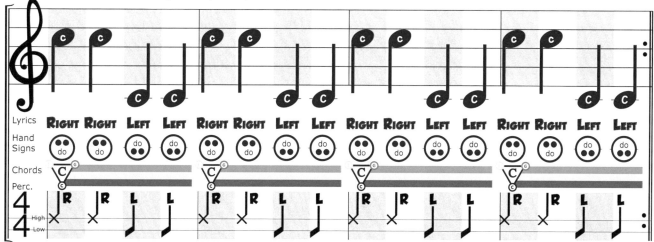

3 Paradiddle
Start slow and speed up as you repeat the paradiddle over and over.

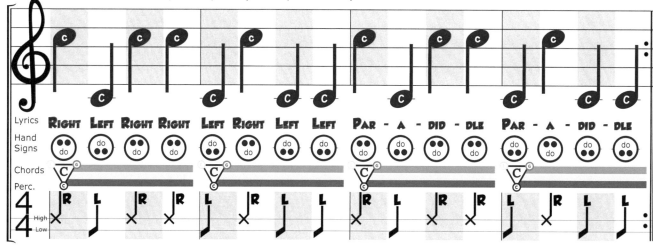

Honu Go Slow
Low & High Studies

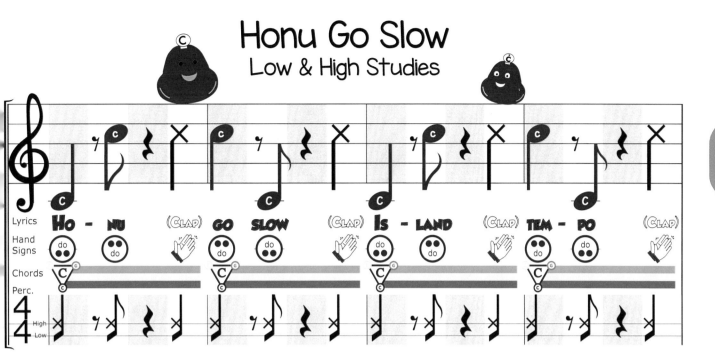

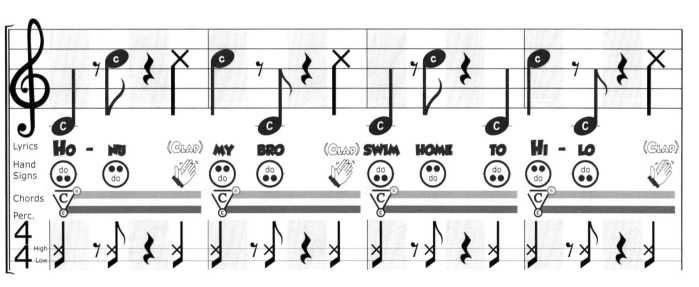

MELODY #1:
Do Re Mi Fa Sol La Ti Do

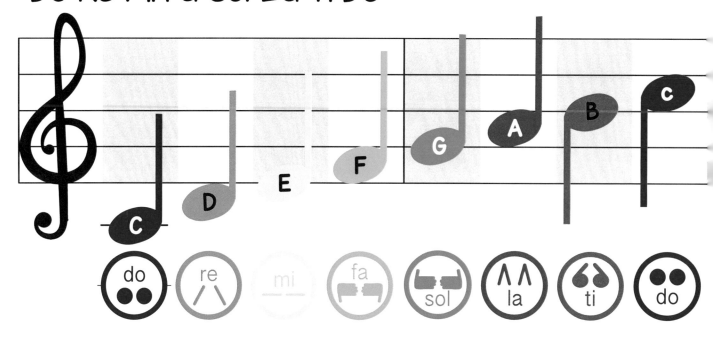

MELODY #2:
Do Ti La Sol Fa Mi Re Do

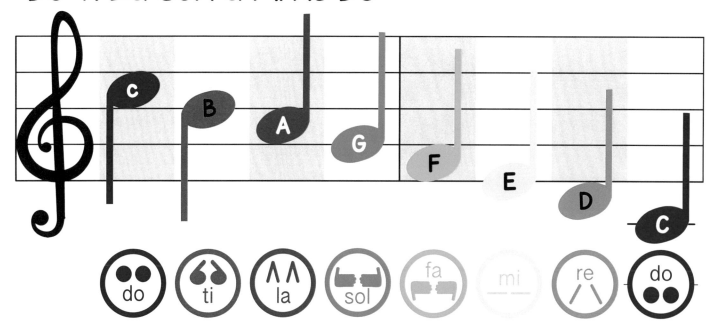

Quiz #1:

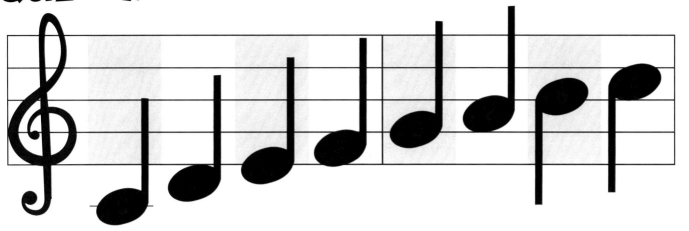

Part 1 : WHICH NOTE?
Write the notes on the blank lines!

___ ___ ___ ___ ___ ___ ___ ___

Part 2 : MIXED UP!
Match the Solfege Hand Signs to the notes above!

Quiz #2:

Part 1 : WHICH NOTE?
Write the notes on the blank lines!

___ ___ ___ ___ ___ ___ ___ ___

Part 2 : MIXED UP!
Match the Solfege Hand Signs to the notes above!

155

Year 1, Week 12

Chapter 2 - Beet & Cherry
LEQ: How are the eighth note and quarter note different?
Week 12 Checklist

	Watched Video	Sang/Played Along	Played Sheet Music 1-3 times	Completed Workbook Activities	Repeat video 2-5 tiunes or as needed for mastery
Activator: Double Stroke Roll	*			N/A	
Core Lesson: Beet & Cherry	*	*	*	*	
Performance: Stomp Stomp Clap	*	*		N/A	
Review: Do, Mi Stars (Extra Practice)			N/A	N/A	

* Suggested Priority Activity

I. Overview: In this lesson, students will add eighth notes to their rhythm practice. Students will practice singing and clapping eighth notes and quarter notes.

II. Objective: By the end of this lesson, students should be able to clap, tap or stomp both a quarter note and an eighth note rhythm.

III. Activator: Students begin by playing "Double Stroke Roll". Students will play both high and low C during this activator. The teacher may want to encourage students to play along with a metronome, and slowly increase the speed as students are ready.

IV. Core Lesson: The teacher should explain to students that they won't need their bells for the core lesson today and instead should clap, tap or stomp along with "Beet & Cherry". Today's lesson is all about rhythm!

After the video, the class should clap, tap or stomp through the sheet music for "Beet & Cherry" as a group (or in smaller stations if that works better for the group). The teacher should lead the students by conducting a slow and steady tempo, or using a metronome at 60-90 BPM to help keep the beat.

Year 1, Week 12

Chapter 2 - Beet & Cherry

LEQ: How are the eighth note and quarter note different?

After playing through the sheet music, students should complete the "Beet & Cherry" worksheet activities that review ta and ti-ti, counting and eighth notes.

V. Performance: As a group (or as assigned homework), students play along with "Stomp, Stomp, Clap", which features scrolling sheet music in the treble clef, as well as a handful of parts for other instruments (percussion, lyrics, hand-signs, chord arrangements, etc.).

VI. Summarizer: If students played the performance track together, the teacher should instruct students to share one thing they liked about the performance with the person next to them (or with the whole group).

Before moving onto the review lesson, the teacher should review today's lesson by asking students some or all of the following questions: *Which note has more claps--eighth or quarter note?; Which note is represented by the word "beet" in this lesson?; Which note is represented by the word "cherry" in this lesson"?*

VII. Review: As a final activity (or as homework), students sing, play and hand-sign along with "Do, Mi Stars" (Extra Practice). This video gives students a chance to bring both Do and Mi into their rhythm practice. This video uses the concept of short and long stars like in Chapter One to give students additional practice with rhythm.

Beet & Cherry

☆★☆☆☆

Sing the chorus to Sweet Beets while tapping a steady beat. Then in the verses, tap, clap or stomp with Beet and Cherry.

CHORUS 1

Sweet Beets, we've got some!

If you want some Sweet Beets, we've got 'em.

If you want Sweet Beets, we've got some,

If you want some Sweet Beets, we've got 'em.

VERSE 1

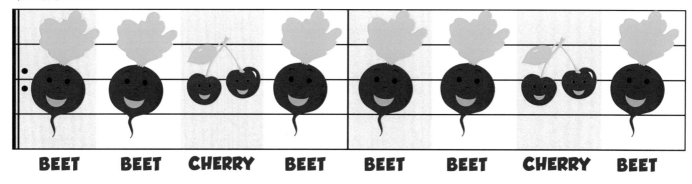

| BEET | BEET | CHERRY | BEET | BEET | BEET | CHERRY | BEET |

REPEAT

| CHERRY | CHERRY | BEET | BEET | CHERRY | CHERRY | BEET | BEET |

CHORUS 2

Sweet Beets, we've got some!
If you want some Sweet Beets, we've got 'em.
If you want Sweet Beets, we've got some,
If you want some Sweet Beets, we've got 'em.

VERSE 2

CHERRY   BEET   CHERRY   BEET   CHERRY   BEET   CHERRY   BEET

REPEAT

CHERRY CHERRY CHERRY BEET   CHERRY CHERRY CHERRY BEET

CHORUS 3

Sweet Beets, we've got some!
If you want some Sweet Beets, we've got 'em.
If you want Sweet Beets, we've got some,
If you want some Sweet Beets, we've got 'em.

VERSE 3

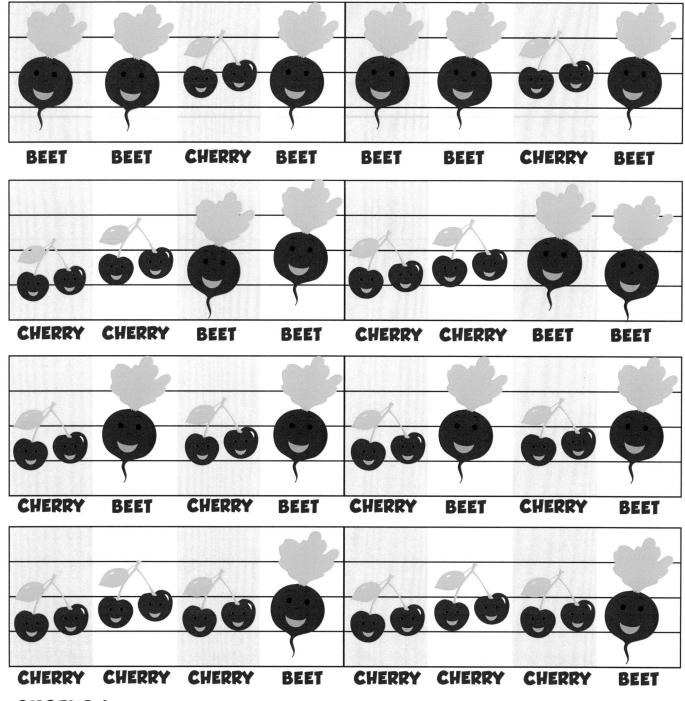

| BEET | BEET | CHERRY | BEET | BEET | BEET | CHERRY | BEET |

| CHERRY | CHERRY | BEET | BEET | CHERRY | CHERRY | BEET | BEET |

| CHERRY | BEET | CHERRY | BEET | CHERRY | BEET | CHERRY | BEET |

| CHERRY | CHERRY | CHERRY | BEET | CHERRY | CHERRY | CHERRY | BEET |

CHORUS 4

Sweet Beets, we've got some!

If you want some Sweet Beets, we've got 'em.

If you want Sweet Beets, we've got some,

If you want some Sweet Beets, we've got 'em.

Tas & Ti-Tis

You can also play rhythms with short syllables like Ta and Ti-Ti. Try singing, tapping, clapping or stomping your way through the rhythms below.

Eighth Notes

Did you notice that the Cherry (Ti Ti) only take up one space in the measure? Even though they make two sounds, they still only take up the space of one Beet (Ta). That's because they are eighth notes.

Eighth notes are a faster type of note. It takes 2 eighth notes to fill one beat and 8 eighth notes to fill one full measure. You may have noticed when we were singing Sweet Beets that we sang and clapped "cherry" faster than "beet".

Practice drawing eighth notes below.

How Many Beats?

Each gray box represents one musical space (beat) in the measure. Most of the measures we'll see have four beats in them, but sometimes there are more or less. Count the number of beats in each measure below and write the number in each space to the right.

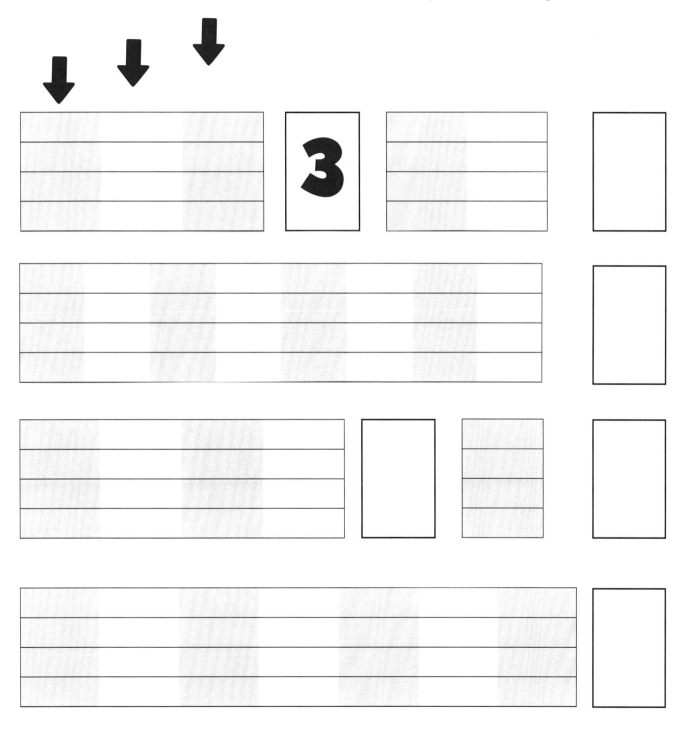

Write Your Own Rhythm

On the staffs below, write your own rhythm practice
using either quarter notes & eighth notes or beets & cherries. Clap,
stomp, beat or snap your rhythm once you've recorded it below.

Stomp Stomp Clap
Low & High Studies

Year 1, Week 13

Chapter 2 - C Sock Slide

LEQ: How can a student differentiate left from right?

Week 13 Checklist

	Watched Video	Sang/Played Along	Played Sheet Music 1-3 times	Completed Workbook Activities	Repeat video 2-5 tiunes or as needed for mastery
Activator: Stomp Stomp Clap	*			N/A	
Core Lesson: C Sock Slide	*	*	*	*	
Performance: Two Foot Stomp	*	*		N/A	
Extenstion: Re Fa Stars (Extra Practice)			N/A	N/A	

* Suggested Priority Activity

I. Overview: In this lesson, students continue to practice with left and right and high and low C, but this time, with their feet.

II. Objective: By the end of this lesson, students should be able to distinguish left from right.

III. Activator: Students begin today's lesson by reviewing the performance from the previous lesson: "Stomp Stomp Clap". This will prime students for today's core lesson in which they play the bells with their feet.

IV. Core Lesson: The teacher should explain to students that they will be playing high and low C a little differently today--with their feet! In "C Sock Slide", students sit in a chair and set the bells below them, so that they can play with their feet.

While this lesson may seem a little silly at first, students will have fun playing with their feet and it is a great opportunity to reinforce left and right with young students.

After the video, students should complete the letter trace and then play the Bell Stomp activity to follow up with "C Sock Slide" as a group (or in smaller stations if that works better for the group). The teacher should lead the students by conducting a slow and steady tempo, or using a metronome at 60-90 BPM to help keep the beat.

Year 1, Week 13

Chapter 2 - C Sock Slide

LEQ: How can a student differentiate left from right?

After playing through the sheet music, students should complete the "C Sock Slide" worksheet activities that review left and right and the C note.

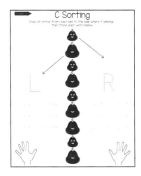
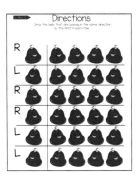
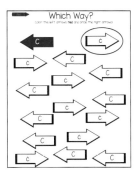
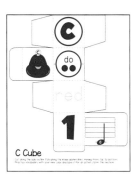

V. Performance: As a group (or as assigned homework), students play along with "Two foot Stomp", which features scrolling sheet music in the treble clef, as well as a handful of parts for other instruments (percussion, lyrics, hand-signs, chord arrangements, etc.).

VI. Summarizer: If students played the performance together, the teacher should instruct students to share one thing they liked about the performance with the person next to them (or with the whole group).

Before moving onto the extension lesson, the teacher should review today's lesson by asking students some or all of the following questions: *Which number represents the high c?; Which number represents the low C?; Which C lives on the left side of the C major scale?; Which C lives on the right side of the C major scale?*

VII. Extension: As a final activity (or as homework), students sing and hand-sign along with "Re Fa Stars". Throughout this chapter, students get a lot of practice with low and high c. In this extension activity, students review the notes D and F.

The teacher can connect this activity to the core lesson by instructing students to play the D bell with their left hand and the F bell with their right. By playing these two other notes in the C Major scale, students have a chance to compare and differentiate the sounds low C and high c with other notes.

C Sock Slide

☆☆☆☆☆

Trace the capital letters L and R, and then play this song with your feet!

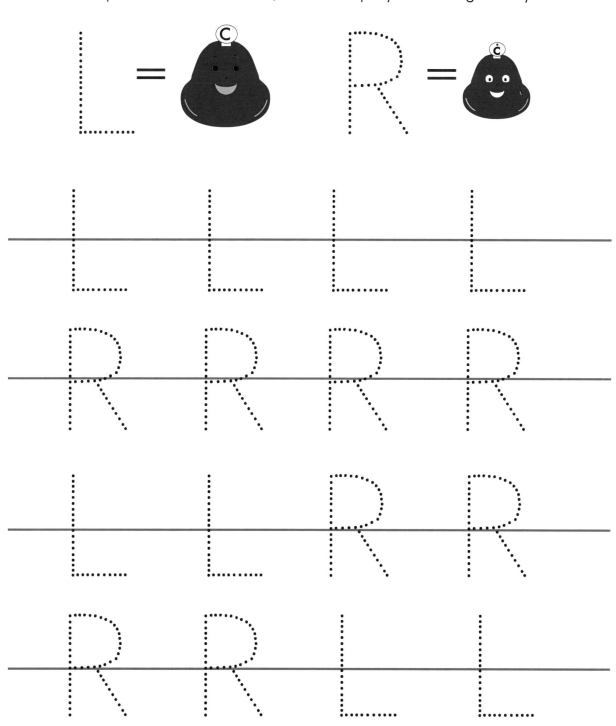

The pattern of left and right on this page is a famous rhythm called the paradiddle.

Can you play and memorize the paraddidle?

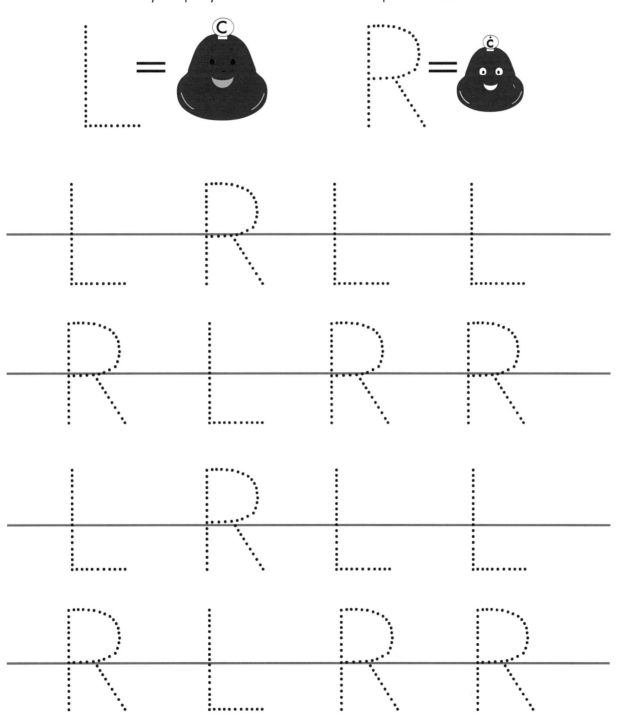

C Sorting

Draw an arrow from each bell to the side where it belongs,
then trace each word below.

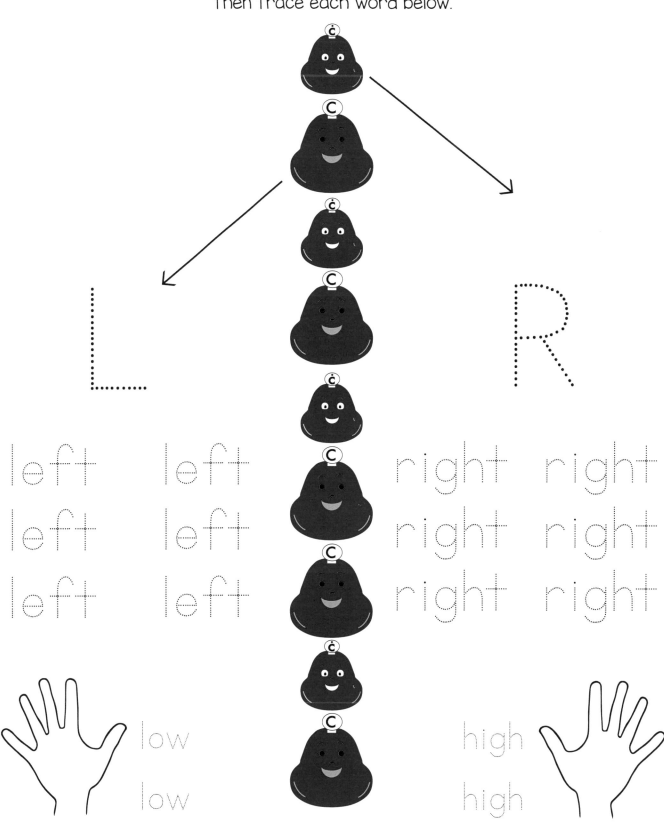

L   R

left   left   right   right
left   left   right   right
left   left   right   right

low   high
low   high

Directions

Circle the bells that are looking in the same direction
as the first in each row.

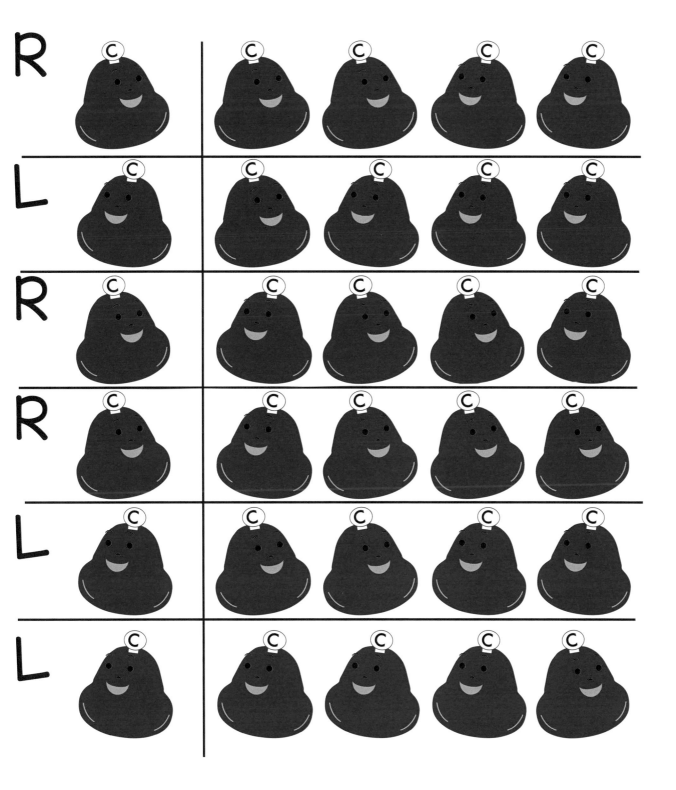

Which Way?

Color the left arrows **red** and circle the right arrows!

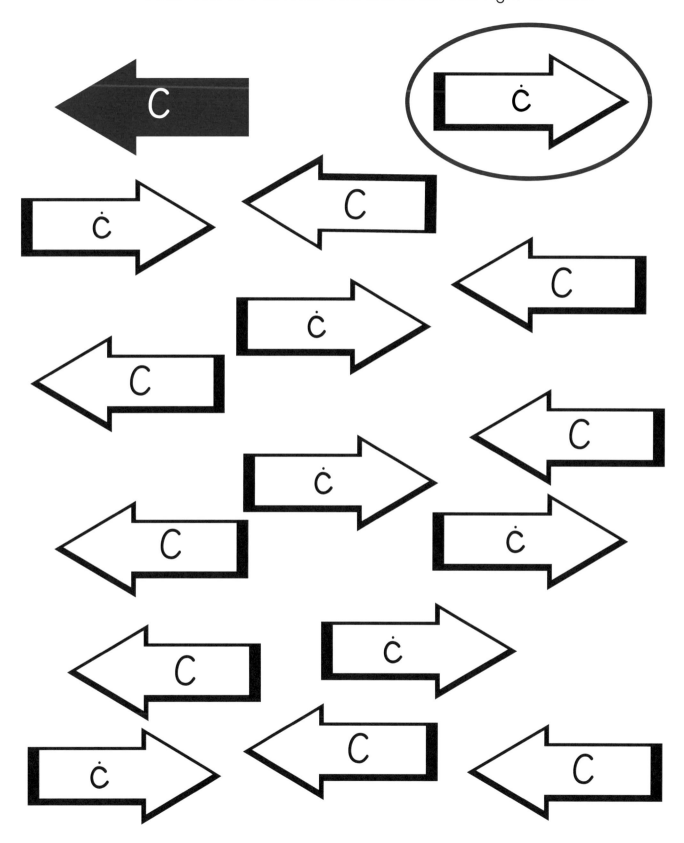

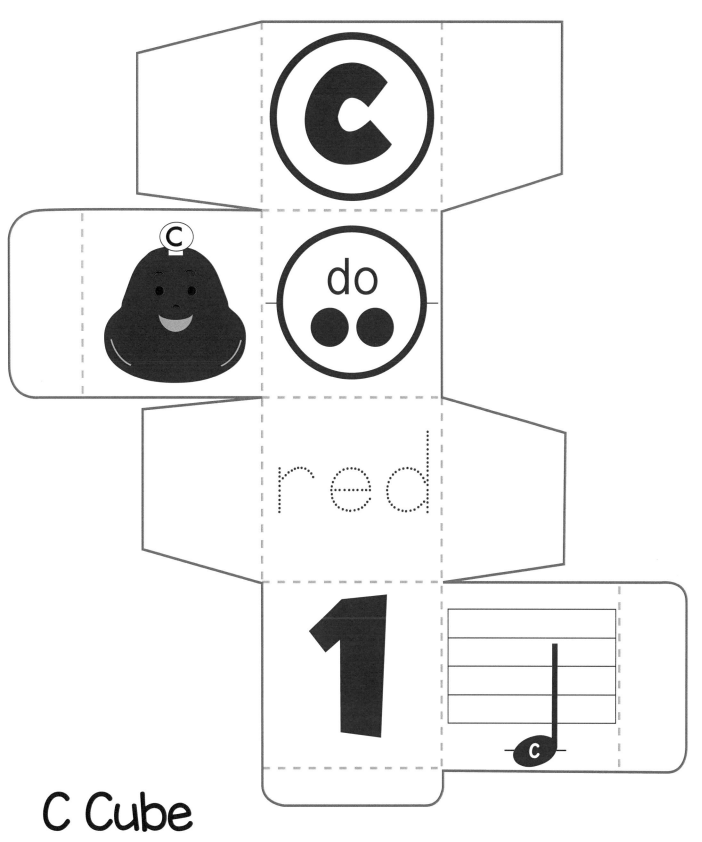

C Cube

Cut along the solid outline. Fold along the inside dashed lines, moving from top to bottom. Practice vocabulary with your new cube and save it for an activity later this section!

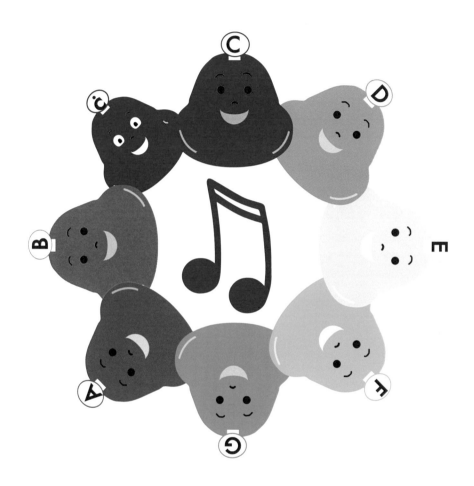

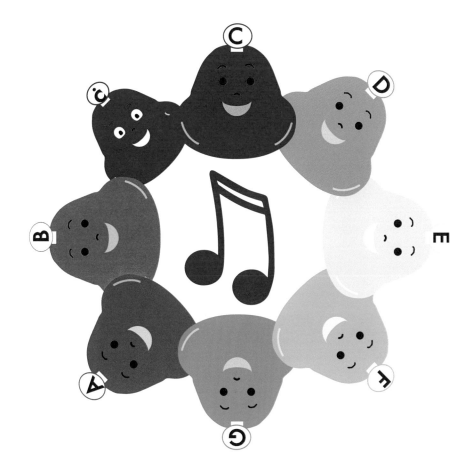

Two Foot Stomp
Low & High Studies

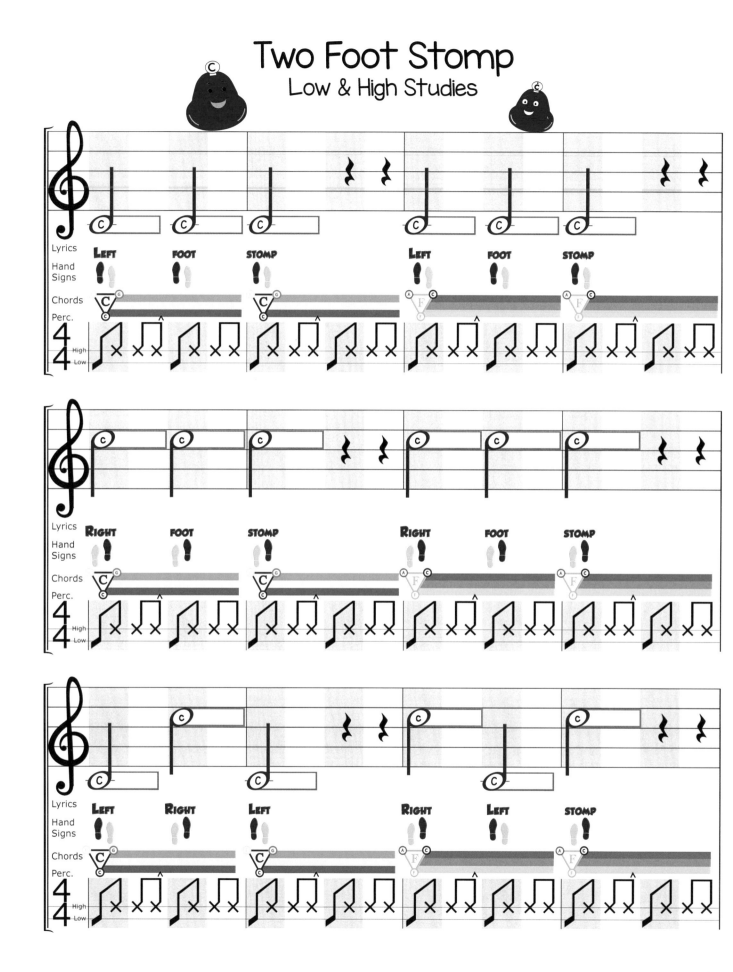

Year 1, Week 14

Chapter 2 - C Chord Slide

LEQ: How can a student build a C Major Chord?

Week 14 Checklist

	Watched Video	Sang/Played Along	Played Sheet Music 1-3 times	Completed Workbook Activities	Repeat video 2-5 tiunes or as needed for mastery
Activator: Do Mi Sol Slide	*		N/A	N/A	
Core Lesson: C Chord Slide	*	*	*	*	
Performance: Mi, Sol Stars (Extra Practice)	*		N/A	N/A	
Review: What Note Is It? # 1	*		N/A	N/A	

＊ Suggested Priority Activity

I. Overview: In this lesson, students review the C Major chord they learned in Chapter One. This time, they add the high c to the C major chord.

II. Objective: By the end of this lesson, students should be able to build a C Major chord and sing with Do, Mi, Sol, and High Do.

III. Activator: Students begin today's lesson by reviewing the video from the Chapter One lesson: "Do Mi Sol Slide". This will activate students' prior knowledge of the C Major chord.

IV. Core Lesson: The teacher should explain to students that they will play the C Major chord today in "C Chord Slide", where they play multiple notes at the same time and expand their understanding of the C Major chord.

Students may need to experiment a bit with the positioning of their hands in order to play multiple bells at one time comfortably. Once students have their 1, 3, 5 & 8 bells out in front them, the teacher should give them a bit to experiment with what feels best.

After the video, students should play along with the sheet music for "C Chord Slide" as a group (or in smaller stations if that works better for the group). The teacher should lead the students by conducting a slow and steady tempo, or using a metronome at 60-90 BPM to help keep the beat.

Year 1, Week 14

Chapter 2 - C Chord Slide

LEQ: How can a student build a C Major Chord?

After playing through the sheet music, students should complete the "C Chord Slide" worksheet activities that review Do, Mi and Sol.

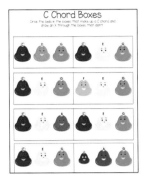 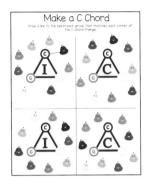  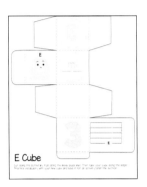

V. Performance: As a group (or as assigned homework), students play along with "Mi, Sol Stars" (Extra Practice). While this isn't one of the usual performances, it gives students a chance to continue practice with Mi and Sol. Alternatively, students can perform the sheet music for "C Chord Slide" in small groups or in front of the whole class.

VI. Summarizer: If students played the performance together, the teacher should instruct students to share one thing they liked about the performance with the person next to them (or with the whole group).

Before moving onto the extension lesson, the teacher should review today's lesson by asking students some or all of the following questions: *Which notes belong in the C chord?; Which color represents the note Mi?; Which number represents the note E?*

VII. Review: As a final activity (or as homework), students play another round of the listening game "What Note Is It? #1". This will test their ear and ability to memorize the notes of the C major chord and be a good warm up for "What Note Is It # 2" in the final lesson in Chapter 2.

Before the students begin the listening activity, the teacher should ask students to think about which note was most difficult to identify last time they participated in this listening activity, and to think about how it may be more or less difficult this time around and why.

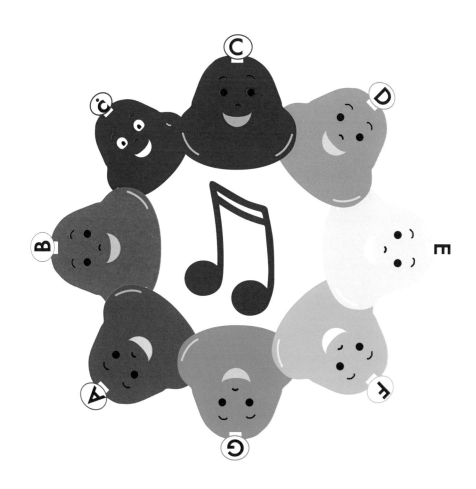

Do Mi Sol do Bell Mat

Use this bell mat when practicing the 2.5 lesson.

C / 1

E / 3

G / 5

C / 8

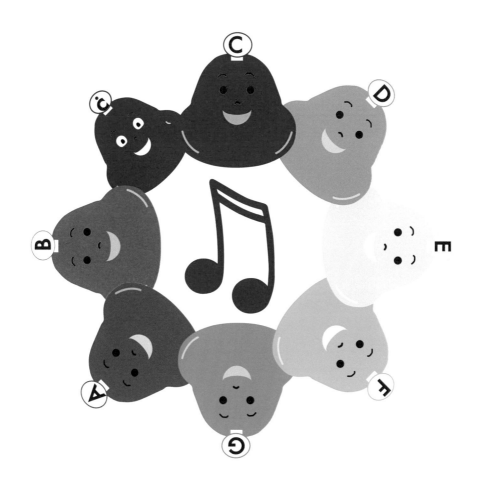

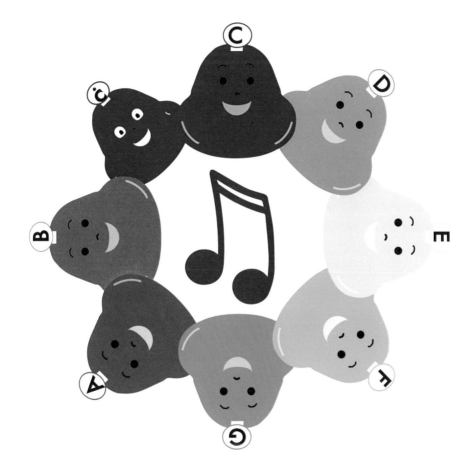

C Chord Slide

Play this song very SLOWLY as you carefully listen to the many different ways of playing the C Major Chord.

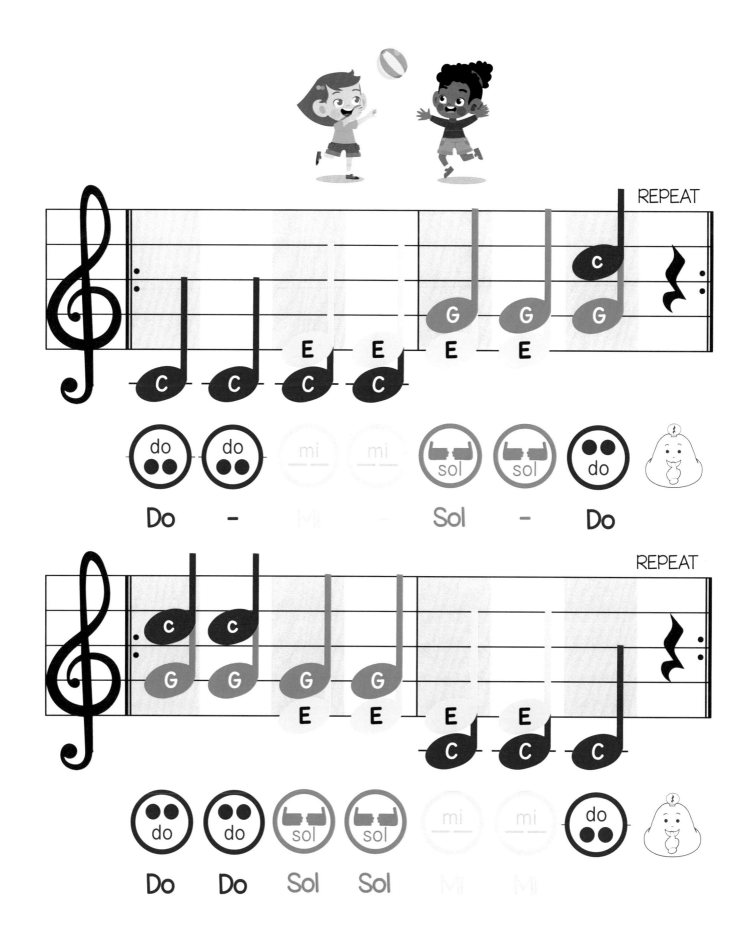

REPEAT

REPEAT

C Chord Boxes

Circle the bells in the boxes that make up a C chord and
draw an X through the boxes that don't.

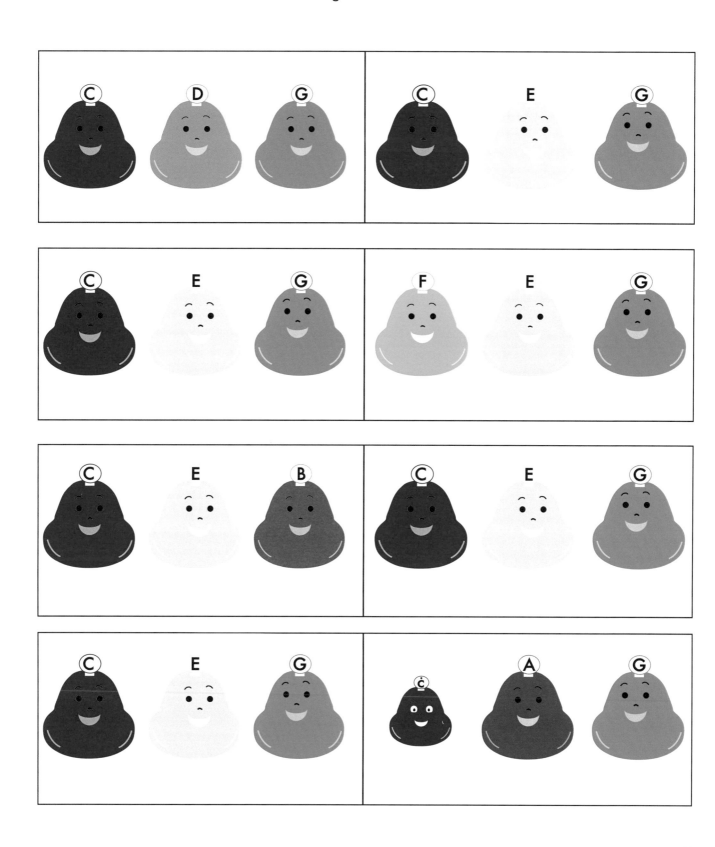

Make a C Chord

Draw a line to the bell in each group that matches each corner of the C chord triangle.

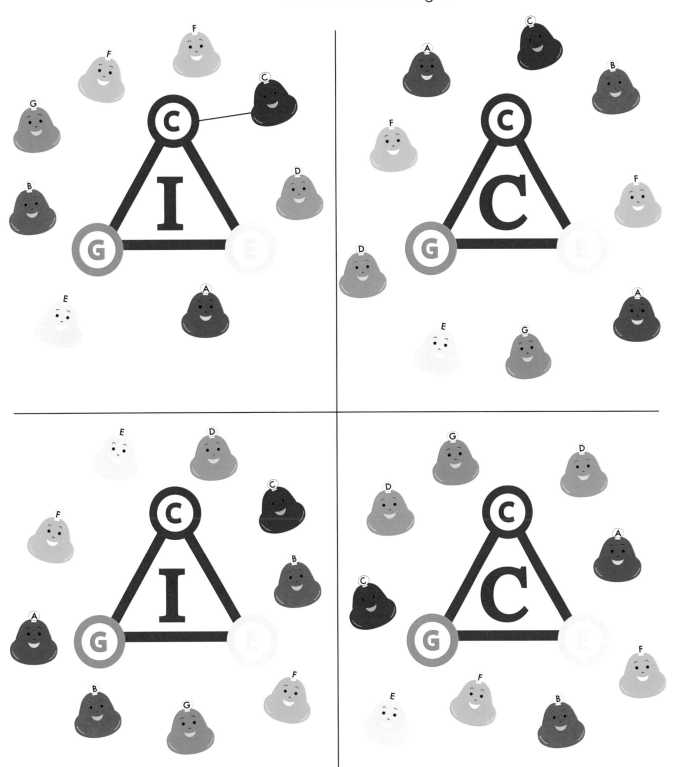

C Chord Trees

Circle the trees that make a C Chord. It's okay if the notes are out of order - they can still make a C chord! Then draw an X through the trees that are not C Chords.

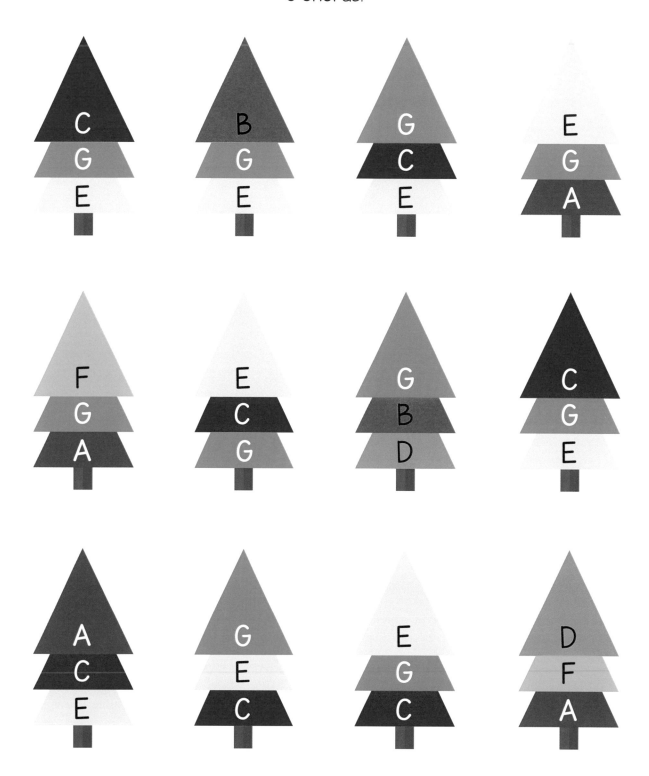

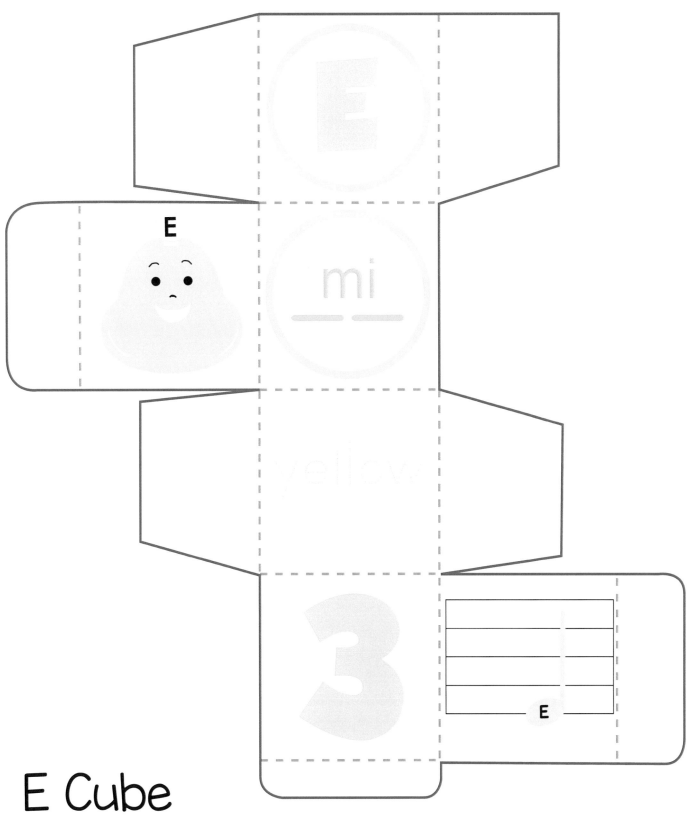

E Cube

Cut along the solid outline. Fold along the inside dashed lines, moving from top to bottom.
Practice vocabulary with your new cube and save it for an activity later this section!t

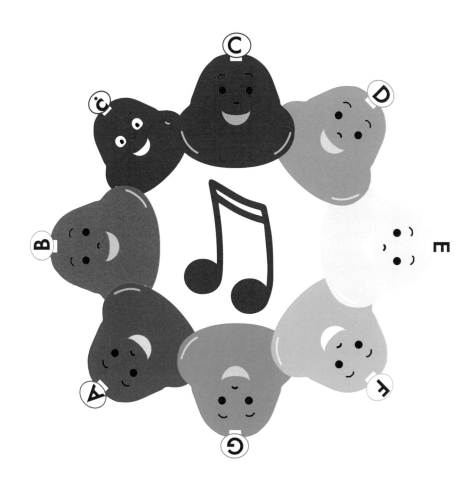

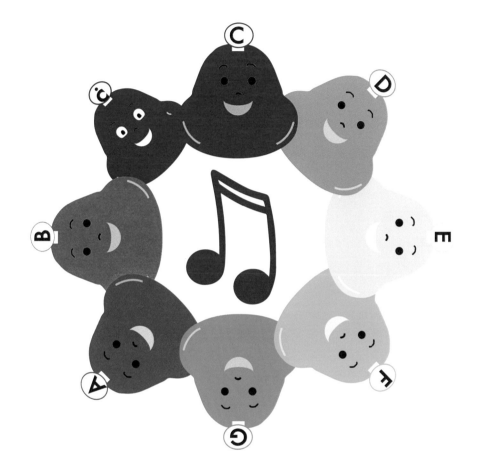

Year 1, Week 15

Chapter 2 - Pipes in C Major
LEQ: How can a student describe the notes of the C Major scale?

Week 15 Checklist

	Watched Video	Sang/Played Along	Played Sheet Music 1-3 times	Completed Workbook Activities	Repeat video 2-5 tiunes or as needed for mastery
Activator: Melodies #2	*			N/A	N/A	
Core Lesson: Pipes in C Major	*	*	*	*	
Performance: Do, Mi; Re, Fa, Mi, Sol Stars (Extra Practice)	*	*	N/A	N/A	
Review: Name That Note #1			N/A		

* Suggested Priority Activity

I. Overview: In this lesson, students play all 8 of their bells, and engage with the colors, letters, numbers and Solfege names of each.

II. Objective: By the end of this lesson, students should recognize each bell's color, letter, number, and Solfege name. They should also understand that each bell has its own place on the staff, even if they can't identify them yet.

III. Activator: Students begin this lesson with the second Melodies video. Melodies is the Prodigies singing and hand-signing series. The teacher should explain to students that before jumping into their main lesson today, they will review all of the hand-signs with Mr. Rob.

IV. Core Lesson: The teacher should explain to students that they will learn about all 8 notes on the C major scale today.

As they watch the video, Mr. Rob will sing about each note name, Solfege name and scale degree. Students should take out all 8 of their deskbells and sing and play along.

After, the class should play through the sheet music for "Pipes in C Major" as a group (or in smaller stations if that works better for the group). The teacher should lead the students by conducting a slow and steady tempo, or use a metronome at 60-90 BPM to help keep the beat.

Year 1, Week 15

Chapter 2 - Pipes in C Major
LEQ: How can a student describe the notes of the
C Major scale?

After playing through the sheet music, students should complete the "Pipes in C Major" workbook activities that incorporate all eight notes from the C major scale.

    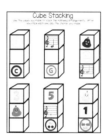

V. Performance: As a group (or as assigned homework), students play along with the Extra Practice performances: "Mi, Sol Stars", Re, Fa Stars", or "Mi, Sol Stars". While these aren't the usual performances, it gives students a chance to continue practice with Mi and Sol. Alternatively, students can perform the sheet music for "Pipes in C Major" in small groups or in front of the whole class.

VI. Summarizer: If students played the performances together, the teacher should instruct students to share one thing they liked about the performance with the person next to them (or with the whole group).

Before moving onto the extension lesson, the teacher should review today's lesson by asking students some or all of the following questions: *what are all eight Solfege names?; what are the colors used to identify each bell?; which number goes with the color teal?*

VII. Review: As a final activity (or as homework), student play another round of the listening game "Name That Note #1". This will test their ears and ability to memorize the notes of the C major scale. Students will complete the next series of listening games in the next lesson, so this review is a good warm up for that.

Before the students begin the listening activity, the teacher should ask students to think about which note was most difficult to identify last time they participated in this listening activity, and to think about how it may be more or less difficult this time around and why.

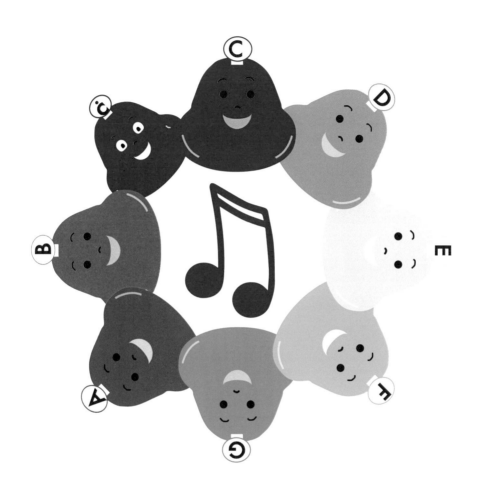

C Major Bell Mat

Use this bell mat for any song that uses all 8 bells!

E / 4 (Green)

E / 3 (Yellow)

Fa

Mi

Re

Do

D / 2 (Orange)

C / 1 (Red)

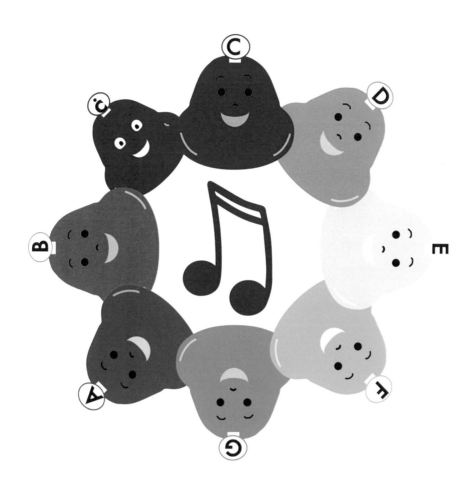

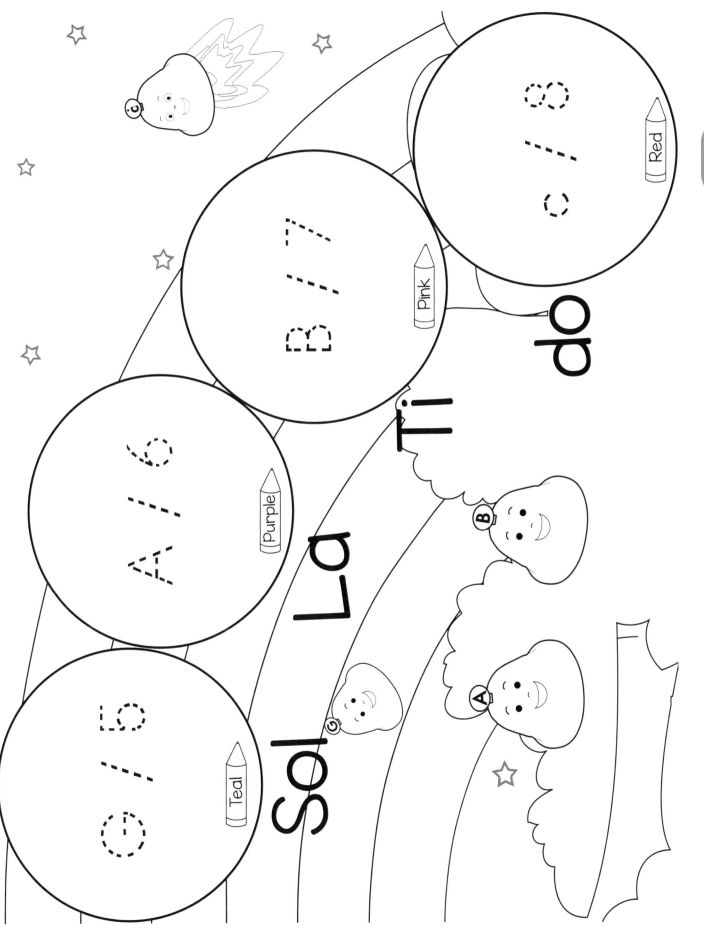

199

C Major Scale

As you play this song, make sure you repeat the song with each different verse.
Try to get comfortable singing with the letter names, the colors and the Solfège syllables while
playing your instrument. And for extra perfect timing, don't forget to use a metronome!

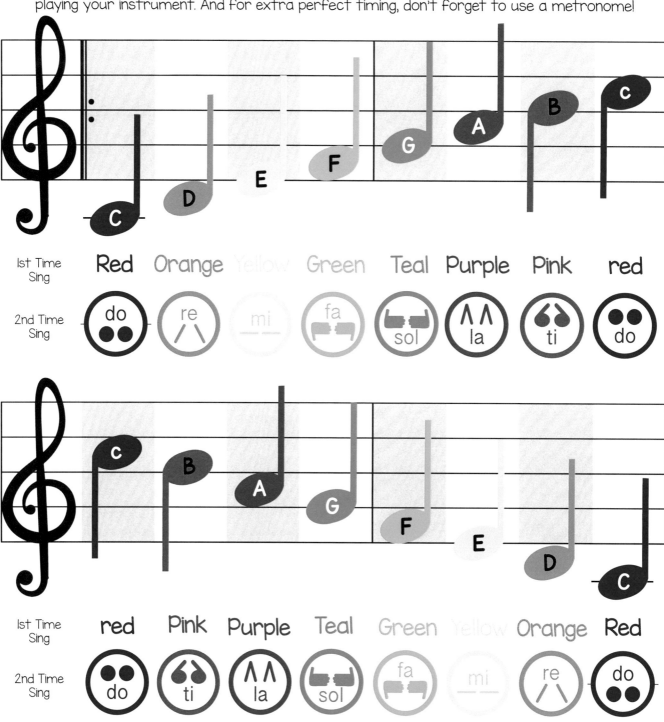

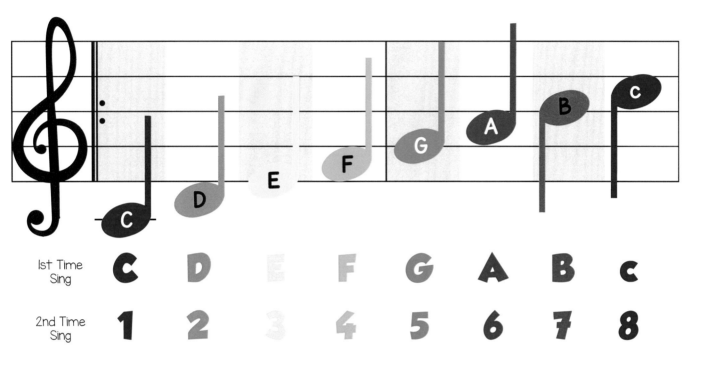

1st Time Sing	C	D	E	F	G	A	B	c
2nd Time Sing	1	2	3	4	5	6	7	8

REPEAT SONG AND SING NEXT LINE

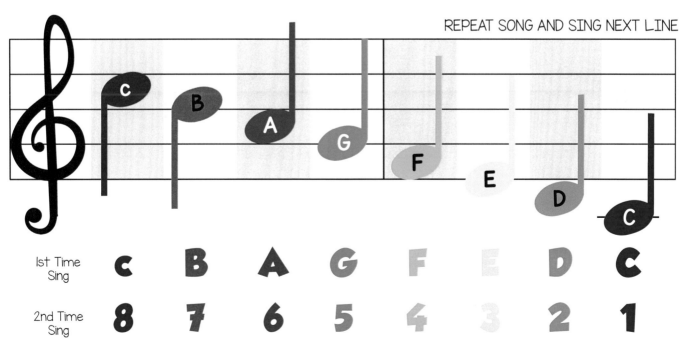

1st Time Sing	c	B	A	G	F	E	D	C
2nd Time Sing	8	7	6	5	4	3	2	1

Bells by Number

Draw a line between each bell its scale degree name.

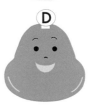

Bells by Solfège

Draw a line between each bell its Solfège name.

Do

Mi

Fa

do

Ti

La

Sol

Re

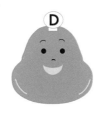

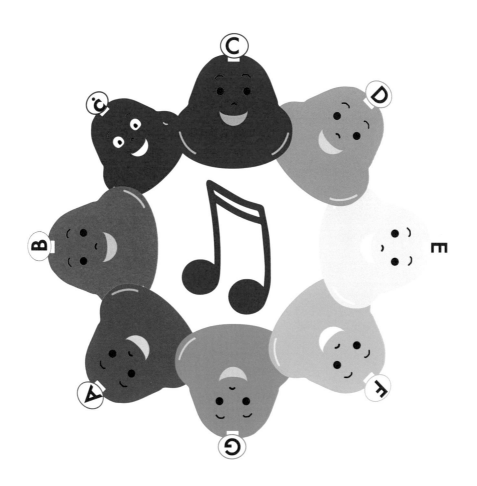

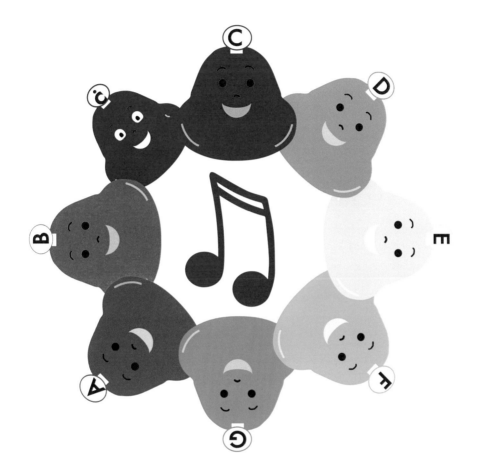

Piano Rainbow
Use the numbers on the piano to color a rainbow!

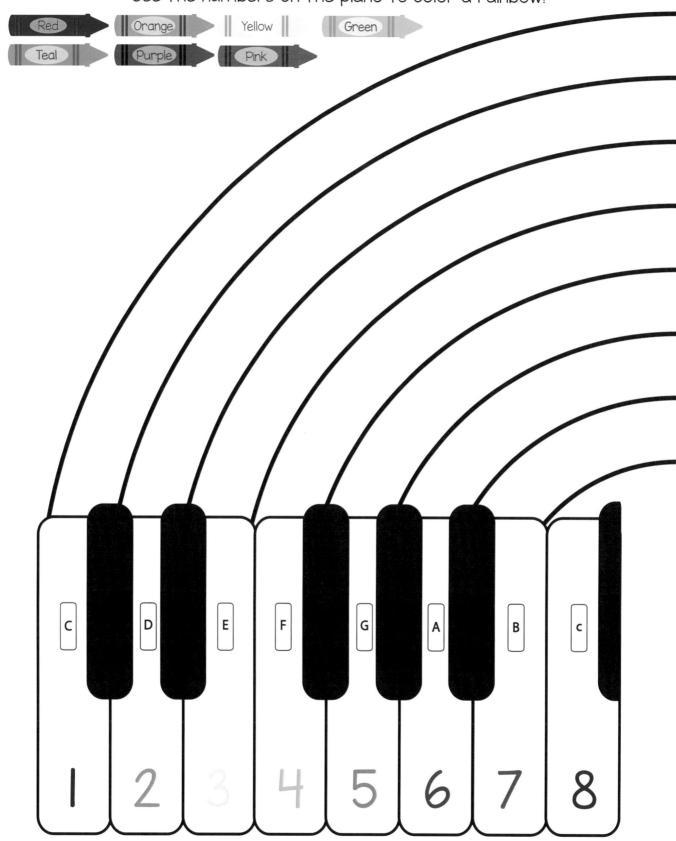

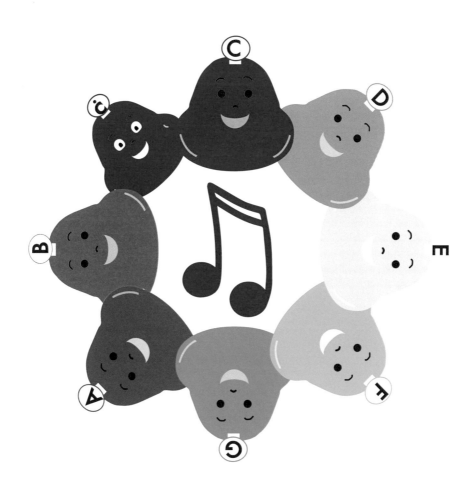

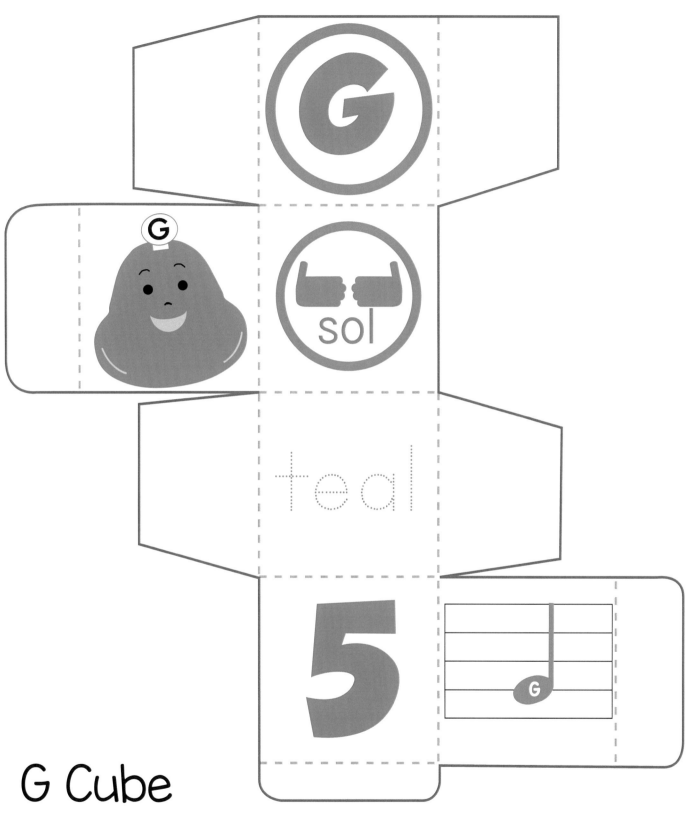

G Cube

Cut along the solid outline. Fold along the inside dashed lines, moving from top to bottom. Practice vocabulary with your new cube and save it for an activity later this section!

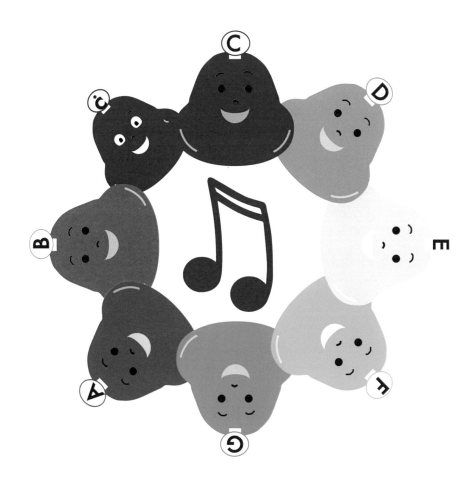

Cube Stacking

Use the cubes you made to stack the following arrangements. After you stack each one, play the chords you made.

Melody #1:
Do Re Mi Fa Sol La Ti Do

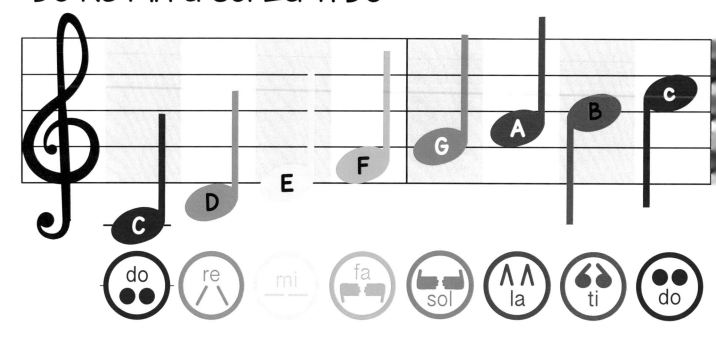

Melody #2:
Do Ti La Sol Fa Mi Re Do

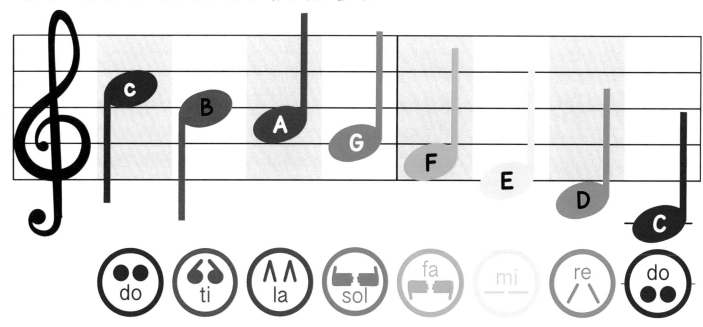

Quiz #1:

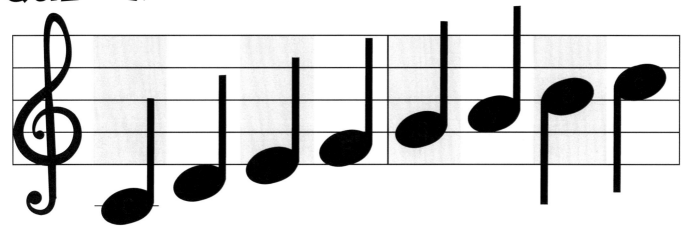

Part 1 : WHICH NOTE?
Write the notes on the blank lines!

___ ___ ___ ___ ___ ___ ___ ___

Part 2 : MIXED UP!
Match the Solfege Hand Signs to the notes above!

Quiz #2:

Part 1 : WHICH NOTE?
Write the notes on the blank lines!

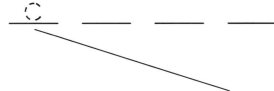

Part 2 : MIXED UP!
Match the Solfege Hand Signs to the notes above!

Year 1, Week 16

Chapter 1 - Perform and Assess
LEQ: How can a student perform and identify the notes in the C major scale?

Week 16 Checklist

	Watched Video	Sang/Played Along	Played Sheet Music 1-3 times	Completed Workbook Activities	Repeat video 2-5 tiunes or as needed for mastery
Activator: Pipes in C Major (Preschool 2.6)	*	*	N/A	N/A	
Performance: Low & High Performance Playlist	*	*		N/A	
Review/Assess: What Note Is It #2 & Name that Note #2	*	*	N/A		
Review/Assess: Interactive Quiz #2			N/A	N/A	

* Suggested Priority Activity

I. Overview: In this lesson, students take turns performing various performance tracks for the class. Then, students attempt to identify notes just by listening.

II. Objective: By the end of this lesson, students should be familiar with all 8 notes in the C major scale and feel comfortable identifying notes that they hear.

III. Activator: To begin today's lesson, students will play along with "Pipes in C Major". This lesson from last week will give students a chance to play with all 8 bells before putting 6 away and just focusing on Low C and High c for today.

IV. Performance: The teacher should explain to students that they will each play a different performance track today in front of the class. Students can play individually, or if it makes more sense, in small groups. Students can play the same part or different parts (hand-signing, percussion, etc.)

There is a playlist of all the performance track on this week's lesson page, so the teacher can scroll through and assign students a performance track, or (if it's possible with this group of students) students can choose the performance track they'd like to perform.

As each student performs, the teacher should play a metronome at 60-90 BPM to keep the beat. The performers can play along with either the video or just the sheet music if they prefer.

Year 1, Week 16

Chapter 2 - Perform and Assess
LEQ: How can a student perform and identify the
notes in the C major scale?

V. Review/Assess: Instead of a performance track today, students will watch two listening games: "What Note Is It?"and "Name that Note".

The teacher should give each student a copy of the "What Note Is It" handout and explain that as students listen, they should not call out their guess, but circle the matching bell on their paper.

The teacher may decide to model the first guess for students if they are unclear about what to do. The host of the listening game will reveal the answer after each question, so students should mark each of their answers right or wrong.

At the end of the video, the teacher should debrief with students: *Which note was easiest to identify?; Which note was most difficult to identify?; Were there any notes that students consistently got wrong?; Were there any notes that students consistently got right?*

Next, students will attempt to identify all 8 notes. For this activity, the teacher should pause the video after each note, and allow students to guess as a class.

If students become frustrated, the teacher should explain that they have 6 more chapters of content to learn before they will really develop their ears, and that they should keep practicing!

VI. Summarizer: The teacher should begin by summarizing the performance part of this week's lesson. The teacher should ask: *What was students' favorite part of the performance?; What were they most impressed by?; What was one thing they were surprised by?; What is one thing that they could do better (personally) next time?*

Since this is the last lesson in Chapter Two, the teacher should ask students to reflect on the chapter. Which lesson was their favorite and if there's time, review the essential questions from each lesson: *how can a student distinguish between high and low sounds?; how can a student distinguish between left and right?; how can a student distinguish between low and high C?; How are the eighth note and quarter note different?; how can a student differentiate left from right?; how can a student build a C Major chord?; how can a student describe the notes of the C Major scale?; how can a student differentiate between high and low C?*

VII. Review/Assess: As a final activity (or as homework), students complete the second interactive quiz directly on the Prodigies site on this week's lesson page.

What Note Is It?

Draw a circle around the bell you hear in each box!

1		**8**	
2		**9**	
3		**10**	
4		**11**	
5		**12**	
6		**13**	
7		**14**	

Low High
Low & High Studies

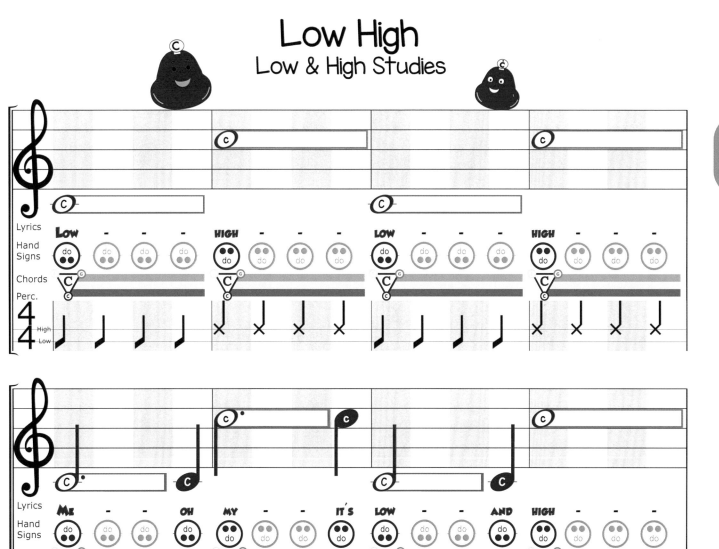

Performance Tip: Play the Low C with your LEFT Hand
& the High c with your RIGHT HAND

Birds Fly
Low & High Studies

18 They're Great
Low & High Studies

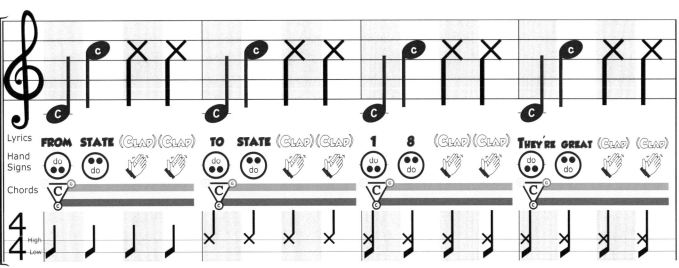

219

3 Key Rudiments with Right (R) & Left (L)

1 Single Stroke Roll
Start slow with A (R L R L), repeating R L over and over. Speed up gradually until you can't go any faster. Then, repeat with B (L R L R).

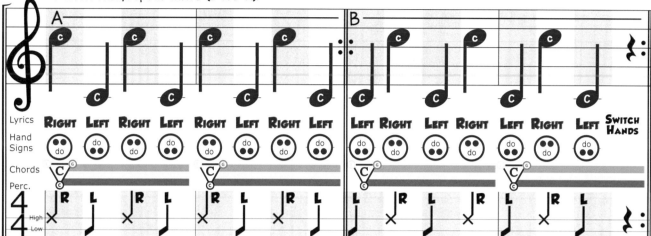

2 Double Stroke Roll
Start slow and speed up as you repeat

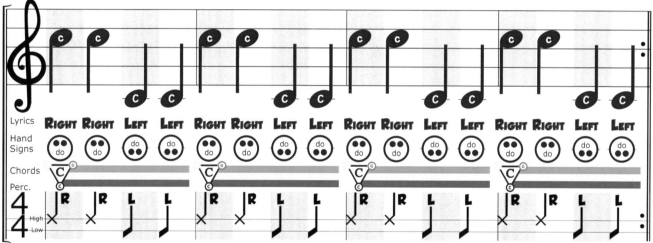

3 Paradiddle
Start slow and speed up as you repeat the paradiddle over and over.

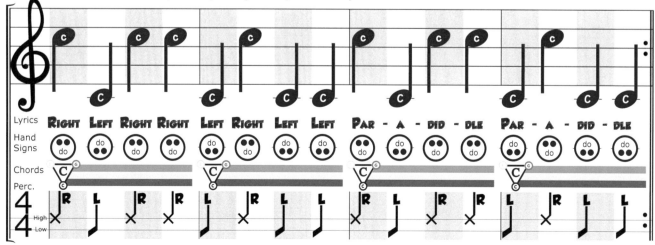

Stomp Stomp Clap
Low & High Studies

Two Foot Stomp
Low & High Studies

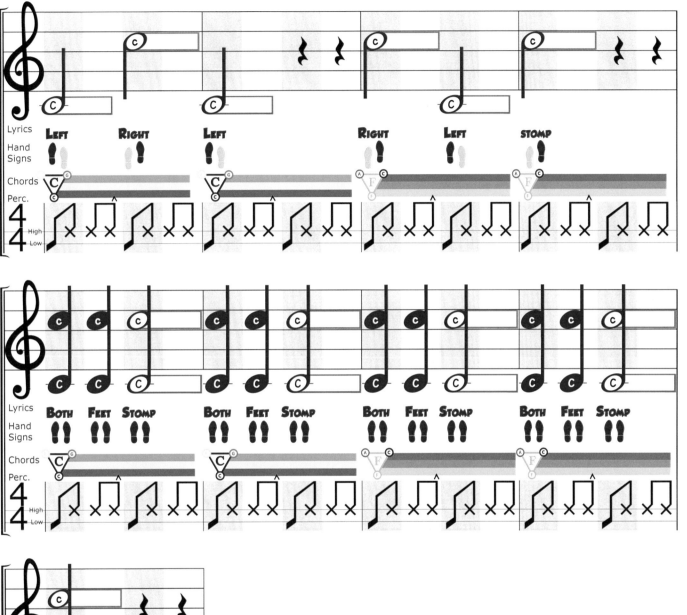

Honu Go Slow
Low & High Studies

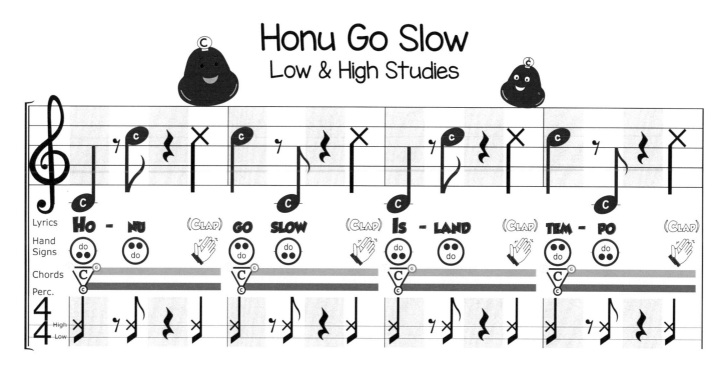

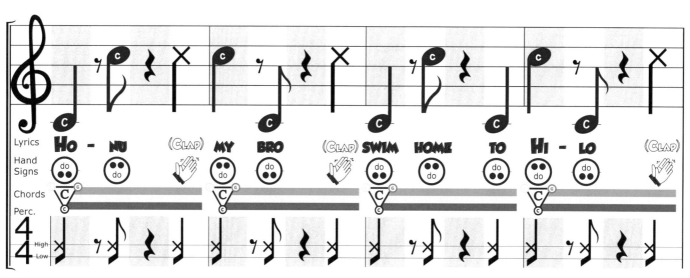

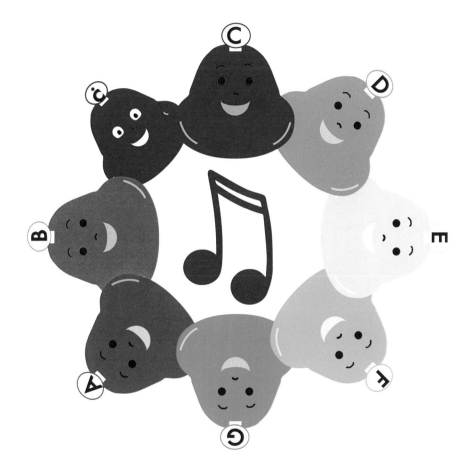

General Music Level 1A Workbook

CHAPTER THREE

Dear families & teachers,

Welcome back to Prodigies Music Lessons! Prepare for more musical fun in Chapter Three!

In this chapter, your learner will learn their second chord, G Major. We'll play both the C Major and G Major chords, compare them with listening games, chord building activities and Roman numeral practice.

Chords are a more difficult concept, and playing more than one musical note at a time can be challenging; however, research and methods surrounding early pitch development show us that early practice with the 3 Major chords (I, IV and V) are essential to developing a strong sense of pitch.

To make approaching chords a little easier for kids, here are a couple tips:

1. If a chord lesson has 5 different notes, split the five bells up among multiple players. Then, children only have to worry about 1 or 2 notes. This will reinforce cooperative play with their peers, turn taking and ensemble playing, while simplifying the physical challenge of playing multiple bells.

2. Don't be afraid to simplify the chord. If a chord is written as 3 notes and you can only play 2, that's okay! Experiment with what pairs you like best.

3. Focus on learning the notes of the chord, but don't get hung up on the order. With the C Major Bells, we only have one octave of notes, so the order of the chord may seem inconsistent or slightly random. Don't fret! The general mood of the chord will still shine through.

4. Use the speed control options inside the Playground videos to slow down any lessons your learner is having trouble with.

As always, encourage your learner to practice consistently and often. Create lots of opportunities to work music into your day and always approach the subject postively.

Happy Musicing!

– Mr. Rob & Prodigies Team

Year 1, Week 17

Chapter 3 - C & G, Best Friends

LEQ: How can a student differentiate between the notes C and G?

Week 17 Checklist

	Watched Video	Sang/Played Along	Played Sheet Music 1-3 times	Completed Workbook Activities	Repeat video 2-5 tiunes or as needed for mastery
Activator: Snow Day	*		N/A	N/A	
Core Lesson: C & G, Bestfriends	*	*	*	*	
Performance: Yankee Doodle	*	*		N/A	
Extension: Beethoven's 5th				N/A	N/A

⋆ Suggested Priority Activity

I. Overview: In this lesson, students explore the notes C and G while incorporating whole notes into their play.

II. Objective: By the end of this lesson, students should be able to differentiate between C and G and be able to play both whole and half notes.

III. Activator: Students begin this lesson with the rhythm song "Snow Day".

Before beginning, the teacher should explain to students that they will sing and clap or tap in response to Mr. Rob. In this lesson, students will practice clapping or tapping quarter notes, eighth notes and sixteenth notes.

At the end of the video, Mr. Rob gives a quick mini-lesson on the notes featured in this song.

IV. Core Lesson: Students take out their C and G bells to play along with "C & G, Best Friends". Students can begin by hand-signing do or sol, or jump right into playing the bells.

Students should tap each bell along with Mr. Rob as the C and G bells appear on the screen.

After the video, the class should play through the sheet music for "C & G, BFFs" as a group (or in smaller stations if that works better for the group). The teacher should lead the students by conducting a slow and steady tempo, or using a metronome at 60-90 BPM to help keep the beat.

Year 1, Week 17

Chapter 3 - C & G, Bestfriends

LEQ: How can a student differentiate between the notes C and G?

After playing through the sheet music, students should complete the "C and G, Bestfriends" worksheet activities that review do and sol, whole and half notes, patterns, and C & G.

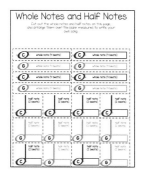 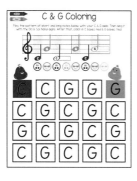 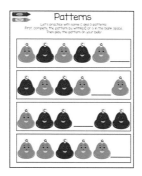 

V. Performance: As a group (or as assigned homework), students play along with "Yankee Doodle", which features scrolling sheet music in the treble clef, as well as a handful of parts for other instruments (percussion, lyrics, hand-signs, chord arrangements, etc).

VI. Summarizer: If students played the performance together, the teacher should instruct students to share one thing they liked about the performance with the person next to them (or with the whole group).

Before moving onto the review lesson, the teacher should review today's lesson by asking students some or all of the following questions: *what color is the G bell?; what color is the G bell?; what is the hand-sign for sol?; how many beats is a half note?; how many beats is a whole note?*

VII. Extension: As a final activity (or as homework), students watch "Beethoven's 5th" featuring Do and Sol. This is a very simple version of this song, and gives students a chance to practice hand-signing Do and Sol.

The teacher should explain to students that they will play or hand-sign along with each note as the bell appears on the screen.

C & G, BFFs

☆☆☆☆☆

Practice singing and playing with Do and Sol in this simple song!

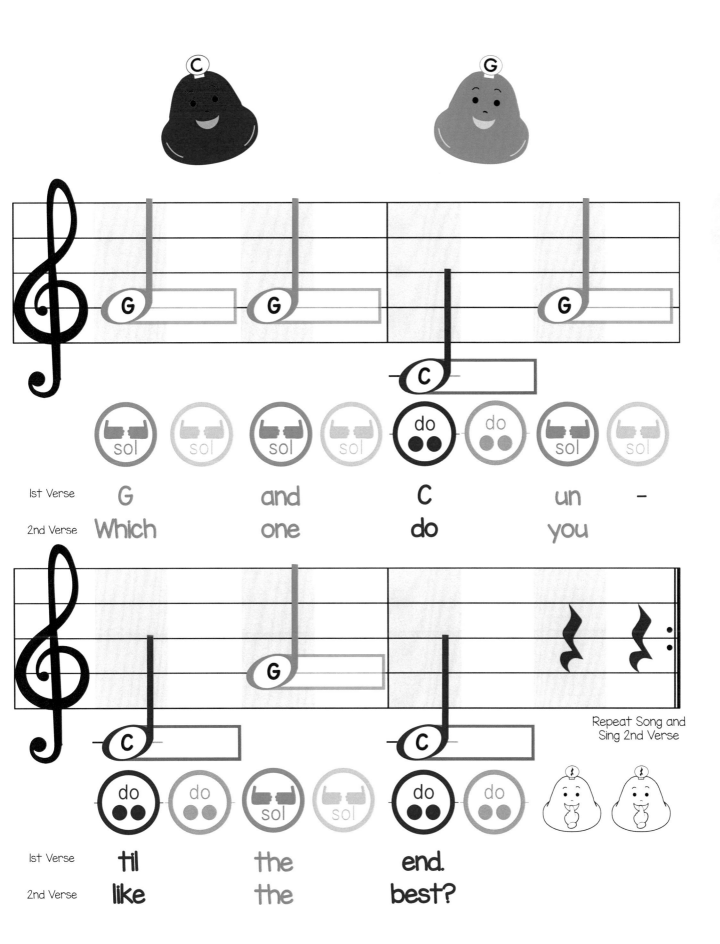

1st Verse   G   and   C   un   –

2nd Verse   Which   one   do   you

Repeat Song and
Sing 2nd Verse

1st Verse   til   the   end.

2nd Verse   like   the   best?

231

Whole Notes and Half Notes

Cut out the whole notes and half notes on the next page, and arrange them over the blank measures to write your own song.

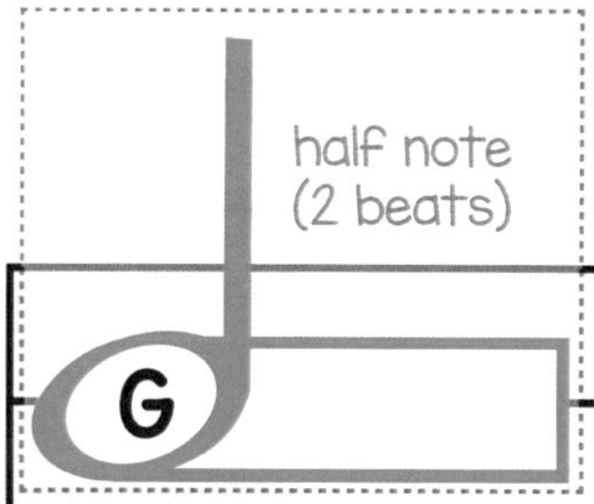

half note
(2 beats)

G

Whole Notes and Half Notes

Cut out the whole notes and half notes on this page,
and arrange them over the blank measures to write your
own song.

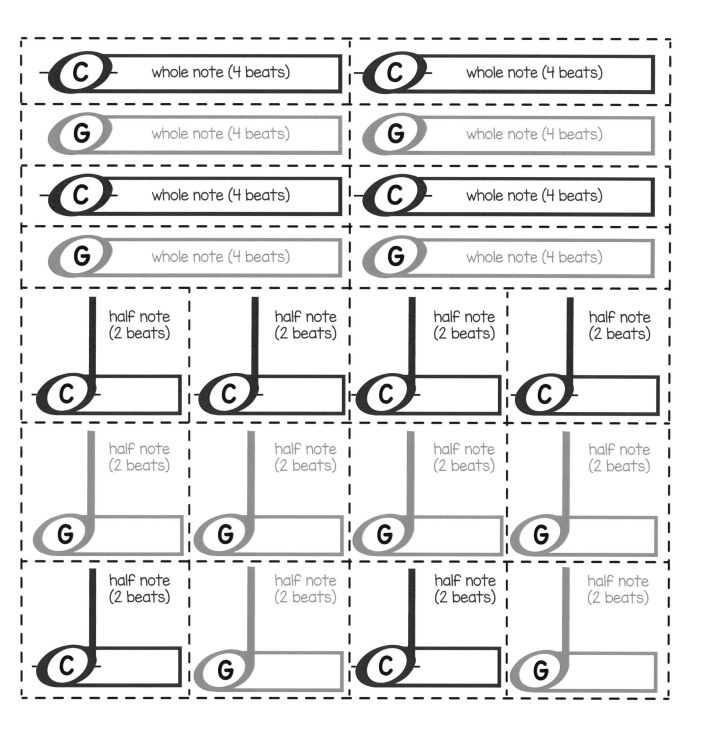

C & G Coloring

Play the pattern of short and long notes below with your C & G bells. Then sing it with the Do & Sol hand-signs. After that, color in C boxes red & G boxes teal.

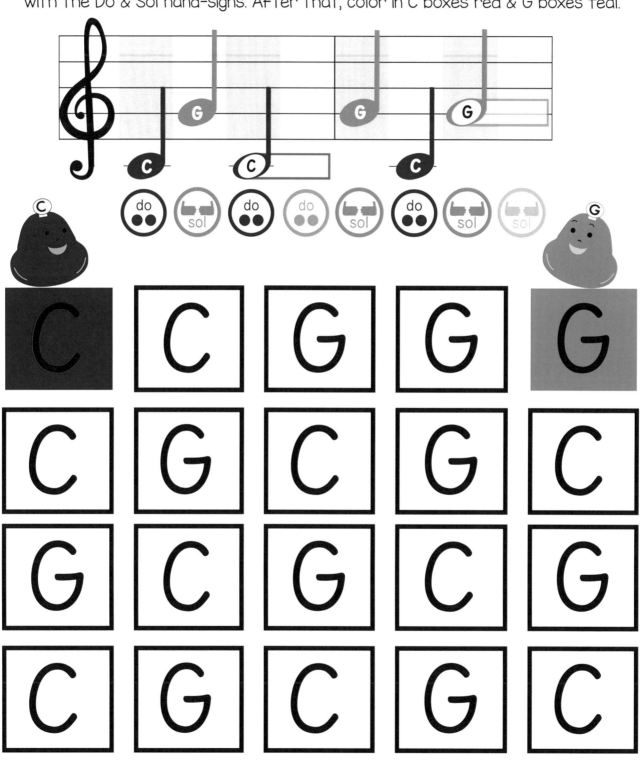

Patterns

Let's practice with some C and G patterns.
First, complete the pattern by writing C or G in the blank space.
Then play the pattern on your bells!

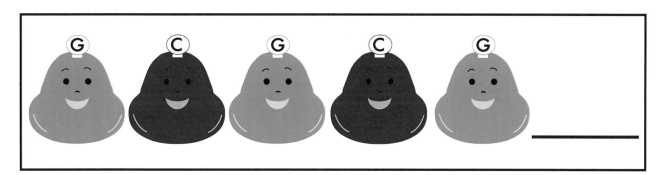

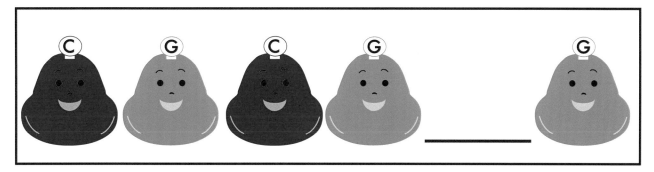

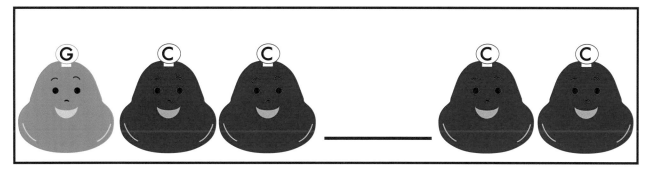

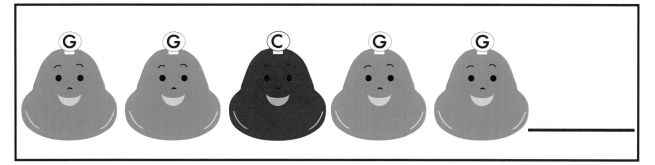

Circle the Gs & Cs

1. Practice writing the words below.
2. Put a **red circle** around the words that start with C.
3. Put a teal circle around the words that start with G.

chick   window   gift

giraffe   coat   street

flower   grass   corn

236

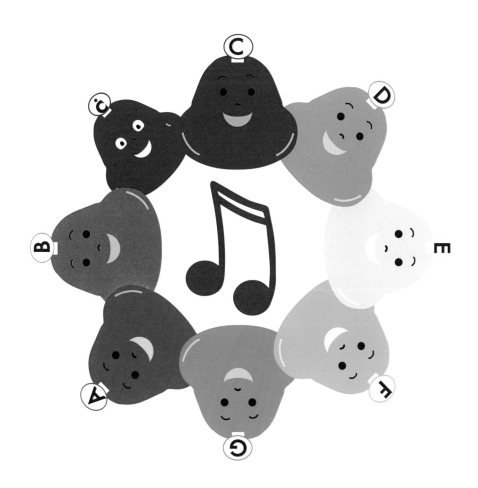

Year 1, Week 18

Chapter 3 - The Wheels on the Bus
LEQ: How can a student use C and G to simplify
"The Wheels on the Bus"?

Week 18 Checklist

	Watched Video	Sang/Played Along	Played Sheet Music 1-3 times	Completed Workbook Activities	Repeat video 2-5 tiunes or as needed for mastery
Activator: Melodies #3	*			N/A	
Core Lesson: The Wheels on the Bus	*	*	*	*	
Performance: Wheels on the Bus	*	*		N/A	
Extension: London Bridge				N/A	

* Suggested Priority Activity

I. Overview: In this lesson, students play a simplified version of "The Wheels on the Bus", using C, G and quarter notes.

II. Objective: By the end of this lesson, students should be able to use C and G to simplify "The Wheels on the Bus".

III. Activator: Students begin this lesson with Melodies # 3. Melodies is the Prodigies singing and hand-signing series. The teacher should explain to students that before jumping into their main lesson today, they will review all of the hand-signs with Mr. Rob.

Students should hand-sign and sing the Solfege names as they scroll across the screen.

IV. Core Lesson: Students take out their C and G bells to play along with "The Wheels on the Bus".

This is a simplified version of "The Wheels on the Bus", and very easy to follow. Students should play the bell as it appears on the screen.

After the video, the class should play through the sheet music for "The Wheels on the Bus" as a group (or in smaller stations if that works better for the group). The teacher should lead the students by conducting a slow and steady tempo, or using a metronome at 60-90 BPM to help keep the beat.

Year 1, Week 18

Chapter 3 - The Wheels on the Bus

LEQ: How can a student use C and G to simplify "The Wheels on the Bus"?

After playing through the sheet music, students should complete the "The Wheels on the Bus" worksheet activities that review left and right.

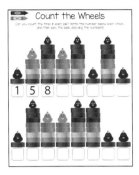   

V. Performance: As a group (or as assigned homework), students play along with "The Wheels on the Bus", which features scrolling sheet music in the treble clef, as well as a handful of parts for other instruments (percussion, lyrics, hand-signs, chord arrangements, etc).

VI. Summarizer: If students played the performance together, the teacher should instruct students to share one thing they liked about the performance with the person next to them (or with the whole group).

Before moving onto the review lesson, the teacher should review today's lesson by asking students some or all of the following questions: *which number represents the low C?; which number represents the high c?; which number represents the G?*

VII. Extension: As a final activity (or as homework), students play along with "London Bridge" featuring C, G and D. This is a fun sing and play-along that gives students a chance to sing a familiar song.

The teacher should explain to students that they should play along with the bells as they appear on the screen, and that students will be playing two bells at one time. Students should set up their bells with the G in the middle, then practice playing C and G at the same time and G and D at the same time.

The Wheels on the Bus

Below is a simple arrangement for the Wheels on the Bus. It may seem easy and different from the full song, but we will get to playing the full song soon! To make sure your ready for the harder version, spend some time practicing this arrangement with a metronome! Try to play along with the beep of the metronome at 80-90 BPM.

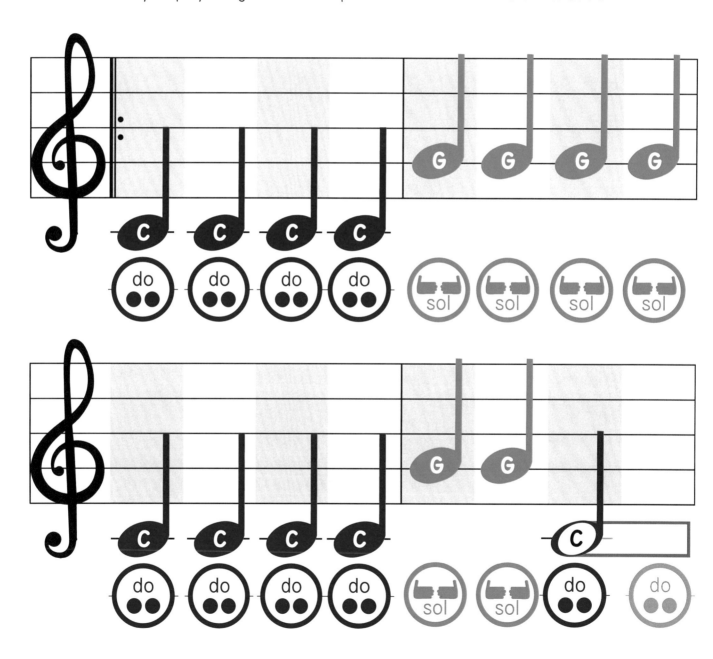

Do and Sol Hand-Signs

Adding hand-signs to our musical notes makes learning, feeling and singing the notes more physical and more fun!

You can hang this hand-sign poster in your music room!
Use it to practice with Do and Sol. Try singing and hand-signing back and forth slowly. Then practice a little bit faster and see just how fast you can go!

Count the Wheels

Can you count the tires in each pile? Write the number below each stack,
and then play the bells and sing the numbers!

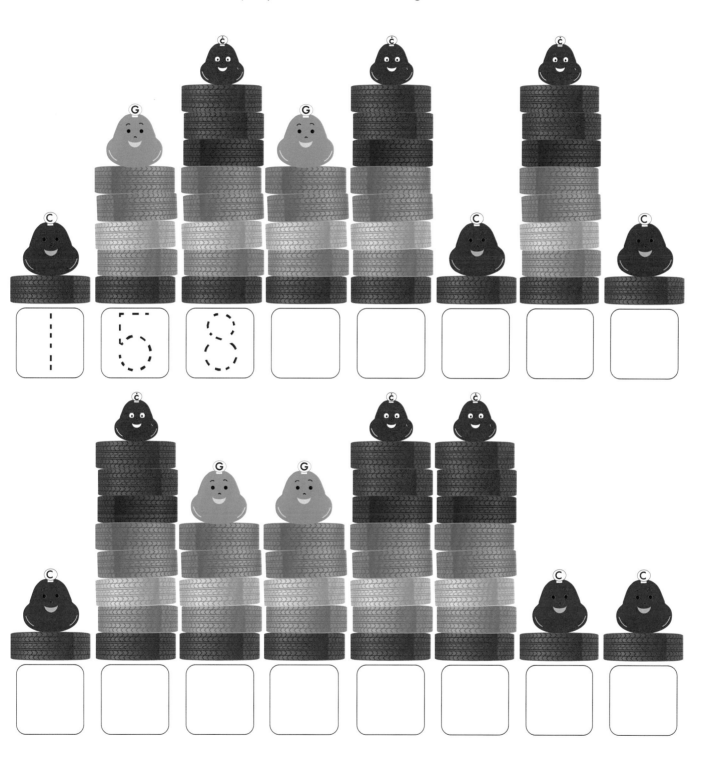

Compose a 1, 5, 8 Song

Practice writing the numbers 1, 5 and 8!

Only put one number in each box! Then try to play your song with your bells.
Challenge: Write the words to a song underneath the numbers and try to sing
it. You can use the different letters of your name instead of words!

Quarter Notes

Have you ever tried to clap and count at the same time? Try it below!

Repeat the top line again! It's a great way to practice keeping a steady beat!

Let's try it again with the Red Bell!

Now let's try it with the **quarter note.**

245

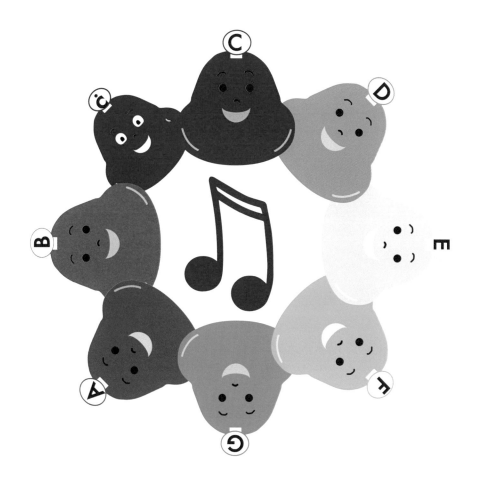

Quarter Notes

Cut out the quarter notes below and paste them on top
of the gray boxes on the previous page to make a quarter note song!

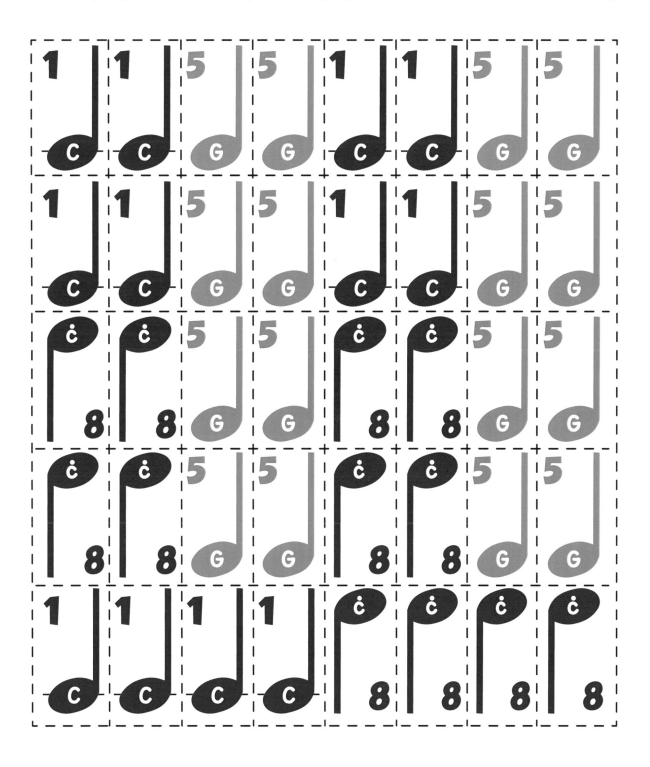

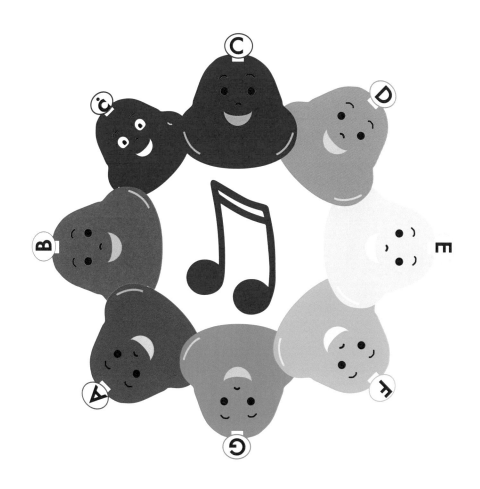

Notes Used:

Wheels on the Bus
C & G Borduns

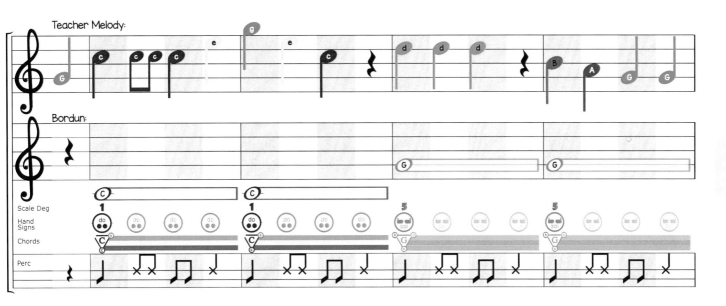

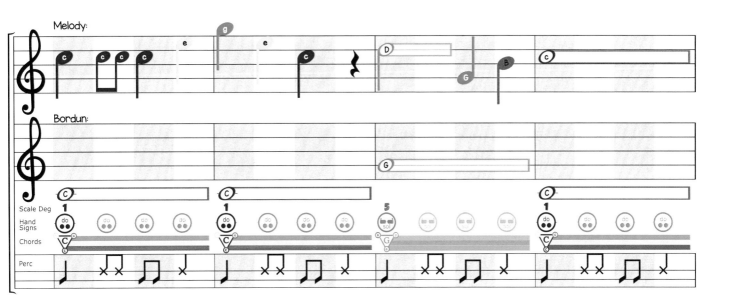

Melody #3:
Do Re Mi Fa Sol Sol Do

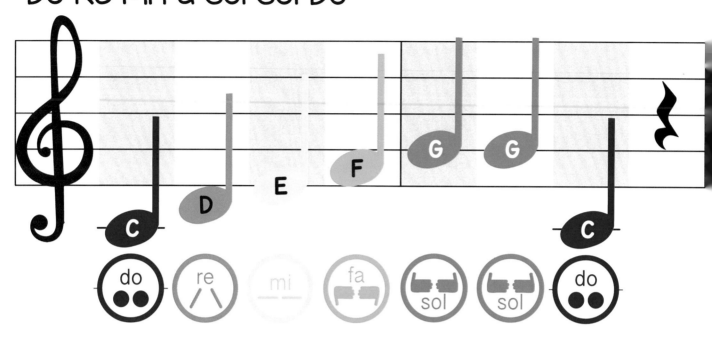

Melody #4:
Do Ti La Sol Do Re Do

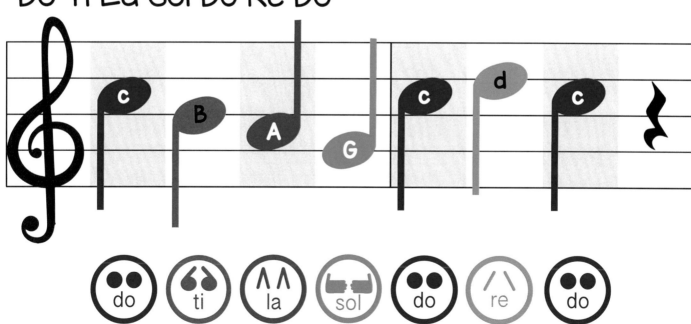

250

Quiz #3:

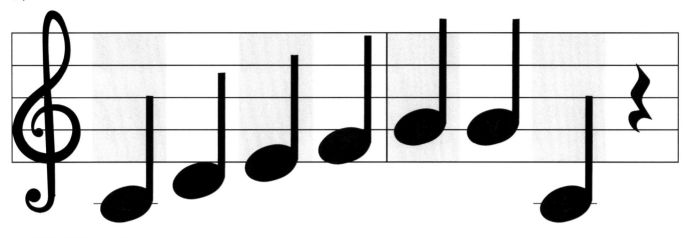

Part 1 : WHICH NOTE?
Write the notes on the blank lines!

__ __ __ __ __ __ __

Part 2 : MIXED UP!
Match the Solfege Hand Signs to the notes above!

Quiz #4:

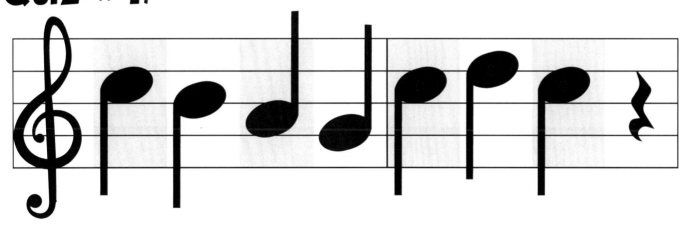

Part 1 : WHICH NOTE?
Write the notes on the blank lines!

__ __ __ __ __ __ __

Part 2 : MIXED UP!
Match the Solfege Hand Signs to the notes above!

Year 1, Week 19

Chapter 3 - C & G Chords

LEQ: How can a student play and reference a C and G Major Chord?

Week 19 Checklist

	Watched Video	Sang/Played Along	Played Sheet Music 1-3 times	Completed Workbook Activities	Repeat video 2-5 times or as needed for mastery
Activator: London Bridge	*		N/A	N/A	
Core Lesson: C Major & G Major Chords	*	*	*	*	
Performance: Frere Jacques	*	*		N/A	
Extension: Sol Ti Re Slide				N/A	

* Suggested Priority Activity

I. Overview: In this lesson, students practice with the C and G Major chords, and learn Roman numbers to reference the I and V chords.

II. Objective: By the end of this lesson, students should be able to both identify the notes in teh C Major Chord and the G Major Chord, and write the Roman numeral for 1 and 5.

III. Activator: Students begin this lesson by reviewing "London Bridge", the extension activity from the previous lesson. This song features C, G and D, and is a great way to warm up playing C and G chords.

Students should put the G bell in the middle of C and D, and practice playing the C and G together and the G and D together.

IV. Core Lesson: The teacher should explain to students that today they will learn chords today! A chord is a group of notes that sounds nice when we play them together. "C & G Chords" uses the notes C, E, G, B and D.

Students will practice playing notes individually and together as chords.

After the video, the class should play through the sheet music for "C & G Chords" as a group (or in smaller stations if that works better for the group). The teacher should lead the students by conducting a slow and steady tempo, or using a metronome at 60-90 BPM to help keep the beat.

Year 1, Week 19

Chapter 3 - C & G Chords

LEQ: How can a student play and reference a C and
G Major Chord?

After playing through the sheet music, students should complete the "C and G Chords"
worksheet activities that review left and right and low and high sounds.

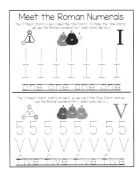
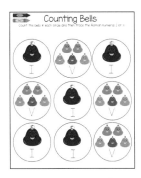
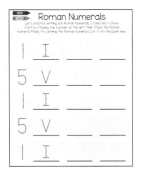
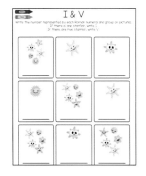

V. Performance: As a group (or as assigned homework), students play along with "Frere
Jacques", which features scrolling sheet music in the treble clef, as well as a handful of parts
for other instruments (percussion, lyrics, hand-signs, chord arrangements, etc).

VI. Summarizer: If students played the performance together, the teacher should
instruct students to share one thing they liked about the performance with the person next to
them (or with the whole group).

Before moving onto the review lesson, the teacher should review today's lesson by asking
students some or all of the following questions: *which notes live in the G chord?; which notes
live in the C chord?; what is the Roman numeral for 1?; what is the Roman numeral for 5?*

VII. Extension: As a final activity (or as homework), students play along with "Sol Ti Re Slide"
featuring G, B and D. This song is a look ahead to chapter 7, and gives students additional
practice with the notes in the G chord.

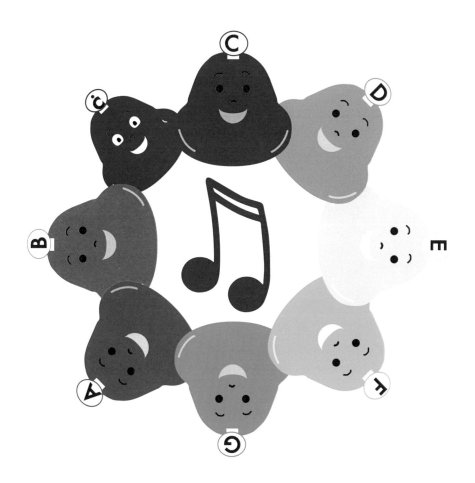

Chord Mat
I – V
C Major & G Major

C / 1

E / 3

G / 5

D / 2

B / 7

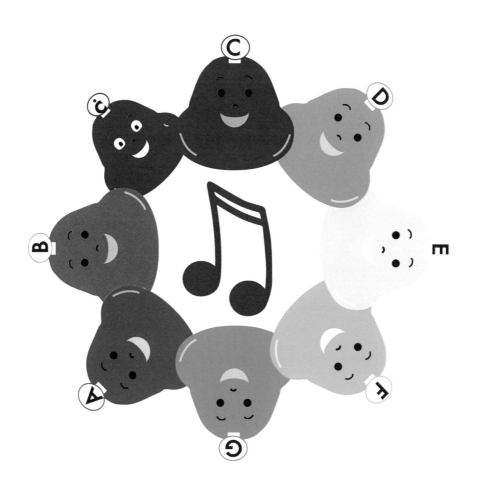

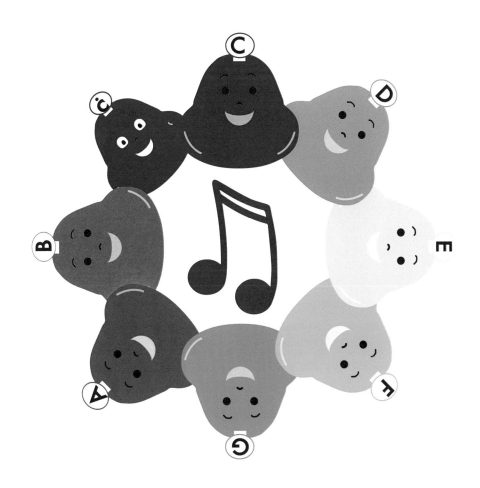

Chords: C and G

☆☆☆☆☆

Try singing the broken chords in this song using the letter names!

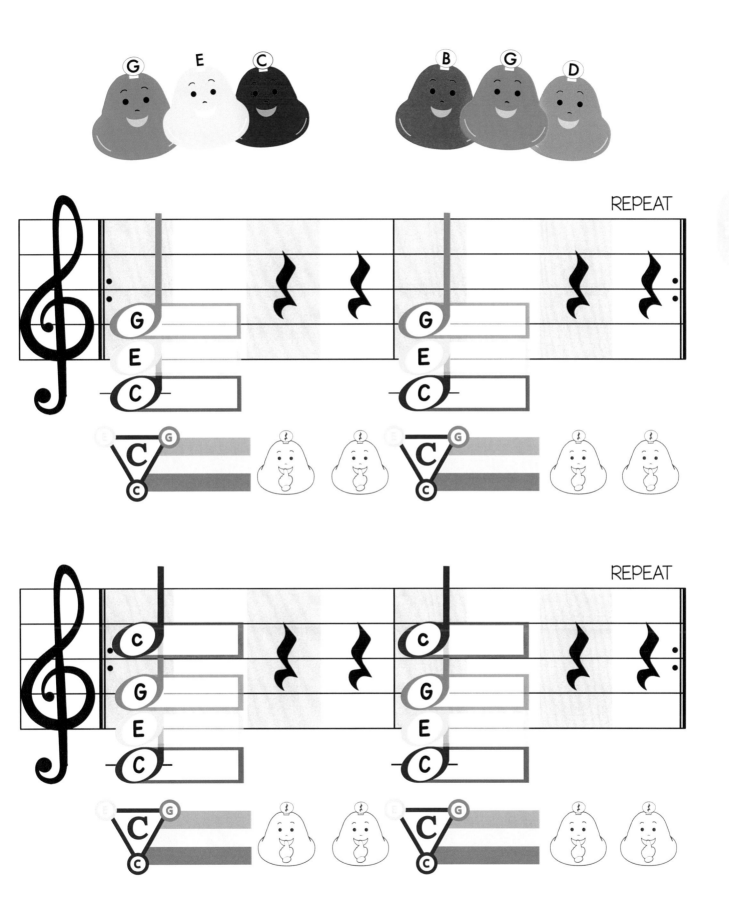

REPEAT

REPEAT

259

Meet the Roman Numerals

The "C Major Chord" is also called the "One Chord." To make the "One Chord,"
we use the Roman numeral for I, which looks like an I.

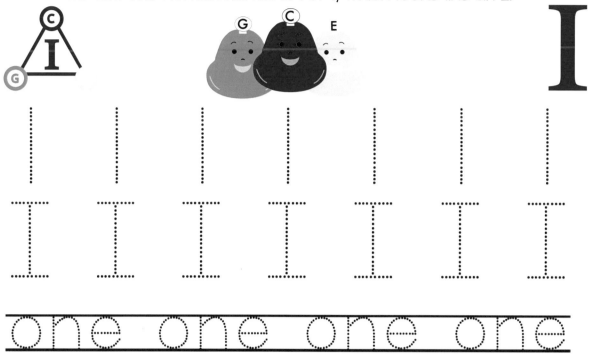

I I I I I I I I I I

I I I I I I

one one one one

The "G Major Chord" starts on bell 5, so we call it the "Five Chord," and we
use the Roman numeral for 5, which looks like a V.

5 5 5 5 5 5 5 5

V V V V V V V

five five five five

Counting Bells

Count the bells in each circle and then trace the Roman numeral I or V.

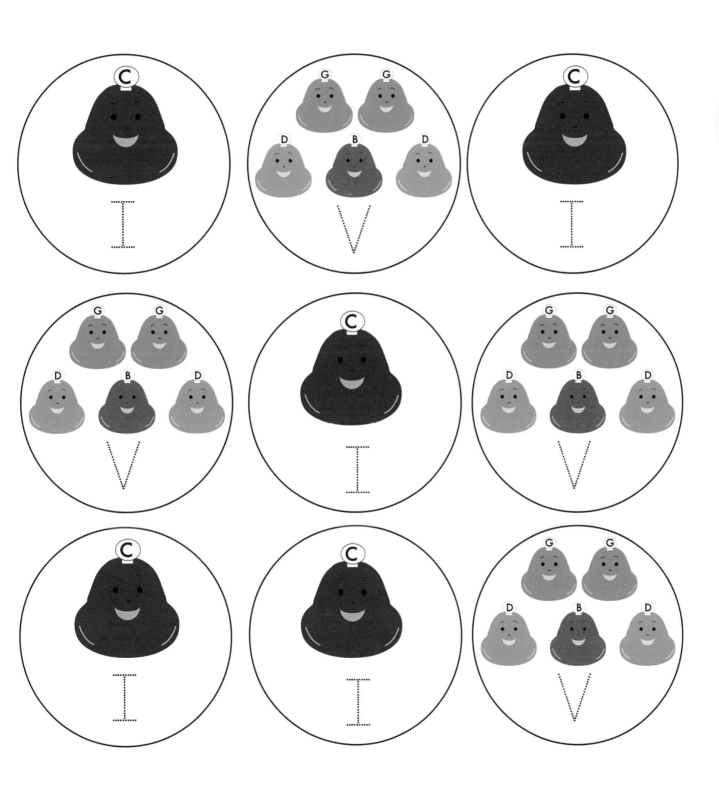

Roman Numerals

Let's practice writing our Roman Numerals, I (one) and V (five). Start by tracing the number on the left. Then trace the Roman numeral. Finally, try writing the Roman numeral (I or V) on the blank lines.

I   I   _____   _____

5   V   _____   _____

I   I   _____   _____

5   V   _____   _____

I   I   _____   _____

I & V

Write the number represented by each Roman numeral and group of pictures.
If there is one starfish, write I.
If there are five starfish, write V.

Notes Used:

Frère Jacques
C & G Borduns

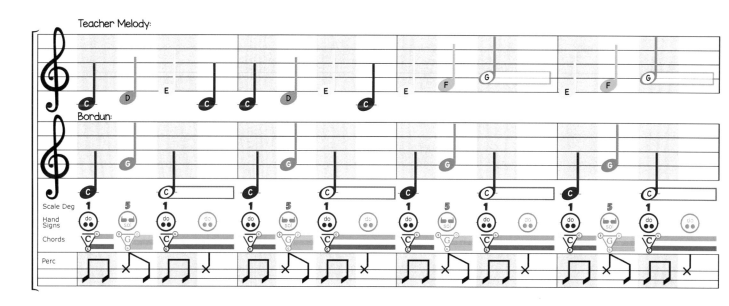

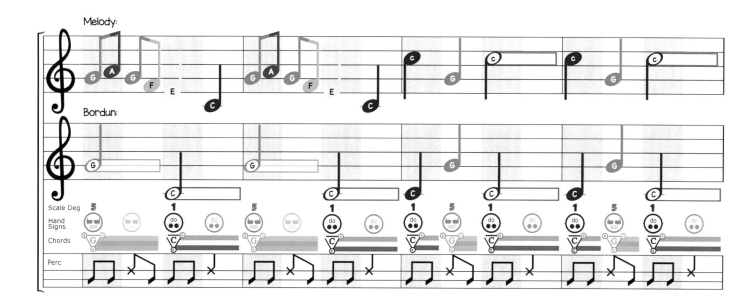

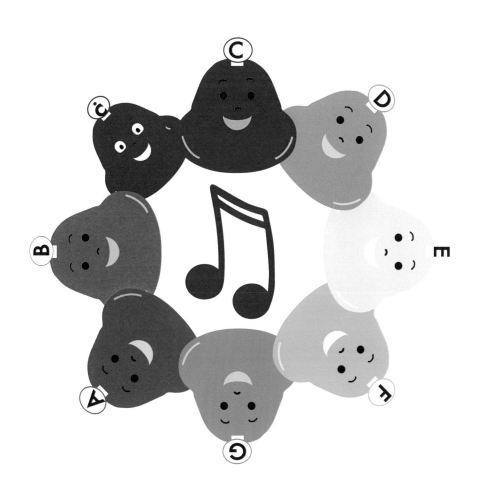

Year 1, Week 20

Chapter 3 - Beet & Cherry

LEQ: How can a student count quarter notes and eighth notes?

Week 20 Checklist

	Watched Video	Sang/Played Along	Played Sheet Music 1-3 times	Completed Workbook Activities	Repeat video 2-5 tiunes or as needed for mastery
Activator: Meteor Man	*		N/A	N/A	
Core Lesson: Beet & Cherry (Harder)	*	*	*	*	
Performance: Yankee Doodle	*	*		N/A	
Extension: Snow Day				N/A	

* Suggested Priority Activity

I. Overview: In this lesson, students will continue to practice eighth and quarter notes. Students will count with beets & cherries, tas & titis, and numbers.

II. Objective: By the end of this lesson, students should be able to clap, tap or stomp both a quarter note and an eighth note rhythm.

III. Activator: Students begin by playing a silly clap-along song call "Meteor Man". The teacher should explain that they will dance along with the video, and when it gets to the chorus, students will clap along with the words (and number of syllables) on the screen.

IV. Core Lesson: The teacher should explain to students that they won't need their bells for the core lesson today and instead should clap, tap or stomp along with "Beet & Cherry". Today's lesson is all about rhythm!

After the video, the class should clap, tap or stomp through the sheet music for "Beet & Cherry" as a group (or in smaller stations if that works better for the group). The teacher should lead the students by conducting a slow and steady tempo, or using a metronome at 60-90 BPM to help keep the beat.

Year 1, Week 20

Chapter 3 - Beet & Cherry

LEQ: How can a student count quarter notes and eighth notes?

After playing through the sheet music, students should complete the "Beet & Cherry" worksheet activities that review ta and ti-ti, counting and eighth notes.

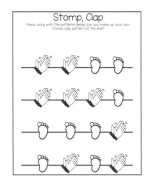

V. Performance: As a group (or as assigned homework), students play along with "Yankee Doodle", which features scrolling sheet music in the treble clef, as well as a handful of parts for other instruments (percussion, lyrics, hand-signs, chord arrangements, etc).

VI. Summarizer: If students played the performance together, the teacher should instruct students to share one thing they liked about the performance with the person next to them (or with the whole group).

Before moving onto the review lesson, the teacher should review today's lesson by asking students some or all of the following questions: *which note has more claps--eighth or quarter note?; which note is represented by the word "beet" in this lesson?; which note is represented by the word "cherry" in this lesson"?*

VII. Extension: As a final activity (or as homework), students sing and clap along with "Snow Day". This video gives students a chance to practice quarter notes, eighth notes and sixteenth notes--with no references to foods!

Beet & Cherry

☆☆☆☆☆

Sing the chorus to Sweet Beets while tapping a steady beat. Then in the verses, tap, clap or stomp with Beet and Cherry.

CHORUS 1

Sweet Beets, we've got some!

If you want some Sweet Beets, we've got 'em.

If you want Sweet Beets, we've got some,

If you want some Sweet Beets, we've got 'em.

VERSE 1

| BEET | BEET | CHERRY | BEET | CHERRY CHERRY | BEET | BEET |

| CHERRY | BEET | CHERRY | BEET | CHERRY CHERRY CHERRY | BEET |

CHORUS 2

Sweet Beets, we've got some!

If you want some Sweet Beets, we've got 'em.

If you want Sweet Beets, we've got some,

If you want some Sweet Beets, we've got 'em.

VERSE 2

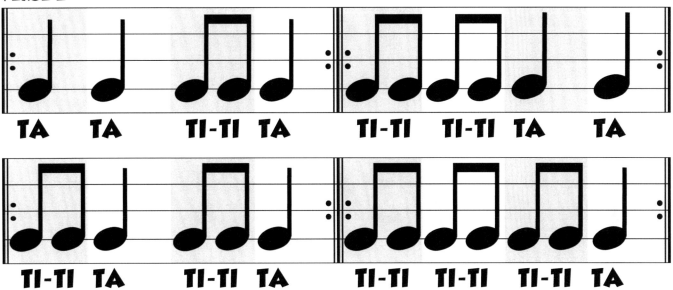

TA   TA   TI-TI   TA   TI-TI   TI-TI   TA   TA

TI-TI   TA   TI-TI   TA   TI-TI   TI-TI   TI-TI   TA

CHORUS 3

Sweet Beets, we've got some!

If you want some Sweet Beets, we've got 'em.

If you want Sweet Beets, we've got some,

If you want some Sweet Beets, we've got 'em.

VERSE 3

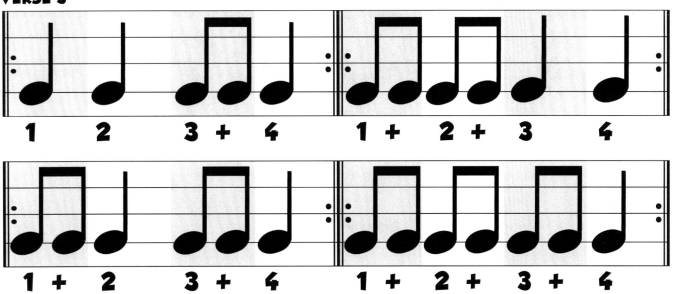

1   2   3 + 4   1 +   2 +   3   4

1 +   2   3 + 4   1 +   2 +   3 +   4

CHORUS 4

Sweet Beets, we've got some!
If you want some Sweet Beets, we've got 'em.
If you want Sweet Beets, we've got some,
If you want some Sweet Beets, we've got 'em.

VERSE 4

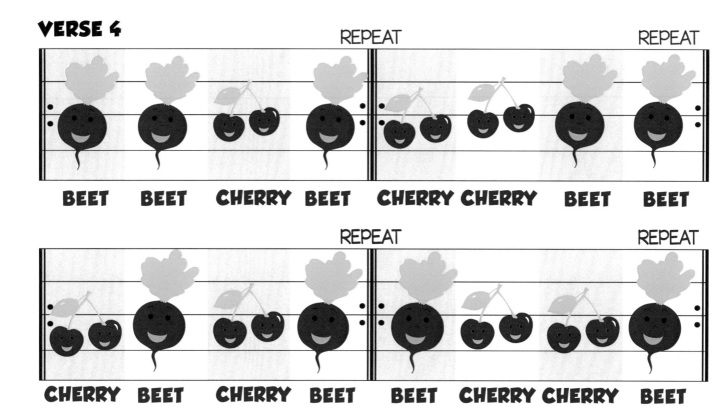

BEET   BEET   CHERRY BEET   CHERRY CHERRY   BEET   BEET

CHERRY BEET   CHERRY BEET   BEET   CHERRY CHERRY   BEET

CHORUS 5

Sweet Beets, we've got some!
If you want some Sweet Beets, we've got 'em.
If you want Sweet Beets, we've got some,
If you want some Sweet Beets, we've got 'em.

Note Math

In each box, count the number of NOTES. You can look for each individual note head ●, or just focus on counting the stems |.

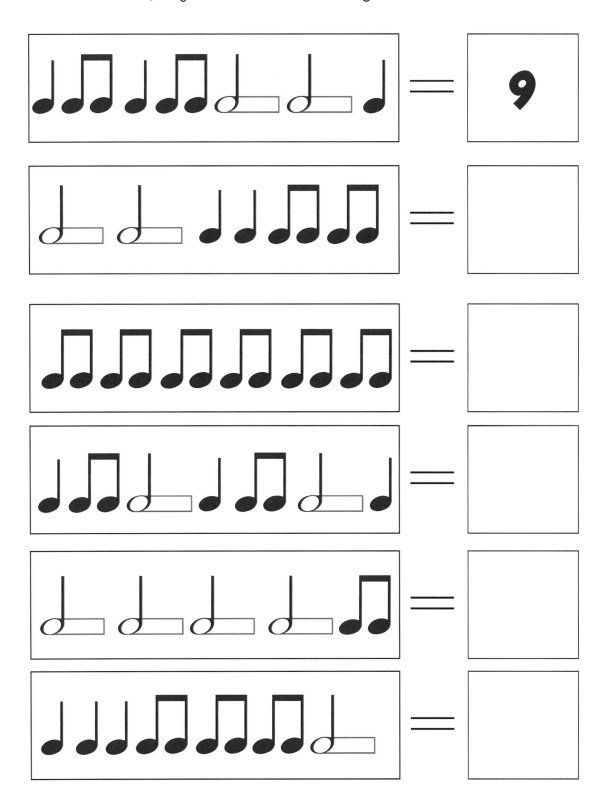

271

Beat Math

In each row, count the number of BEATS. The Half Note takes up 2 beats. The quarter note takes up 1 beat. It takes 2 Eighth Notes to fill 1 beat.

Stomp, Clap

Follow along with the patterns below; can you make up your own stomp, clap pattern at the end?

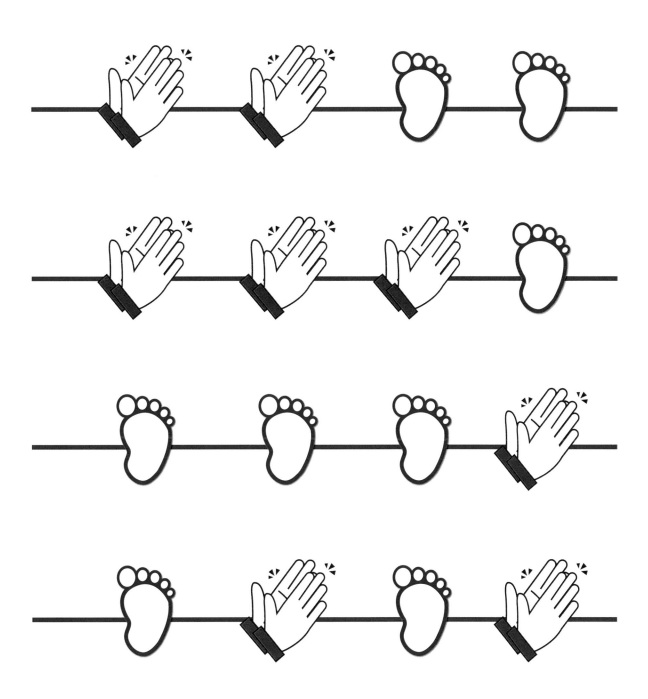

Eighth Notes

You practiced counting quarter notes. Can you count eighth notes at twice the speed?

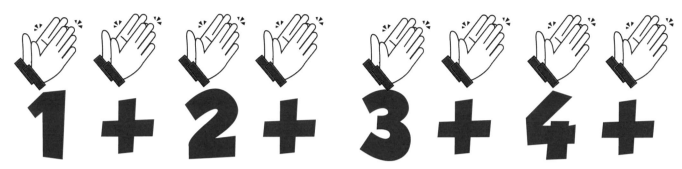

Repeat the top line again! It's a great way to practice keeping a steady beat!

Let's try it again with the Red Bell!

Now let's try it with the **eighth note.**

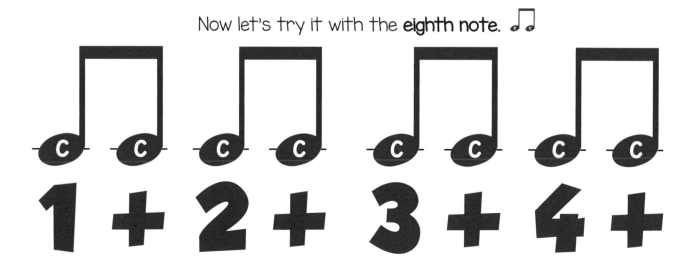

Yankee Doodle
C & G Borduns

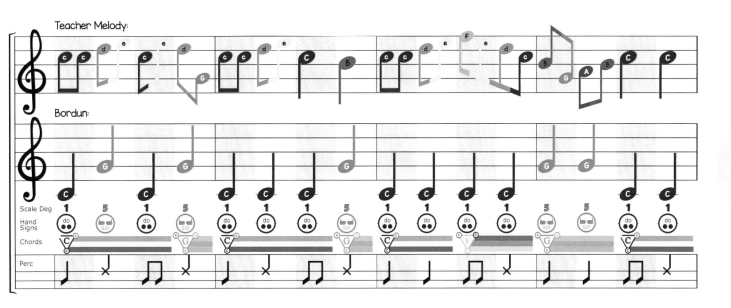

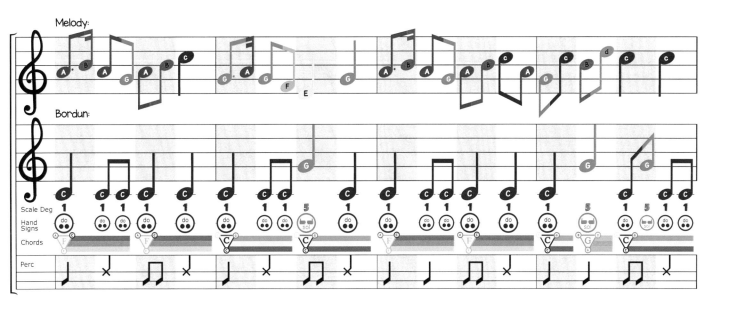

275

Year 1, Week 21

Chapter 3 - The Chords on the Bus

LEQ: How can a student play a simplified version of "The Wheels on the Bus" using chords?

Week 21 Checklist

	Watched Video	Sang/Played Along	Played Sheet Music 1-3 times	Completed Workbook Activities	Repeat video 2-5 tiunes or as needed for mastery
Activator: The Wheels on the Bus	*			N/A	
Core Lesson: The Chords on the Bus	*	*	*	*	
Performance: Row Your Boat	*	*		N/A	
Extension: Melodies #4			N/A	N/A	

* Suggested Priority Activity

I. Overview: In this lesson, students modify chords to play "The Wheels on the Bus".

II. Objective: By the end of this lesson, students should be able to play "The Wheels on the Bus" using the I Chord and the V Chord.

III. Activator: Students begin this lesson with a review of "The Wheels on the Bus". The teacher should explain to students that in their main lesson today, they will play "The Wheels on the Bus" using multiple notes at one time, or chords!

To warm up, students will begin with the simplified version of "The Wheels on the Bus" that they played in Chapter 3, Week 20.

IV. Core Lesson: The teacher should explain to students that they will play simplified versions of the C and G chord to play "The Wheels on the Bus".

Students should practice playing the G and B together and the C and E together to represent each chord.

After the video, students should complete the letter trace and then play the Bell Stomp activity to follow up with "C Sock Slide" as a group (or in smaller stations if that works better for the group). The teacher should lead the students by conducting a slow and steady tempo, or using a metronome at 60-90 BPM to help keep the beat.

Year 1, Week 21

Chapter 3 - The Chords on the Bus

LEQ: How can a student play a simplified version of
"The Wheels on the Bus" using chords?

After playing through the sheet music, students should complete the "The Chords on the Bus" worksheet activities that review the C and G chord.

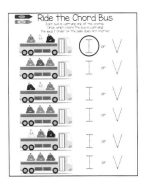
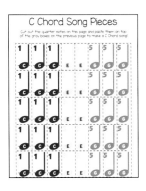

V. Performance: As a group (or as assigned homework), students play along with "Row your Boat", which features scrolling sheet music in the treble clef, as well as a handful of parts for other instruments (percussion, lyrics, hand-signs, chord arrangements, etc).

VI. Summarizer: If students played the performance together, the teacher should instruct students to share one thing they liked about the performance with the person next to them (or with the whole group).

Before moving onto the extension lesson, the teacher should review today's lesson by asking students some or all of the following questions: *which colors make up the G chord?; which colors make up the C chord?; how can a musician modify the C chord?; how can a musician modify the G chord?; which chords are used to play "The Wheels on the Bus"?*

VII. Review: As a final activity (or as homework), students play sing and hand-sign along with Melodies # 4. Melodies is the Prodigies singing and hand-signing series. The teacher should explain to students that before jumping into their main lesson today, they will review all of the hand-signs with Mr. Rob.

Students should hand-sign and sing the Solfege names as they scroll across the screen.

Wheels on the Bus

The wheels on the bus go round and round,

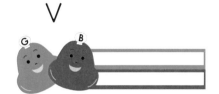 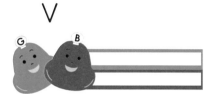

round and round, round and round.

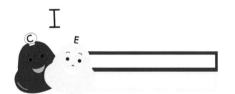 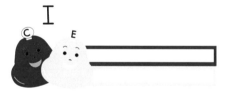

The wheels on the bus go round and round,

all through the town.

The mommies on the bus go shh, shh, shh,

shh, shh, shh,   shh, shh, shh.

The mommies on the bus go shh, shh, shh,

all through the town.

The bells on the bus go Do Mi Sol,

Sol Ti Re, Sol Ti Re.

The bells on the bus go Do Mi Sol,

Sol Ti Re through the town.

Ride the Chord Bus

Each bus is carrying one of the chords.
Circle which chord the bus is carrying!
The exact order of the bells does not matter.

C Chord Song

Cut out the quarter notes on the next page and paste them on top
of the gray boxes below to make a quarter note song!

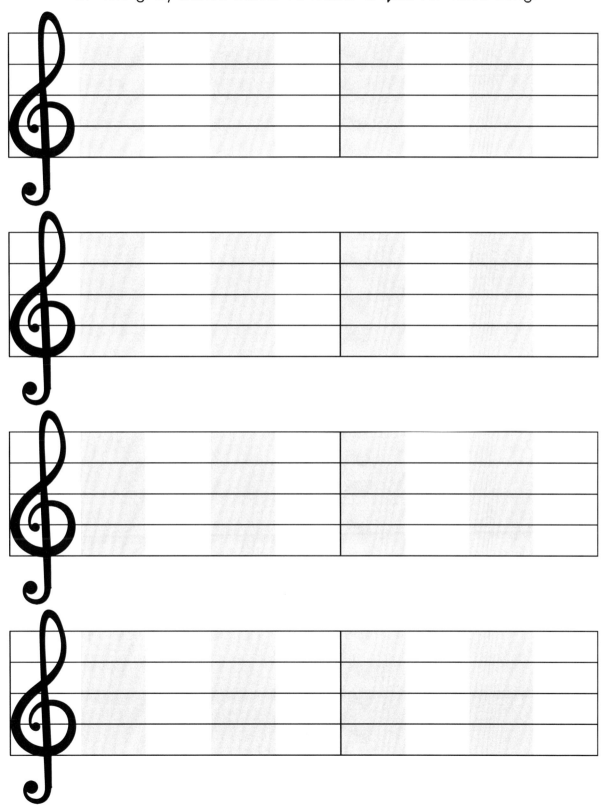

C Chord Song Pieces

Cut out the quarter notes on this page and paste them on top of the gray boxes on the previous page to make a C Chord song!

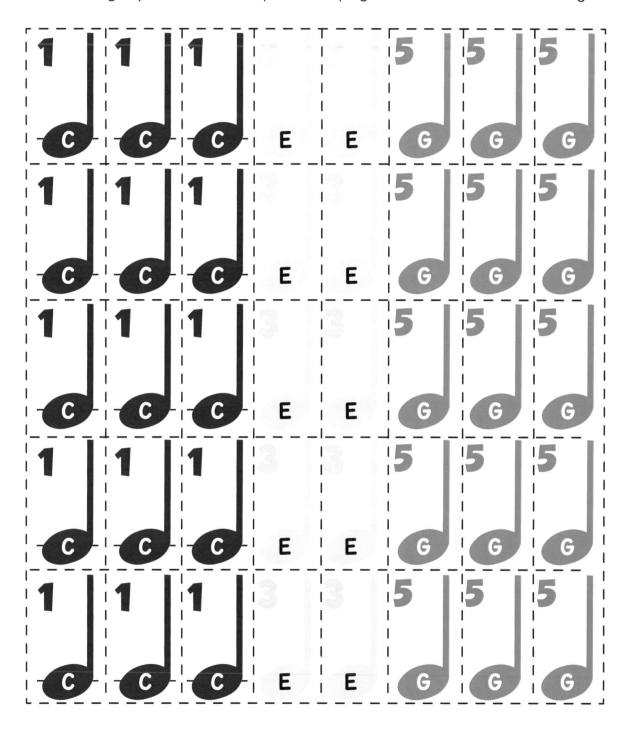

G Major Wheels

Can you count the tires in each pile? Write the number
below each stack, and then grab your bells and play the number song!

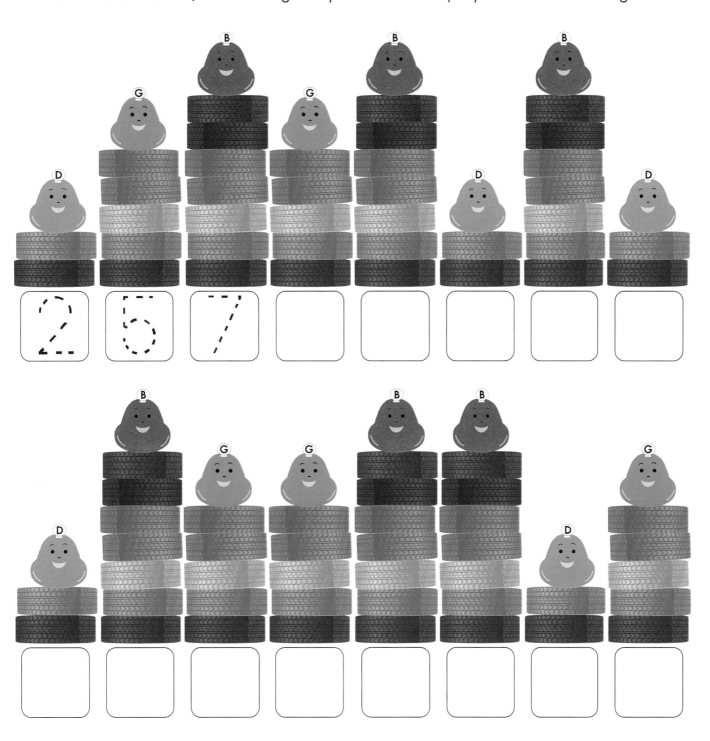

2 5 7

283

Compose a 2, 5, 7 Song

Practice writing the numbers 2, 5 and 7!
Only put one number in each box! Then try to play your song with your bells.
Challenge: Write the words to a song underneath the numbers and try to sing
your new song. You can use the different letters of your name instead of words!

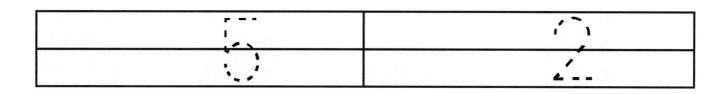

Row Your Boat
C & G Borduns

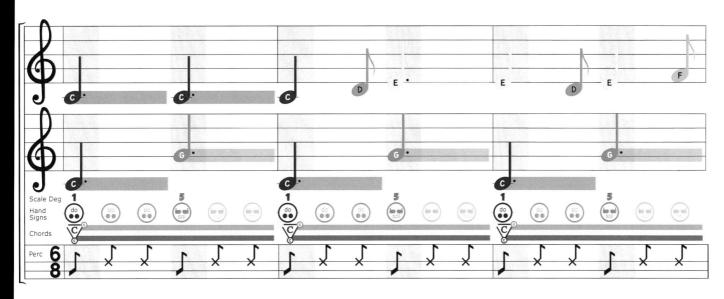

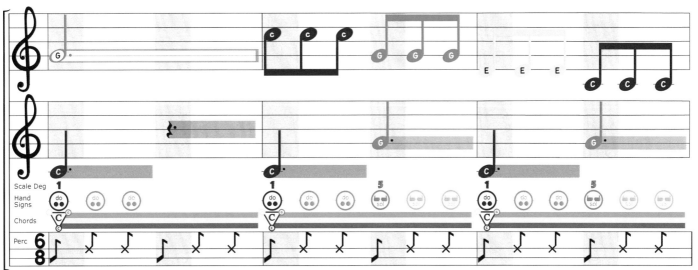

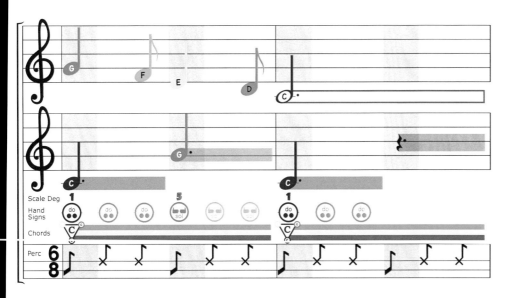

MELODY #3:
Do Re Mi Fa Sol Sol Do

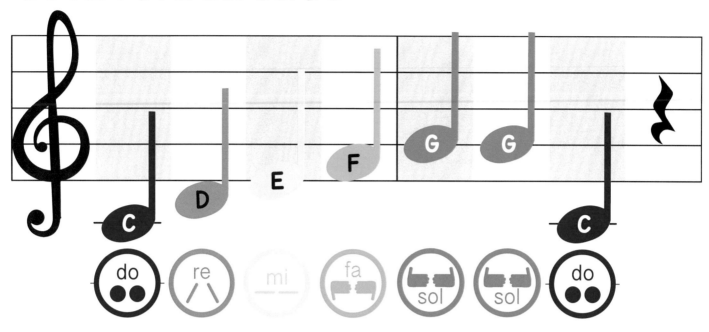

MELODY #4:
Do Ti La Sol Do Re Do

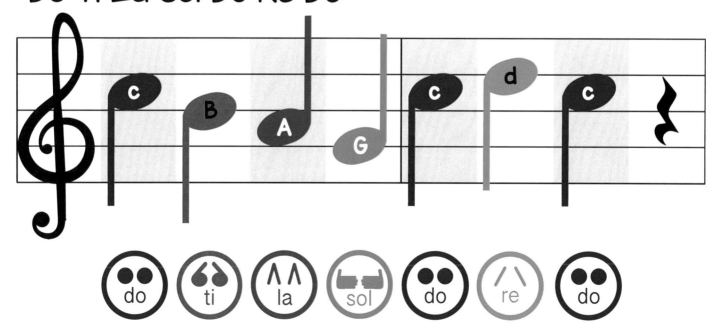

Quiz #3:

Part 1 : WHICH NOTE?
Write the notes on
the blank lines!

Part 2 : MIXED UP!
Match the Solfege
Hand Signs to the
notes above!

Quiz #4:

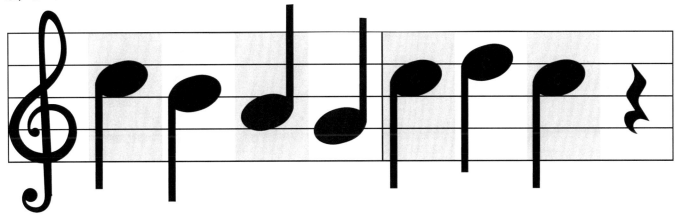

Part 1 : WHICH NOTE?
Write the notes on
the blank lines!

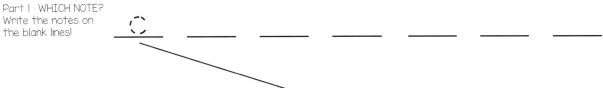

Part 2 : MIXED UP!
Match the Solfege
Hand Signs to the
notes above!

Year 1, Week 22

Chapter 3 - Chord Watching #2

LEQ: How can a student identify the C and G chords?

Week 22 Checklist

	Watched Video	Sang/Played Along	Played Sheet Music 1-3 times	Completed Workbook Activities	Repeat video 2-5 tiunes or as needed for mastery
Activator: Chord Watching #1	⋆		N/A	N/A	
Core Lesson: Chord Watching #2	⋆	⋆	⋆	⋆	
Performance: Beethoven's Minuet No.2	⋆		N/A	N/A	
Extension: Beethoven's 5th	⋆		N/A	N/A	

⋆ Suggested Priority Activity

I. Overview: In this lesson, students continue to practice with the C and G chords, specifically identifying each note by ear.

II. Objective: By the end of this lesson, students should be able to distinguish between the C and G Major Chords.

III. Activator: Students begin today's lesson by reviewing the first chord watching video from Chapter 1. In this video, students listen and determine whether they hear a C chord or a non-musical sound.

IV. Core Lesson: Once students have warmed up identifying the C chord, students watch and listen to Chord Watching # 2.

The teacher should explain that students will not play their bells today, and instead will listen and try to identify the G chord and C chord. The teacher can review both chords at this time to help the students warm up their listening ears.

After the video, students should play along with the sheet music for "Chord Watching # 2" as a group (or in smaller stations if that works better for the group). The teacher should lead the students by conducting a slow and steady tempo, or using a metronome at 60-90 BPM to help keep the beat.

Year 1, Week 22

Chapter 3 - Chord Watching #2

LEQ: How can a student distinguish the C and G chords?

After playing through the sheet music, students should complete the "Chord Watching #2" worksheet activities that review Roman numerals, the C major chord and the G major chord.

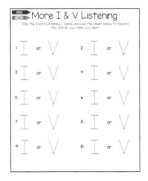   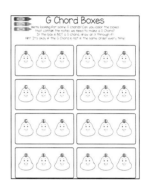

V. Performance: As a group (or as assigned homework), students play along with "Beethoven's Minuet No. 2" which features scrolling sheet music in the treble clef, as well as a handful of parts for other instruments (percussion, lyrics, hand-signs, chord arrangements, etc).

VI. Summarizer: If students played the performance together, the teacher should instruct students to share one thing they liked about the performance with the person next to them (or with the whole group).

Before moving onto the extension lesson, the teacher should review today's lesson by asking students some or all of the following questions: *which notes belong in the C chord?; which notes belong in the G chord?; which colors are associated with the G chord?; which colors are associated with the C chord?*

VII. Extension: As a final activity (or as homework), students play along with "Beethoven's 5th. This C and G performance gives students the chance to continue practice with C and G.

C and G Chord Practice

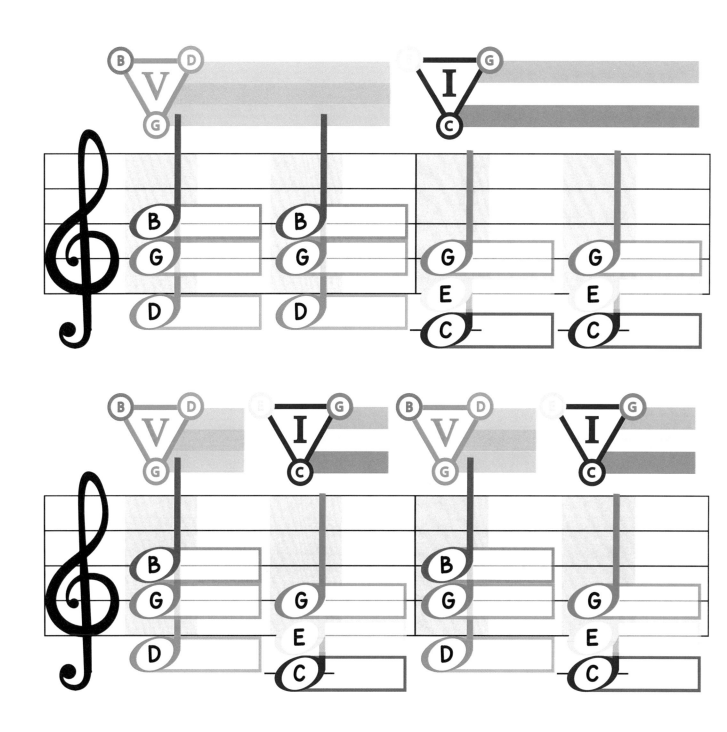

Chord Listening 2

Listening to chords and knowing what chord you are listening to is a big part of building a musical ear!

Cut out the chord cards below and play a listening game. Player 1 takes the bells and the cards. Player 2 closes their eyes.

Then Player 1 plays EITHER the C Major Card OR the G Major Card.

Player 2 listens and tries to guess which Chord Card they heard. Record your answers as you play on the next page!

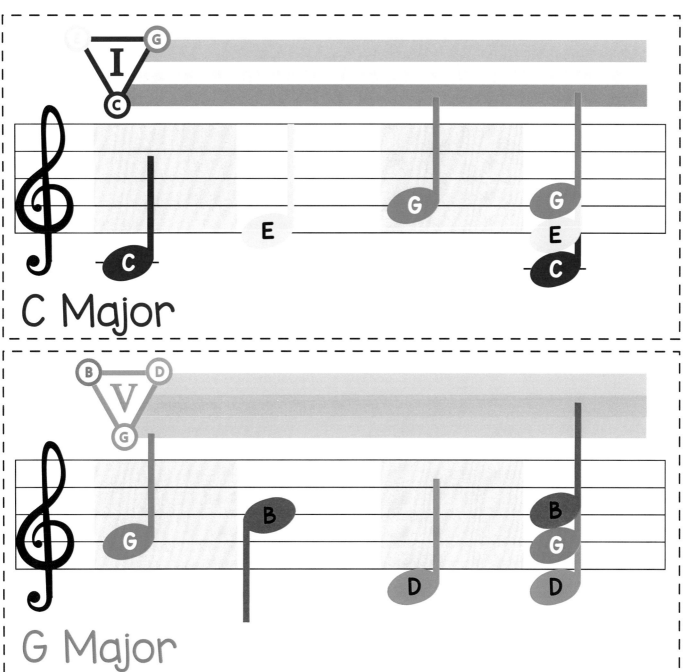

C Major

G Major

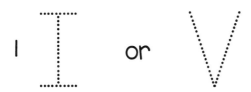

More I & V Listening

Play the Chord Listening 2 Game and use the sheet below to record
the chords you think you hear!

1 I or V   2 I or V

3 I or V   4 I or V

5 I or V   6 I or V

7 I or V   8 I or V

9 I or V   10 I or V

Chord Clouds

Draw a oval around the (G Chords.) Draw a rectangle around the [C Chords.]

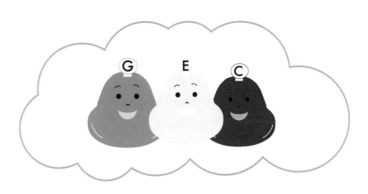

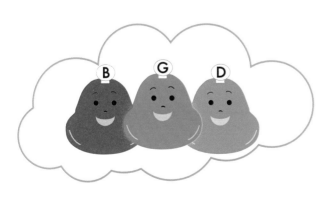

I and V Matching

Draw a line to the bell in each group that matches each corner of the I and V Chords.

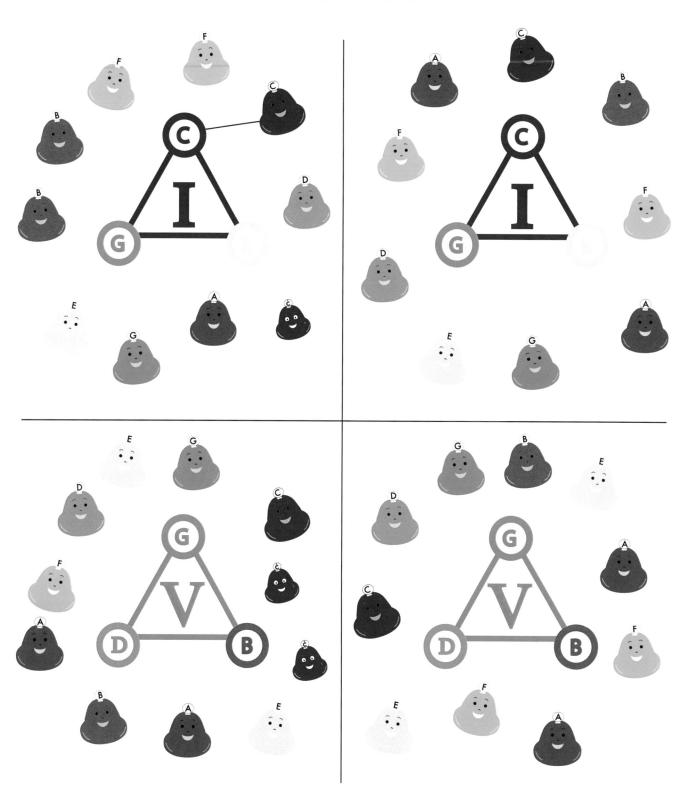

G Chord Boxes

We're looking for some G chords! Can you color the boxes
that contain the notes we need to make a G Chord?
If the box is NOT a G chord, draw an X through it!
Hint: It's okay if the G Chord is not in the same order every time!

 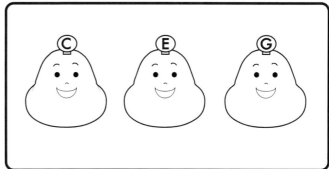

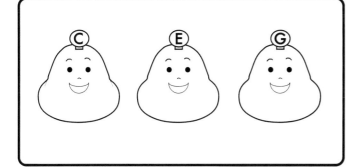 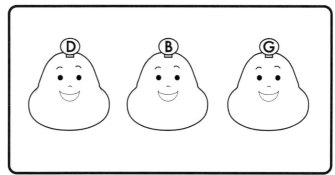

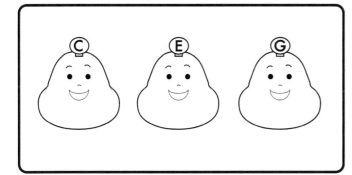 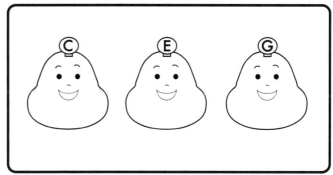

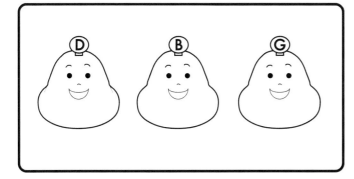 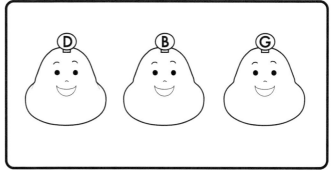

Year 1, Week 23

Chapter 3 - C & G Review
LEQ: How can a student distinguish the notes C and G?

Week 23 Checklist

	Watched Video	Sang/Played Along	Played Sheet Music 1-3 times	Completed Workbook Activities	Repeat video 2-5 tiunes or as needed for mastery
Activator: C Major & G Major Chords	*			N/A	N/A
Core Lesson: Which Witch?	*	*	*	*	
Performance: Vivaldi's Spring	*	*		N/A	N/A
Review: Chord Watching #2				N/A	

* Suggested Priority Activity

 I. **Overview:** In this lesson, students listen and try to identify the notes C and G by ear.

II. **Objective:** By the end of this lesson, students should be able to identify C and G and differentiate between those two notes.

III. **Activator:** Students begin this lesson by reviewing the C and G Chords lesson. The teacher should instruct students to take out their C, D, E, G & B bells to play along with the video.

Once students have warmed up with the chords, they can put away all bells except for C and G to prepare for the core lesson.

IV. **Core Lesson:** The teacher should explain to students that they will continue to practice identifying the C and G bell.

There are two options to conduct this review of C and G: follow along with the Witch Which video, or play along with the Bell Balloon Bananza sheet music.

When this video was originally made, it was intended for use around Halloween. If that doesn't make sense with your calendar, or if witches are not appropriate for your class, then cut out the hot air balloons in the workbook activities, glue them to popsicle sticks and play your own review game with hot air balloons.

After, the class should play through the sheet music for "Bell Balloon Bananza" as a group (or in smaller stations if that works better for the group). The teacher should lead the students by conducting a slow and steady tempo, or use a metronome at 60-90 BPM to help keep the beat.

Year 1, Week 23

Chapter 3 - C & G Review
LEQ: How can a student distinguish the notes C and G?

After playing through the sheet music, students should complete the "Bell Balloon Bananza" workbook activities that review left and right and G & C.

 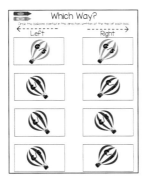  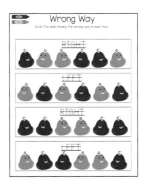

V. Performance: As a group (or as assigned homework), students play along with the Performance track "Vivaldi's Spring" which features scrolling sheet music in the treble clef, as well as a handful of parts for other instruments (percussion, lyrics, hand-signs, chord arrangements, etc).

VI. Summarizer: If students played the performances together, the teacher should instruct students to share one thing they liked about the performance with the person next to them (or with the whole group).

Before moving onto the extension lesson, the teacher should review today's lesson by asking students some or all of the following questions: *which direction is left?; which direction is right?; what number is associated with high C?*

VII. Review: As a final activity (or as homework), student play another round of Chord Watching #2". This will test their ears and ability to memorize the C and G chords. Students can keep their C and G bells out from the core lesson in order to indicate their guess, or make the hand-sign for C or G to indicate the C or G chord.

Bell Balloon Bananza

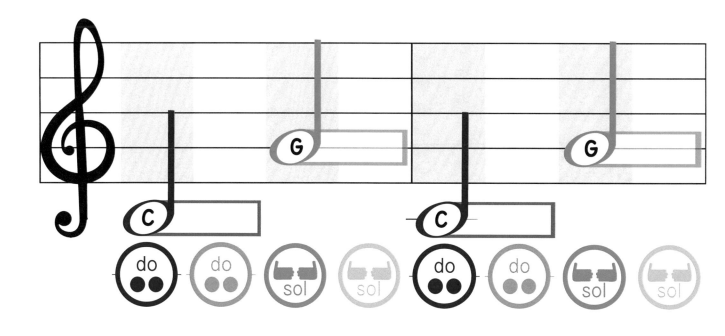

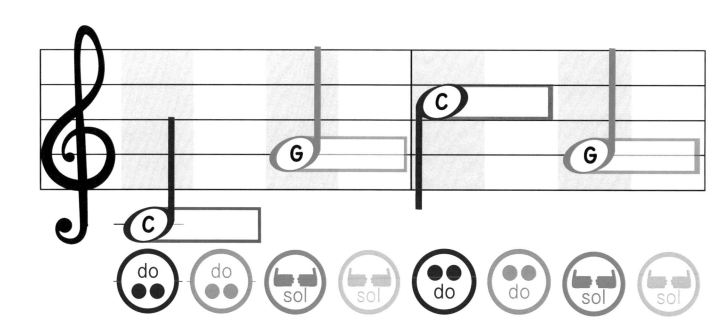

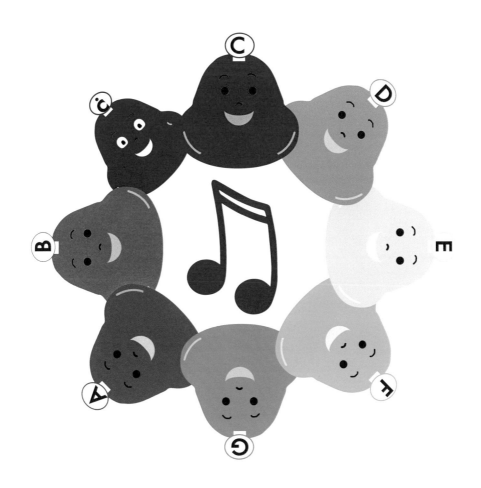

Balloon Puppets

1. Cut out each balloon, and tape or glue it to a popsicle stick.
2. With the bells hidden from the child's view, play one bell at a time and ask the child, "which bell balloon is it?
3. Child identifies the bell verbally OR with the popsicle stick balloons.

If they pick the WRONG note, play them the sound they chose and the correct sound and ask them… "Are these two sounds the same?"

Guide them toward the correct answer and then try again!

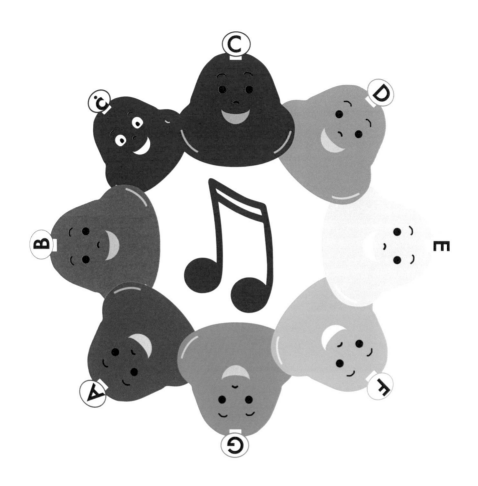

Which Way?

Circle the balloons pointed in the direction written at the top of each box.

← ---------
Left

--------- →
Right

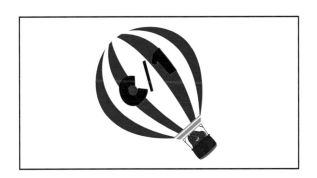

Hot Air Balloon Maze

Follow the balloons to make it all the way to the end of this maze!

Start here!

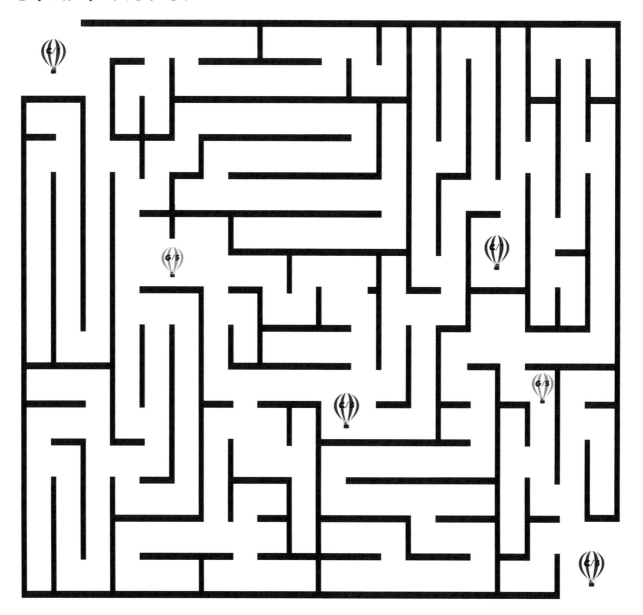

You Made it!

Balloons and Bells

Draw a line between each bell and the balloon with the correct description for that bell.

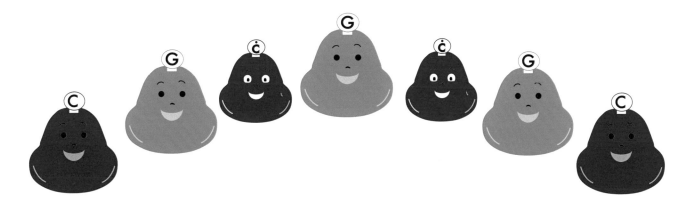

305

Wrong Way

Circle the bells facing the wrong way in each box.

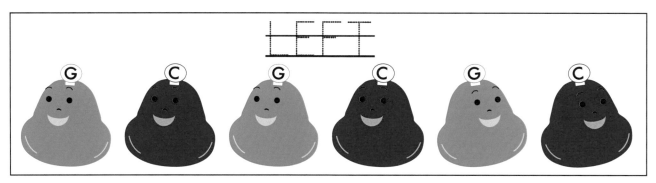

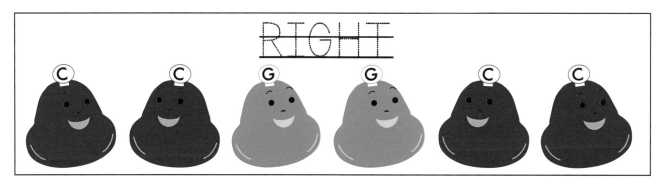

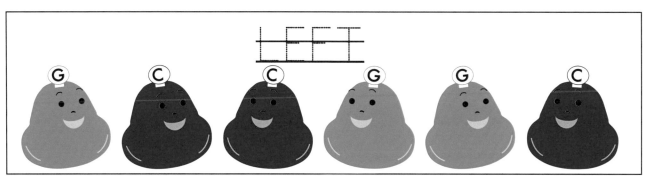

Hidden Bells

Can you find all of the C and G Bells? Write the correct number
next to each big bell below!

Year 1, Week 24

Chapter 3 - Perform and Assess

LEQ: How can a student differentiate between the notes in the G chord and the notes in the C chord?

Week 24 Checklist

	Watched Video	Sang/Played Along	Played Sheet Music 1-3 times	Completed Workbook Activities	Repeat video 2-5 tiunes or as needed for mastery
Activator: Chord Watching #2	*	*	N/A	N/A	
Performance: Do & Sol Performance Playlist	*	*		N/A	
Review/Assess: What Note Is It #1 & What Note Is It #3	*	*	N/A		
Review/Assess: Interactive Quiz #3			N/A	N/A	

* Suggested Priority Activity

I. Overview: In this lesson, students take turns performing various performance tracks for the class. Then students attempt to identify notes just by listening.

II. Objective: By the end of this lesson, students should be able to play a C and G performance track alone or in a small group, and be able to identify the notes of the C and G chords.

III. Activator: To begin today's lesson, students will follow along with "Chord Watching #2". This lesson from last week will give students a chance to review the C and G chords before jumping into their performances.

IV. Performance: The teacher should explain to students that they will each play a different performance today in front of the class. Students can play individually, or if it makes more sense, in small groups. Students can play the same part or various parts (hand-signing, percussion, etc.).

For tracks without sheet music, students should play along with the video accompaniment. This will make the track more recognizable and serve as a scaffold for students.

There is a playlist of all the performance on this week's lesson page, so the teacher can scroll through and assign students a performance track, or (if it's possible with this group of students) students can choose the performance they'd like to perform.

As each student performs, the teacher should play a metronome at 60-90 BPM to keep the beat. The performers can play along with either the video or just the sheet music if they prefer.

Year 1, Week 24

Chapter 3 - Perform and Assess

LEQ: How can a student differentiate between the notes in the G chord and the notes in the C chord?

V. Review/Assess: Instead of a performance today, students will watch two listening games: "What Note Is It?" numbers 1 & 3--the C chord and the G chord.

The teacher should give each student a copy of the "What Note Is It" handouts and explain that as students listen, they should not call out their guess, but circle the matching bell on their paper.

The teacher may decide to model the first guess for students if they are unclear about what to do. The host of the listening game will reveal the answer after each question, so students should mark each of their answers right or wrong.

At the end of each video, the teacher should debrief with students: *Which note was easiest to identify?; Which note was most difficult to identify?; Were there any notes that students consistently got wrong?; Were there any notes that students consistently got right?.*

If students become frustrated, the teacher should explain that they have 5 more chapters of content to learn before they will really develop their ears, and that they should keep practicing! If students have a device at home, they can download the free Prodigies Bell App for continued practice at home.

VI. Summarizer: The teacher should begin by summarizing the performance part of this week's lesson. The teacher should ask: *what was students' favorite part of the performance?; what were they most impressed by?; what was one thing they were surprised by?; what is one thing that they could do better (personally) next time?*

Since this is the last lesson in Chapter Three, the teacher should ask students to reflect on the chapter. Which lesson was their favorite and if there's time, review the essential questions from each lesson: *how can a student differentiate between the notes C and G?; how can a student use C and G to simplify "The Wheels on the Bus?; how can a student play and reference a C and G Major Chord?; how can a student count quarter and eighth notes?; how can a student play a simplified version of chords?; how can a student identify the C and G chords?; how can a student distinguish the notes C and G?; how can a student differentiate between the notes in the G chord and the notes in the C chord?*

VII. Review/Assess: As a final activity (or as homework), students complete the third interactive quiz directly on the Prodigies site on this week's lesson page.

What Note Is It?

Draw a circle around the bell you hear!

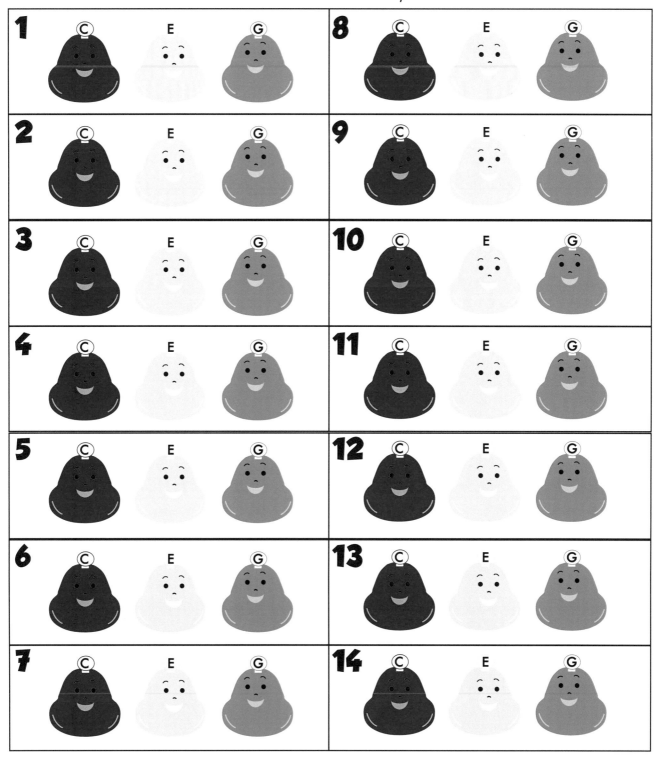

Bonus: What chord is it? _____

What Note Is It?

Draw a circle around the bell you hear in each box!

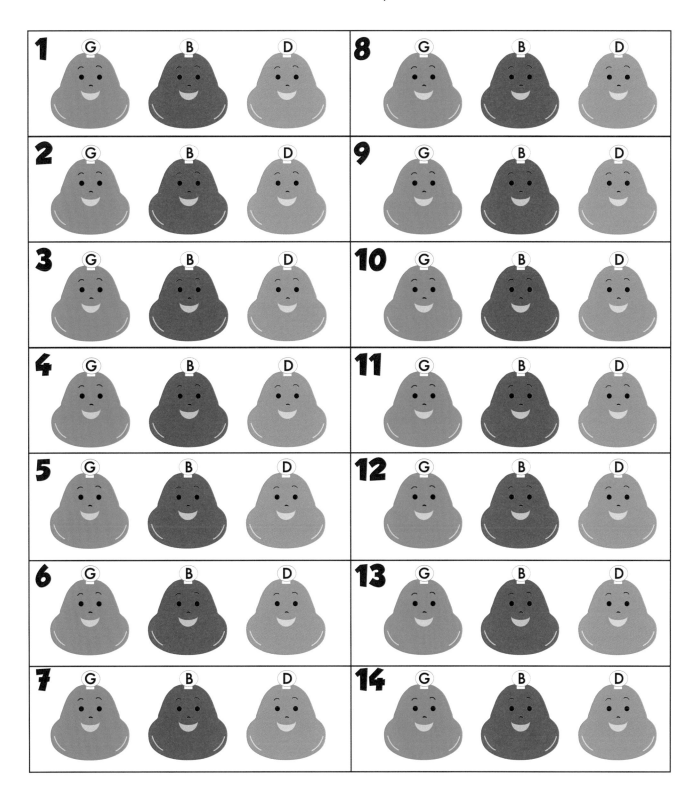

Yankee Doodle
C & G Borduns

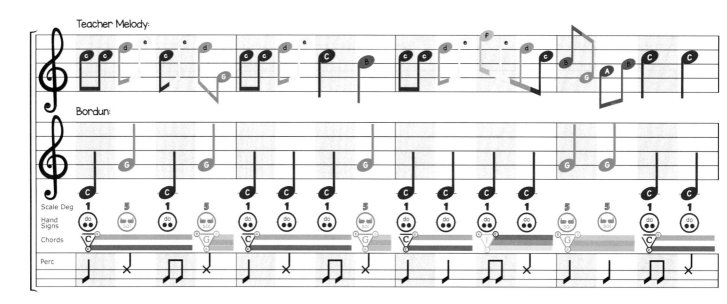

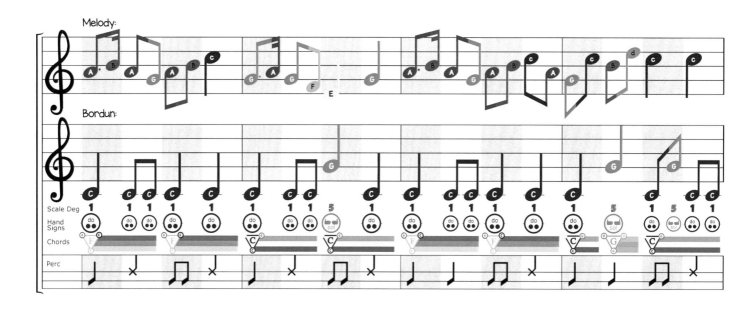

Notes Used:

Frère Jacques
C & G Borduns

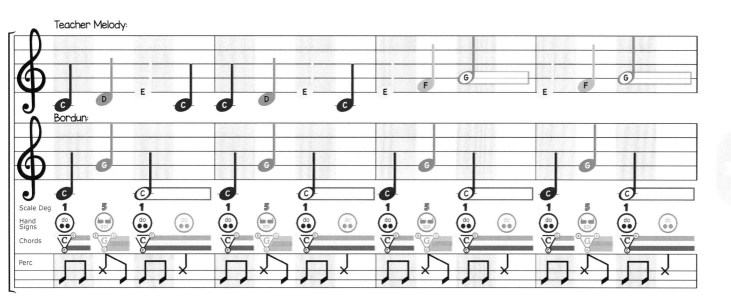

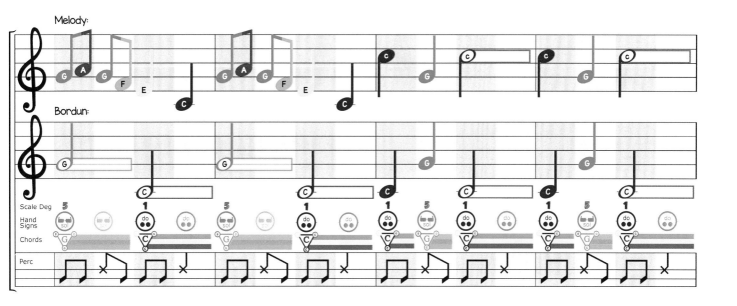

Wheels on the Bus
C & G Borduns

Notes Used:

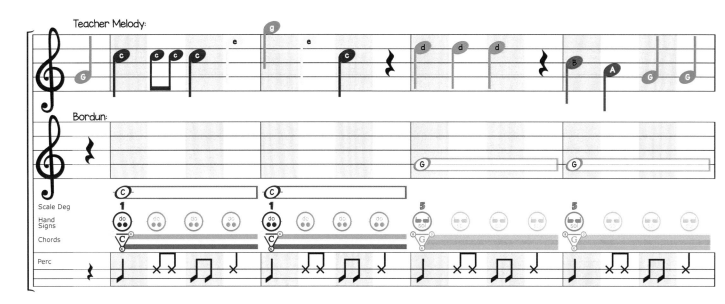

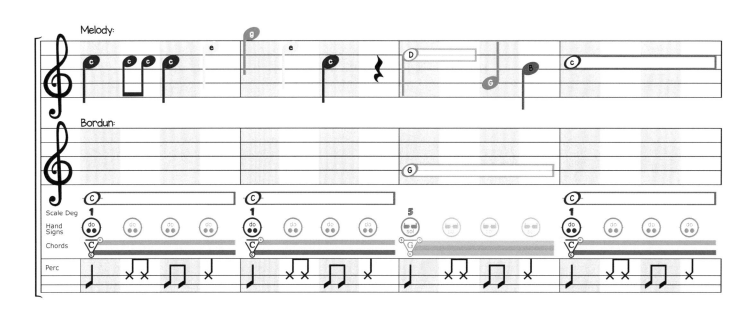

Notes Used:

Row Your Boat
C & G Borduns

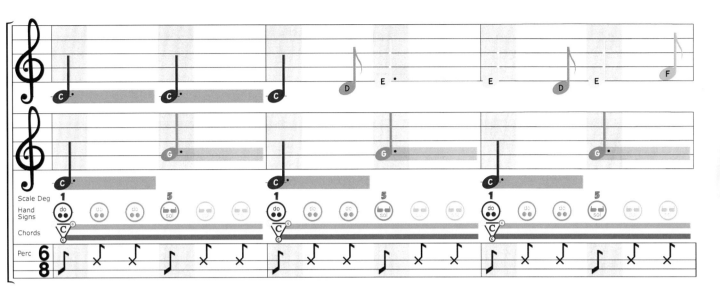

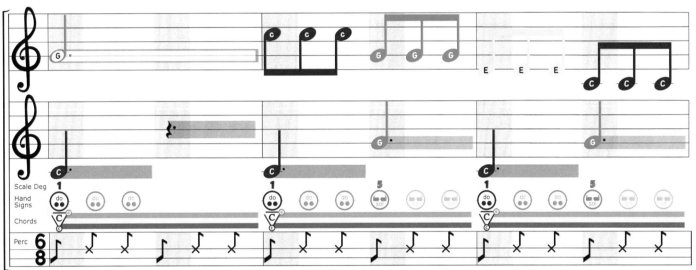

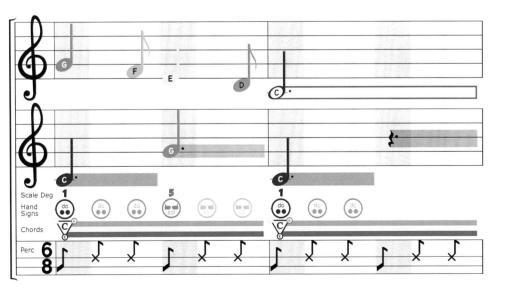

315

Spring
E & B Borduns

Antoni Vivaldi

Notes Used:

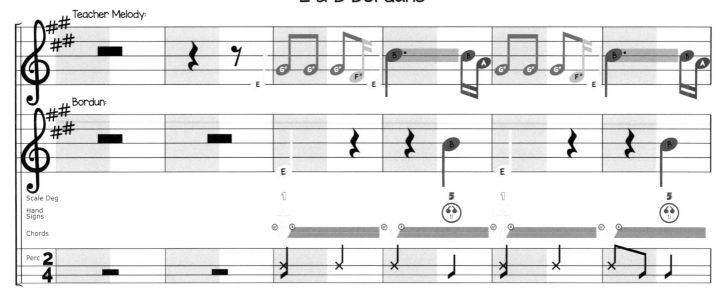

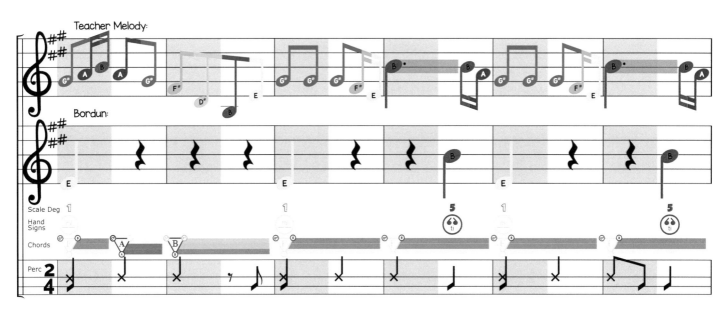

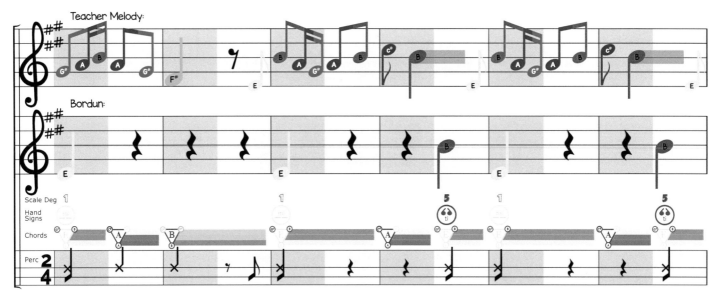

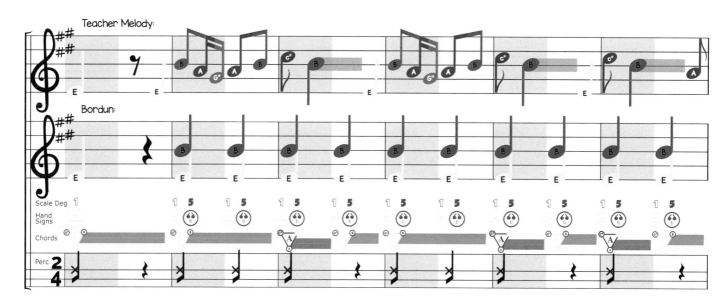

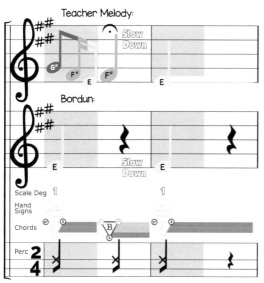

General Music Level 1A Workbook

CHAPTER FOUR

Dear families & teachers,

Welcome back to more musical fun with Prodigies Music Lessons!
In Chapter 4, we'll focus a lot on the first three musical notes: Do, Re & Mi.

Using Do, Re and Mi, we'll start playing some popular songs like Hot Cross Buns and Mary Had a Little Lamb. Make sure your learners are singing along as they play their instrument. We want them to continue connecting the pitch they hear to the pitch they sing, so they sing more in tune and learn to memorize the sound.

Also, be sure sing and sign with the hand-signs in each song! You can do it with the video to start, or you can do it all along to help your learner work their sense of memorized pitch.

As always, strive for a music practice that is positive and memorable. You may know some of the songs in the beginning of each section, so jump in and play or sing along with your learner(s). Playing along with your learner may be an opportunity for a positve music memory and teacher-student bonding.

As you become familiar with Do, Re, Mi, encourage your learner to make up his or her own songs using these three notes. Get silly with it if it will help them stay engaged and having fun!

As always, if you have any questions about the books or video content, please contact us at Hello@Prodigies.com

Happy Musicing!

- Mr. Rob & the Prodigies Team

Rhythms in this Chapter

Quarter Note = 1 Beat

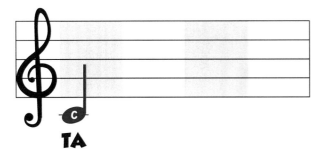

To review, the quarter notes take up one BEAT. It takes four quarter notes to fill up a measure. In other words, it takes up one-quarter of the measure!

Half Note = 2 Beats

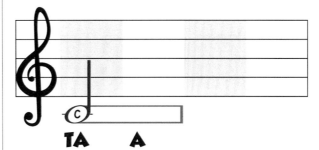

Some notes take up 2 BEATS. We call those HALF NOTES, because they take up one-half of our measure. How many half notes does it take to fill our measure?

Two Eighth Notes = 1 Beat

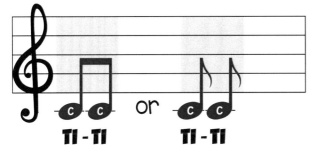

No matter how they are printed, eighth notes are played at twice the speed of quarter notes.
If you sing Ta Ta Ti-Ti Ta, the Ti-Ti is the speed of the eighth notes!

Triplet = 1 Quarter Note

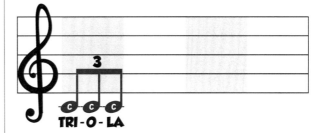

Even faster than the eighth note is the triplet! It takes 3 of these small notes to fill the space of one quarter note. The triplet is a more advanced rhythm. It feels different from our other rhythms because it has an ODD number of notes. That's okay though, we'll still have fun with it when we meet Pineapple later this chapter.

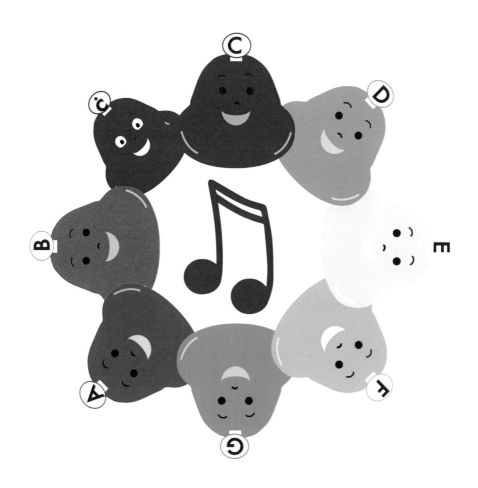

Do Re Mi Bell Mat

Use this bell mat when practicing Do, Re, Mi and when playing along with Chapter 4.

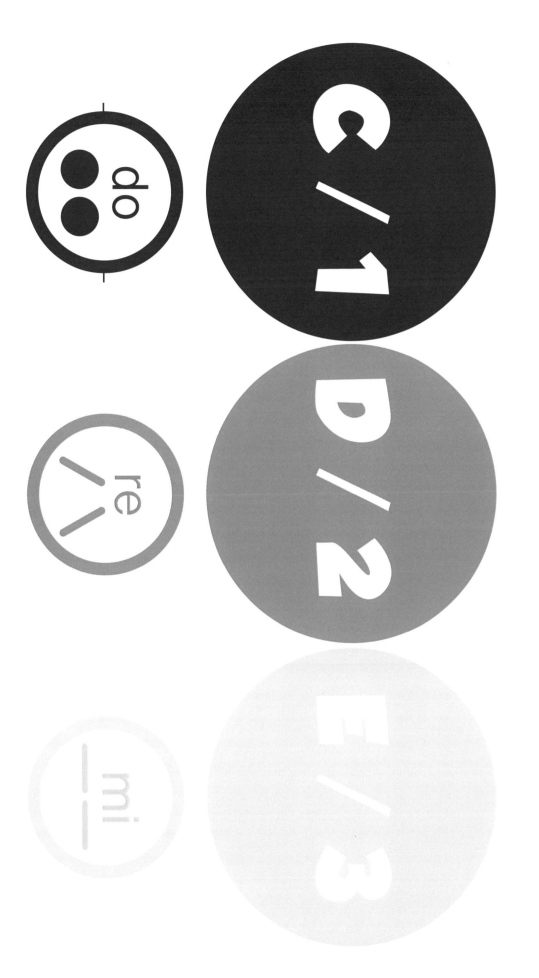

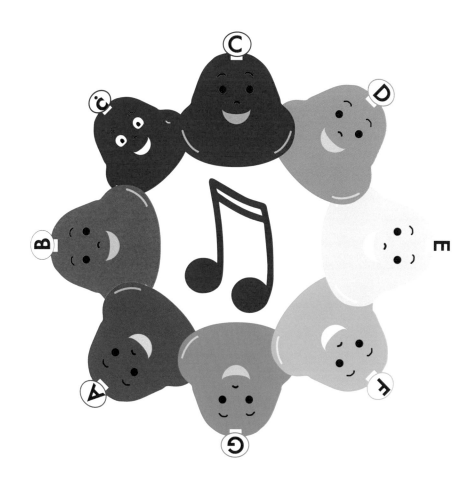

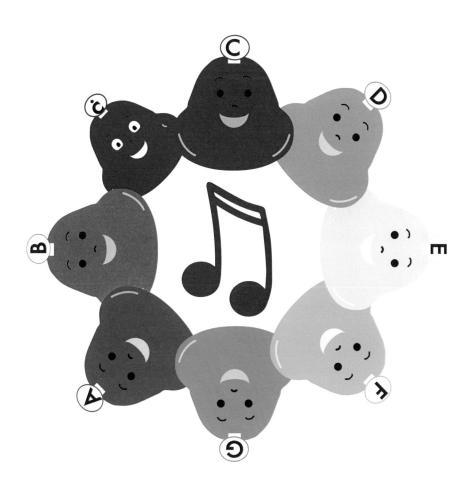

Year 1, Week 25

Chapter 4 - Do, Re, Mi Warm Up

LEQ: How can a student perform the hand-signs for C, D and E?

Week 25 Checklist

	Watched Video	Sang/Played Along	Played Sheet Music 1-3 times	Completed Workbook Activities	Repeat video 2-5 times or as needed for mastery
Activator: Campfire Song	*		N/A	N/A	
Core Lesson: Do, Re, Mi Intro	*	*	*	*	
Performance: Warm Up #1	*	*		N/A	
Extension: Warm Up #2				N/A	

⋆ Suggested Priority Activity

I. Overview: In this lesson, students study the Solfege hand-signs for C, D and E.

II. Objective: By the end of this lesson, students should be able to differentiate between the hand-signs for C, D and E.

III. Activator: Students begin this lesson with the sing-along "Campfire Song".

Before beginning, the teacher should explain to students that they will sing and sign along as Mr. Rob sings about Do, Re and Mi.

Students can sing along with the lyrics as they appear on the screen, or just sing and sign along with the Solfege in the chorus.

IV. Core Lesson: Students take out their C, D and E bells to play along with "Do, Re, Mi Intro". Students begin by playing along on the bells, and then hand-sign along.

After the video, the class should play through the sheet music for "Do, Re Mi Intro" as a group (or in smaller stations if that works better for the group). The teacher should lead the students by conducting a slow and steady tempo, or using a metronome at 60-90 BPM to help keep the beat.

Year 1, Week 25

Chapter 4 - Do, Re, Mi Intro

LEQ: How can a student perform the hand-signs for C, D and E?

After playing through the sheet music, students should complete the "Do, Re, Mi Intro" worksheet activities that review hand-signs and give students a song-writing opportunity.

V. Performance: As a group (or as assigned homework), students play along with "Warm Up #1", which features scrolling sheet music in the treble clef, as well as a handful of parts for other instruments (percussion, lyrics, hand-signs, chord arrangements, etc.).

VI. Summarizer: If students played the performance together, the teacher should instruct students to share one thing they liked about the performance with the person next to them (or with the whole group).

Before moving onto the review lesson, the teacher should review today's lesson by asking students some or all of the following questions: *What is the hand-sign for Do?; What is the hand-sign for Re?; What is the hand-sign for Mi?; What are the scale degrees associated with Do, Re and Mi?*

VII. Extension: As a final activity (or as homework), students play along with the Performance "Warm Up #2". This Performance warm up uses Do, Re and Mi, but adds more

Do Re Mi Warm Up

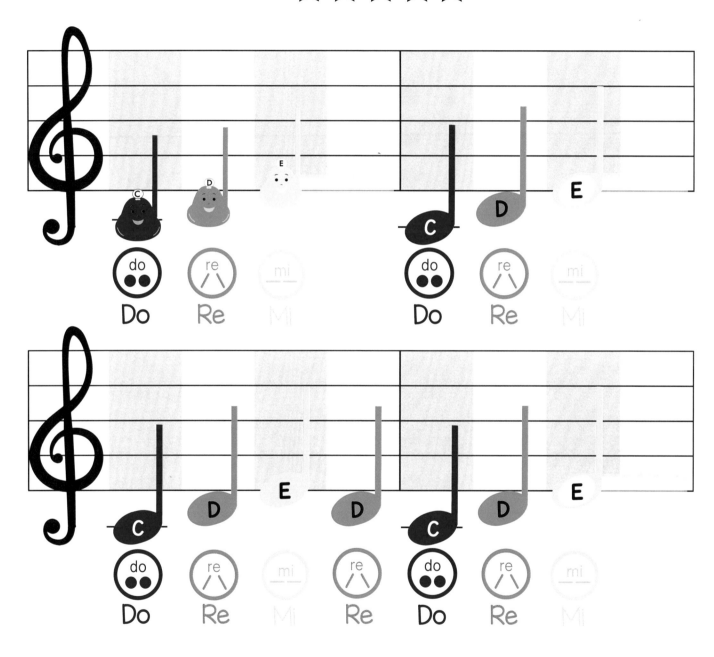

Do Re Mi Hand-Signs

Adding hand-signs to our musical notes makes learning, feeling and singing the notes more physical and more fun!

In this chapter, we'll learn and practice the hand-signs for the first three musical notes: Do, Re and Mi. The signs will make it easier for you and your learner to feel the different sensations of each note.

The detailed drawings of the hand-signs are visible here.

In the middle are some of the simplified versions that we use inside the Playground videos.

The simplified signs are easier to write on a board if you're a teacher and easy enough for kids to draw.

For extra practice, try playing a bell (Red, Orange or Yellow) and then singing the Solfège while making the hand-sign. Have your learner sing and sign along, or even have them play a bell and then sing and sign.

Do Re Mi Hand-Signs

Point and Sign Poster

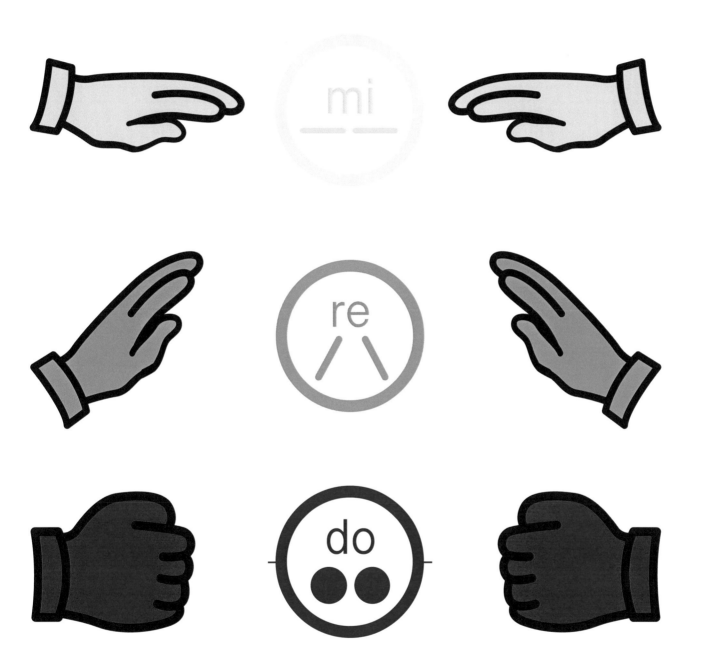

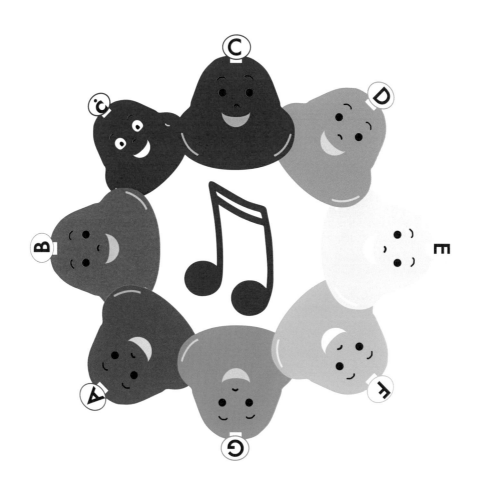

Hand-Sign Cut-Outs

Cut out these twelve hand-signs. Then, arrange them in different orders to make up your own song!

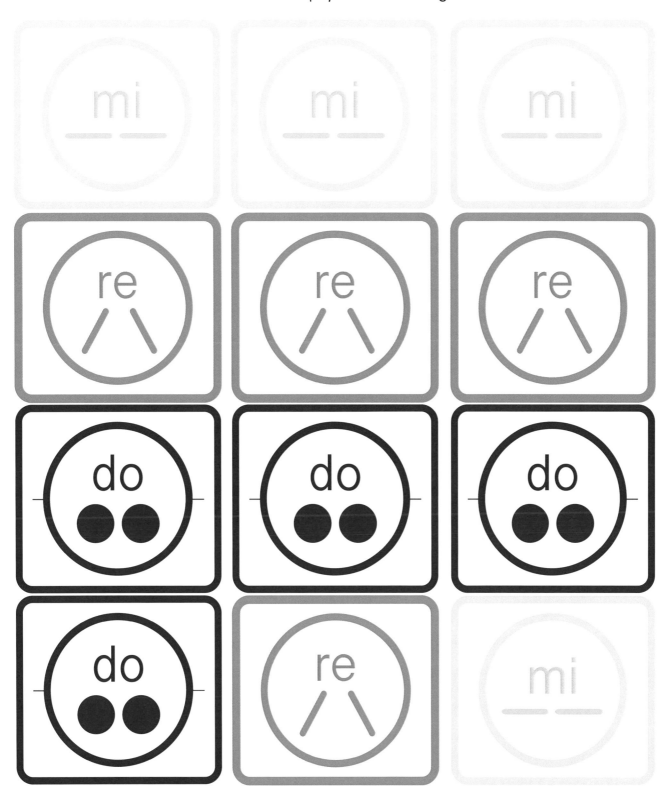

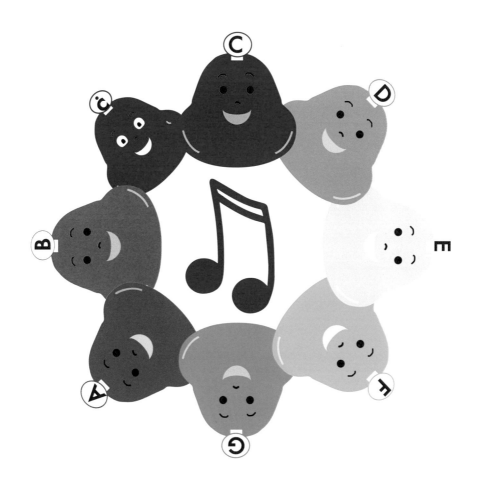

Write a Song Using

Title	Composer

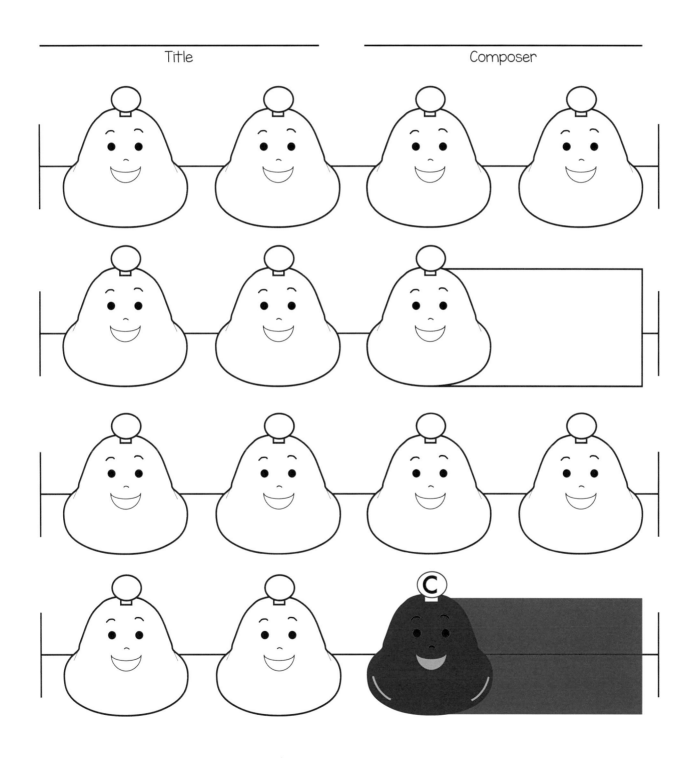

Warm Up #1
C Major

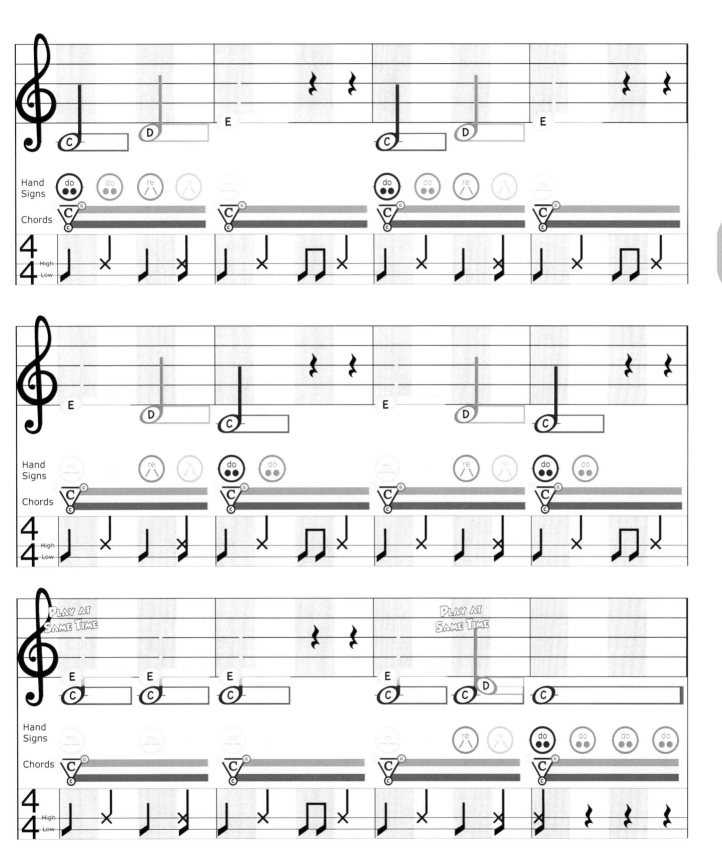

Notes Used:

Warm Up #2
C Major

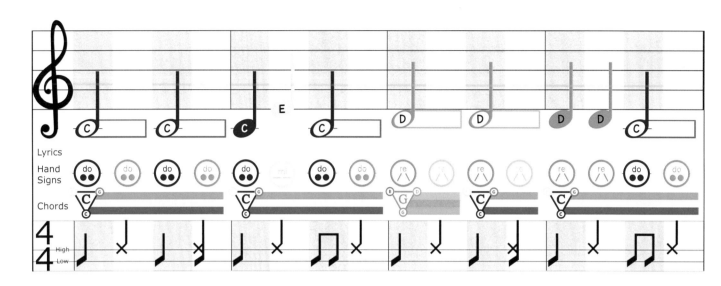

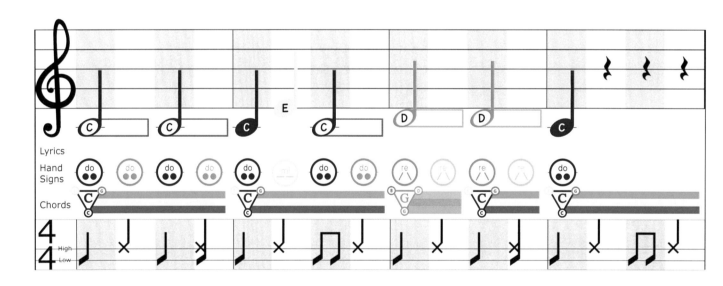

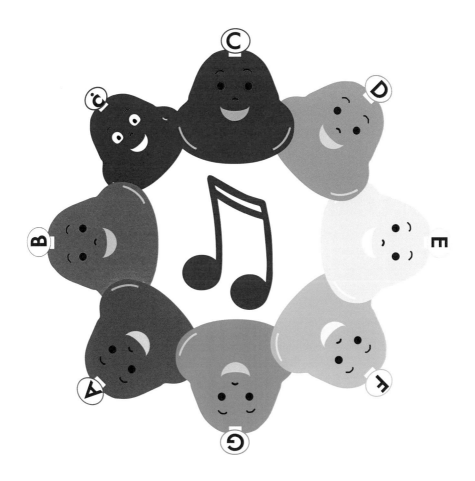

Year 1, Week 26

Chapter 4 - Mary Had a Little Lamb

LEQ: How can a student identify C, D and E?

Week 26 Checklist

	Watched Video	Sang/Played Along	Played Sheet Music 1-3 times	Completed Workbook Activities	Repeat video 2-5 tiunes or as needed for mastery
Activator: Melodies # 3	*			N/A	
Core Lesson: Mary Had a Little Lamb	*	*	*	*	
Performance: Mary Had a Little Lamb	*	*		N/A	
Extension: Campfire Song			N/A	N/A	

* Suggested Priority Activity

  I. Overview: In this lesson, students identify the sound and various elements of C, D and E.

  II. Objective: By the end of this lesson, students should be able to identify the notes C, D and E, and play, sing and hand-sign along with "Mary Had a Little Lamb".

  III. Activator: Students begin this lesson by reviewing hand-signs and Do, Re, Mi with Melodies # 3. The teacher should explain to students that before jumping into their main lesson today, they will review all of the hand-signs with Mr. Rob.

Students should hand-sign and sing the Solfege names as they scroll across the screen.

  IV. Core Lesson: Students take out their C, D and E bells to play along with "Mary Had a Little Lamb". The teacher may decide to have students hand-sign and sing along once through, before playing along with the bells.

After the video, the class should play through the sheet music for "Mary Had a Little Lamb" as a group (or in smaller stations if that works better for the group). The teacher should lead the students by conducting a slow and steady tempo, or using a metronome at 60-90 BPM to help keep the beat.

Year 1, Week 26

Chapter 4 - Mary Had a Little Lamb

LEQ: How can a student identify C, D and E?

After playing through the sheet music, students should complete the "Mary Had a Little Lamb" worksheet activities that review Do, Re, Mi.

V. Performance: As a group (or as assigned homework), students play along with "Mary Had a Little Lamb", which features scrolling sheet music in the treble clef, as well as a handful of parts for other instruments (percussion, lyrics, hand-signs, chord arrangements, etc.).

VI. Summarizer: If students played the performance together, the teacher should instruct students to share one thing they liked about the performance with the person next to them (or with the whole group).

Before moving onto the review lesson, the teacher should review today's lesson by asking students some or all of the following questions: *Which number represents C?; Which number represents D?; Which number represents E?*

VII. Extension: As a final activity (or as homework), students sing and sign along with "Campfire Song" featuring C, D and E. Since students may have sang and signed along in previous lessons, students should be able to follow along.

Mary Had a Little Lamb

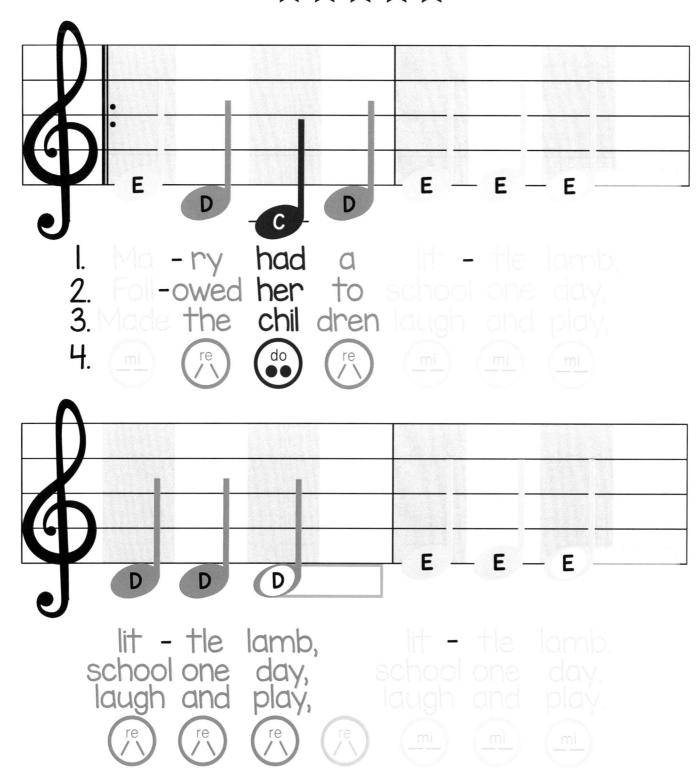

343

Listening Game

In this activity, you will play the C, D & E bells while the student records what they hear you play!

Allow the student to see what bells you're playing at first. Then try playing the same notes and hiding the bells from view. You will most likely need to guide them to the correct answers, but the process will develop both their sense of absolute and relative pitch.

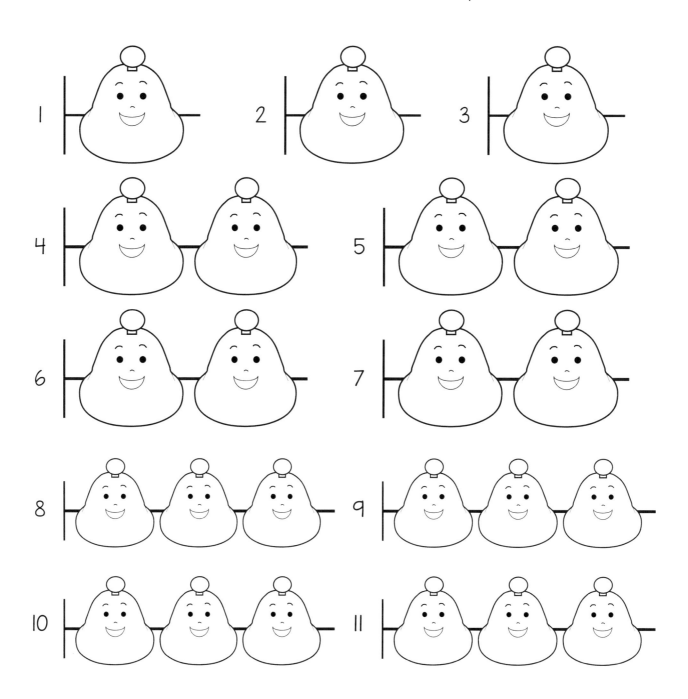

Music Matching

We have lots of different ways to talk about our musical notes, and sometimes they get mixed up!

Can you connect the Solfège words to the scale degrees (numbers), hand-signs and bells?

Music Matching 2

Our musical names got mixed up again! This time, connect the scale degrees, hand-signs, and Solfège names to the bells they match!

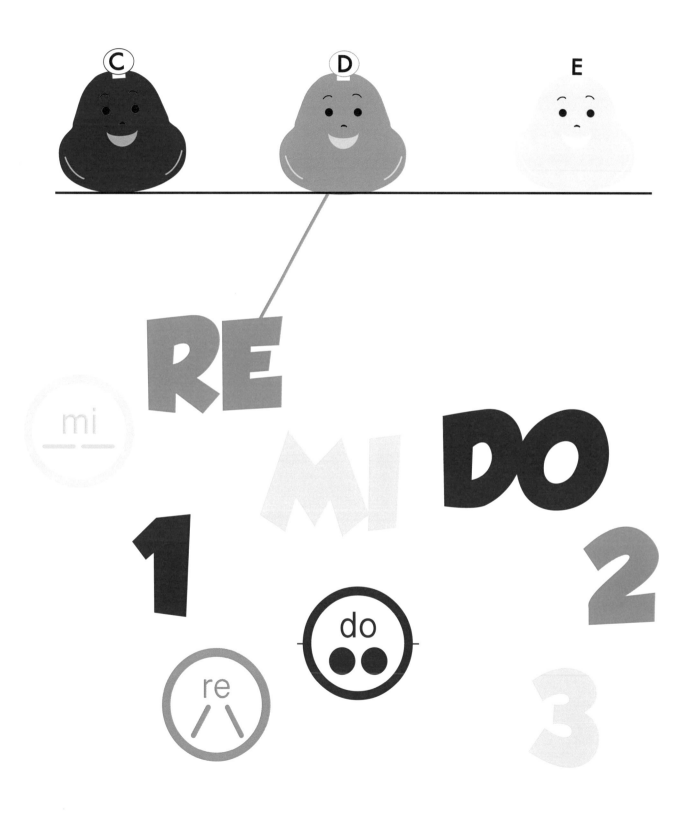

Write a Song Using

1 2 3

Write a song using the numbers and then play it on your bells!

_____ Title   _____ Composer

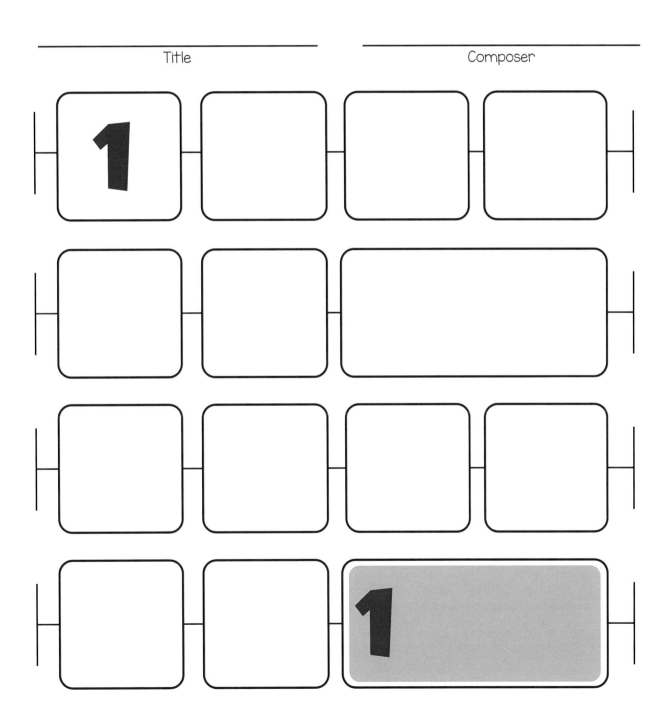

Mary Had a Little Lamb
C Major

Notes Used:

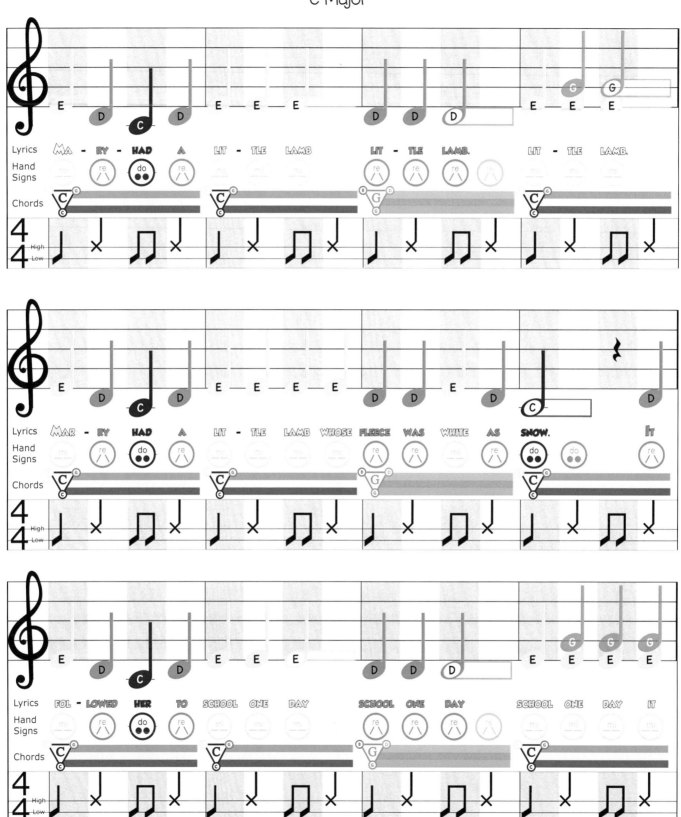

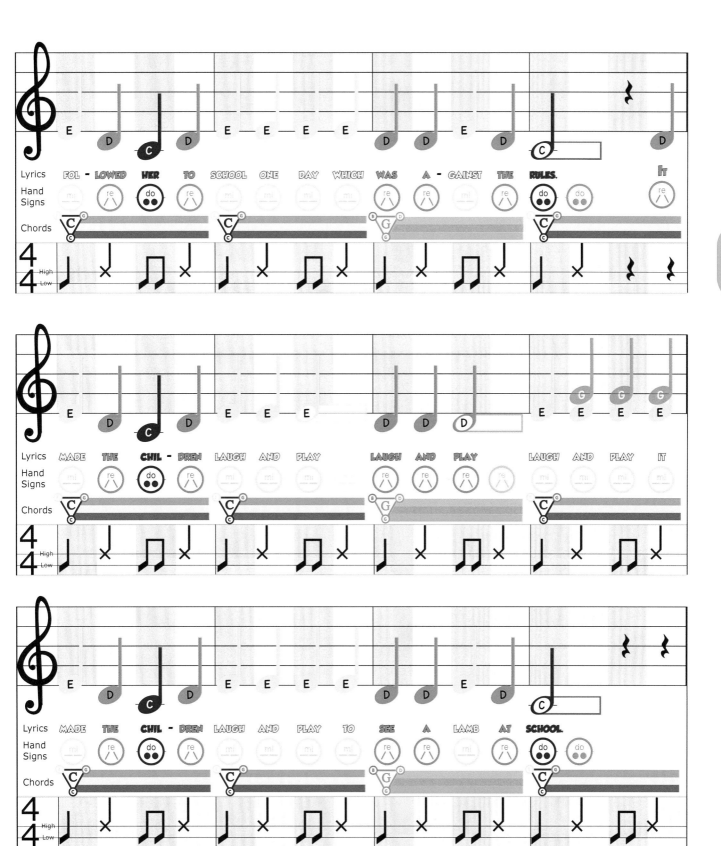

Melody #3:
Do Re Mi Fa Sol Sol Do

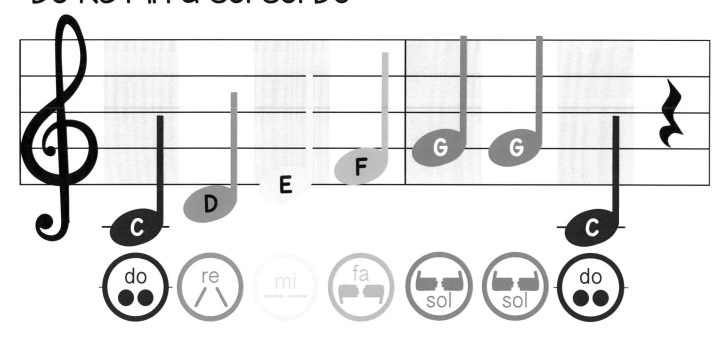

Melody #4:
Do Ti La Sol Do Re Do

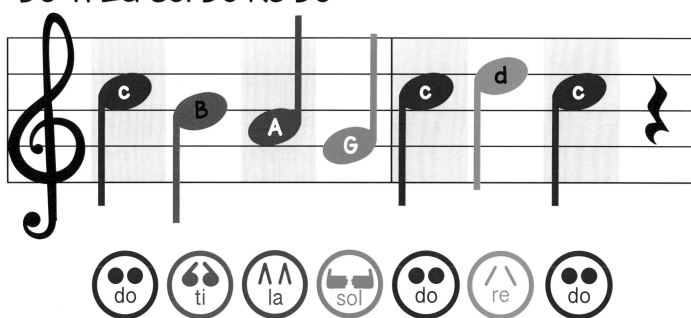

Quiz #3:

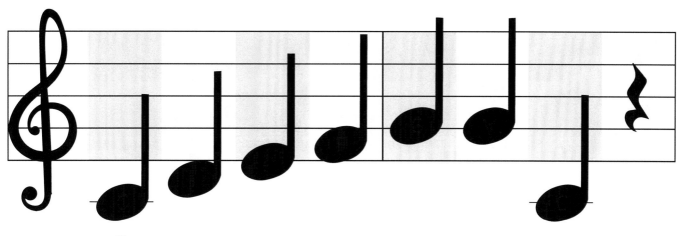

Part 1 : WHICH NOTE?
Write the notes on
the blank lines!

____ ____ ____ ____ ____ ____ ____

Part 2 : MIXED UP!
Match the Solfege
Hand Signs to the
notes above!

Quiz #4:

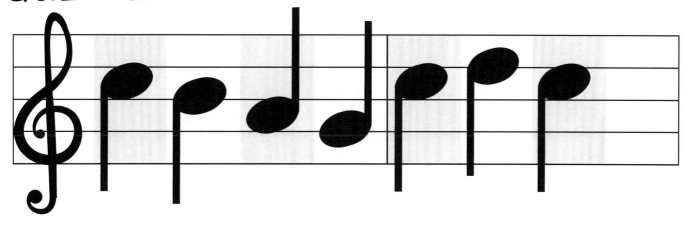

Part 1 : WHICH NOTE?
Write the notes on
the blank lines!

____ ____ ____ ____ ____ ____ ____

Part 2 : MIXED UP!
Match the Solfege
Hand Signs to the
notes above!

Year 1, Week 27

Chapter 4 - Hot Cross Buns

LEQ: How can a student refer to neighboring notes?

Week 27 Checklist

	Watched Video	Sang/Played Along	Played Sheet Music 1-3 times	Completed Workbook Activities	Repeat video 2-5 tiunes or as needed for mastery
Activator: Melodies #5	*			N/A	
Core Lesson: Hot Cross Buns	*	*	*	*	
Performance: Hot Cross Buns	*	*		N/A	
Extension: Hot Cross Buns *Harder				N/A	

* Suggested Priority Activity

I. Overview: In this lesson, students learn to refer to neighboring notes as musical steps and play the classic "Hot Cross Buns".

II. Objective: By the end of this lesson, students should be able to identify neighboring notes as musical steps and play along with Hot Cross Buns.

III. Activator: Students begin this lesson with Melodies #5. This episode of Melodies reviews the hand-signs for Do, Re & Mi, in addition to a few other notes. The teacher should explain to students that today's lesson will focus on Do, Re & Mi, and the distance between each note.

Before playing the video, students should review the hand-signs for Do, Re, Mi.

IV. Core Lesson: The teacher should explain to students that today they will learn Hot Cross Buns and play with the C, D & E bells today! A chord is a group of notes that sounds nice when we play them together. "Hot Cross Buns" uses the notes C, D and E, which are each one space apart.

Students will learn the term "musical step" and study the distance between notes in this lesson's workbook activities.

After the video, the class should play through the sheet music for "Hot Cross Buns" as a group (or in smaller stations if that works better for the group). The teacher should lead the students by conducting a slow and steady tempo, or using a metronome at 60-90 BPM to help keep the beat.

Year 1, Week 27

Chapter 4 - Hot Cross Buns

LEQ: How can a student refer to neighboring notes?

After playing through the sheet music, students should complete the "Hot Cross Buns" worksheet activities that review C, D & E and musical steps.

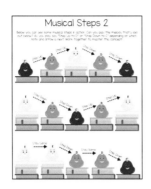

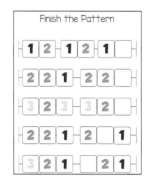

V. Performance: As a group (or as assigned homework), students play along with "Hot Cross Buns", which features scrolling sheet music in the treble clef, as well as a handful of parts for other instruments (percussion, lyrics, hand-signs, chord arrangements, etc.).

VI. Summarizer: If students played the performance together, the teacher should instruct students to share one thing they liked about the performance with the person next to them (or with the whole group).

Before moving onto the review lesson, the teacher should review today's lesson by asking students some or all of the following questions: *Which number is associated with the low C?; Which number is associated with the note D?; Which number is associated with the note E?; How many spaces are between a musical step?*

VII. Extension: As a final activity (or as homework), students play along with "Hot Cross Buns (Harder)" in Performance Prodigies Chapter 4. This song gives students the opportunity to continue practicing "Hot Cross Buns", this time with a more challenging set of notes.

Hot Cross Buns

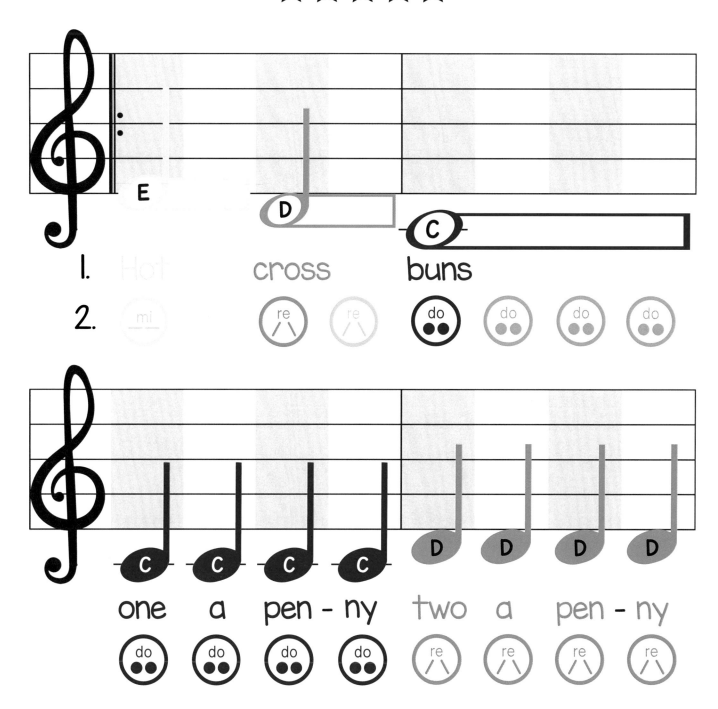

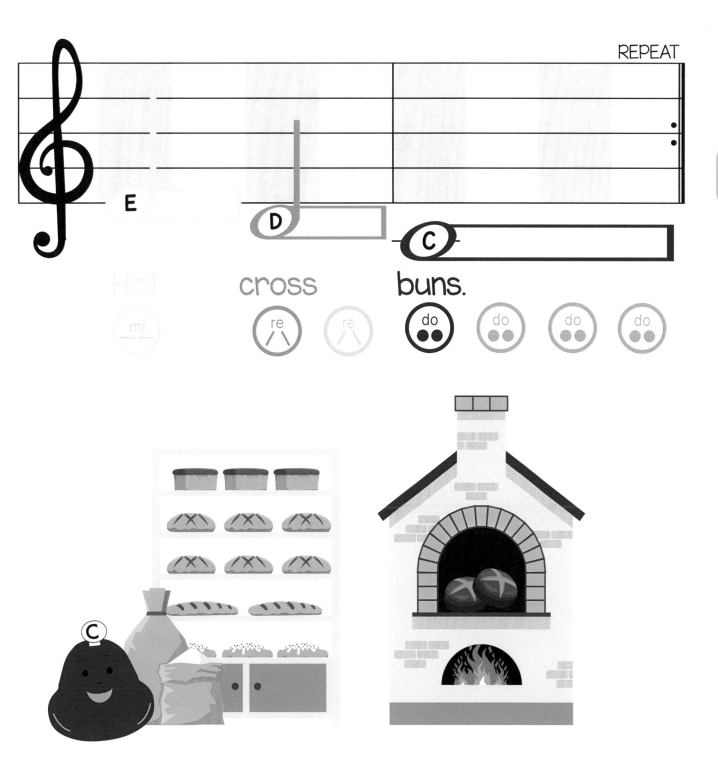

REPEAT

E

Hot

cross

buns.

Musical Steps I

In music, when we go from one note to a neighboring note, we call this a step.

For instance, you can STEP UP from C to D or STEP DOWN from E to D.

You can place the bells on actual steps to see the concept for yourself! Or use some books to make a miniature staircase on your desk.

With this set up, try playing "Hot Cross Buns" or any of the other Do, Re, Mi songs.

As you point to the music, emphasize when you're stepping up versus stepping down. You can have some extra fun by playing the bells with your feet again

We will talk about SKIPPING in a later chapter (from C to E).
For now focus on STEPPING UP and STEPPING DOWN with Do, Re and Mi.

Musical Steps 2

Below you can see some musical steps in action. Can you play the melody that's laid out below? As you play, say "Step Up to D" or "Step Down to C" depending on which note and arrow is next. Work together to master this concept!

Musical Steps 3

Now it's your turn to draw some musical steps!
Draw a straight arrow in between the bells going UP or DOWN, just like we
saw on the previous page.

Finish the Pattern

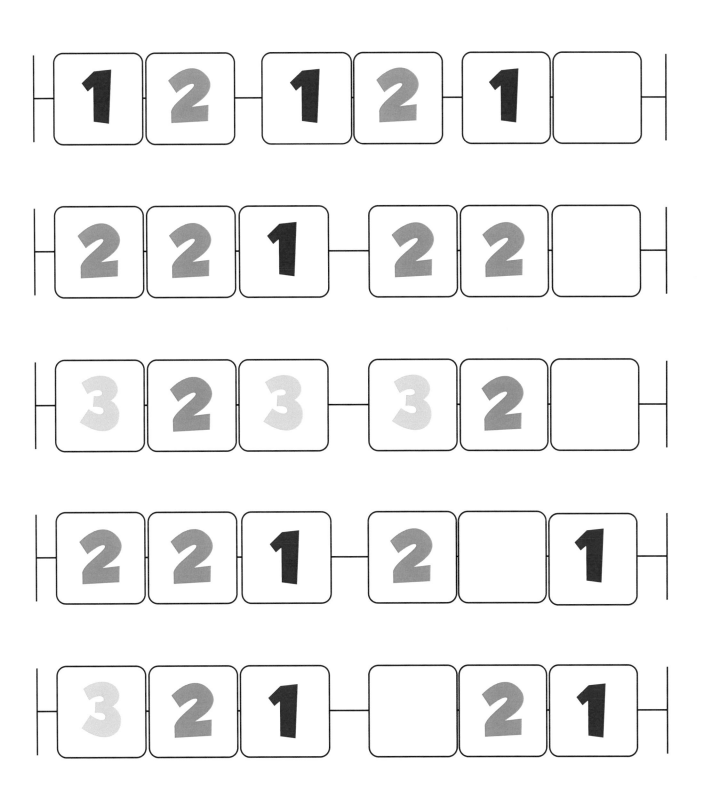

1 2 1 2 1 ___

2 2 1 2 2 ___

3 2 3 3 2 ___

2 2 1 2 ___ 1

3 2 1 ___ 2 1

Hot Cross Buns (easy)
C Major

Notes Used:

Hot Cross Buns (hard)
C Major

Notes Used:

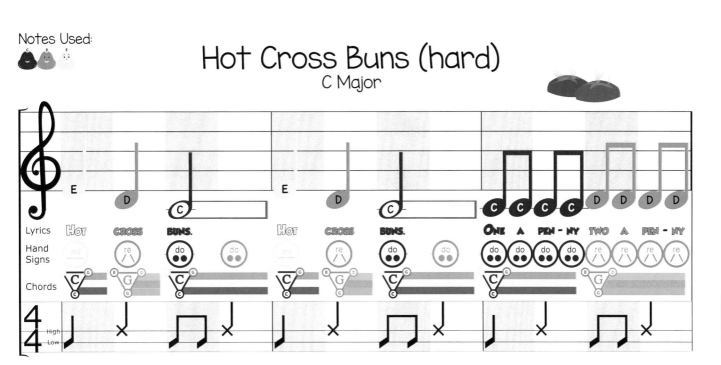

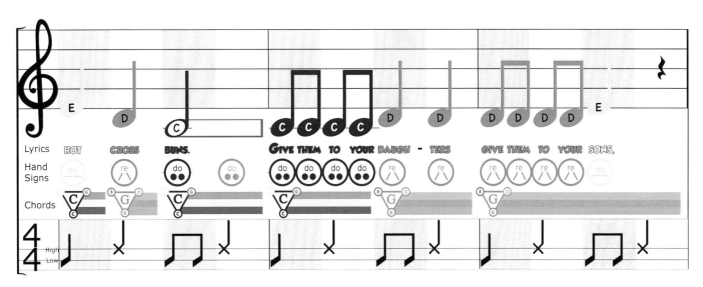

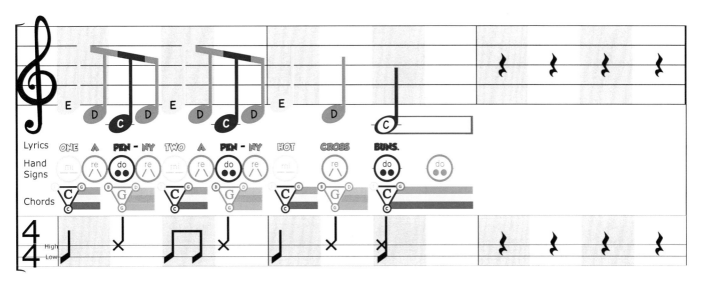

Melody #5:
Do Re Mi Fa Do Ti Do

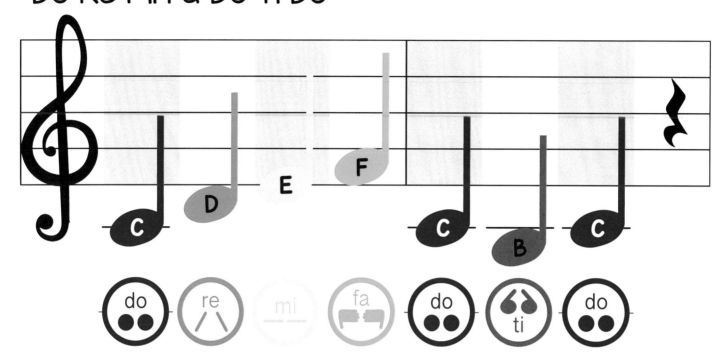

Melody #6:
Sol Fa Mi Re Do Ti Do

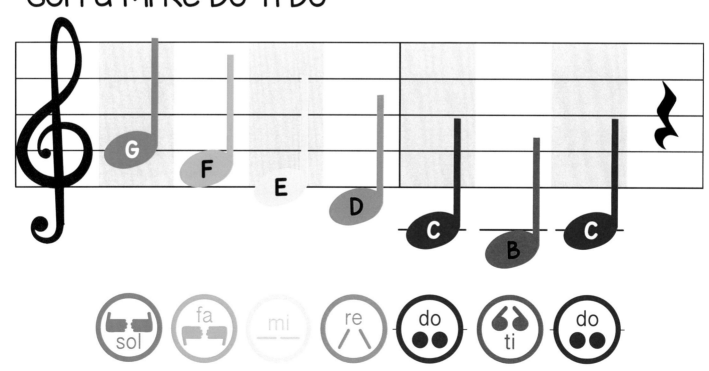

Quiz #5:

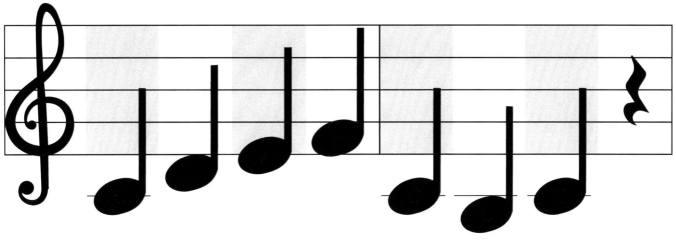

Part 1 : WHICH NOTE?
Write the notes on
the blank lines!

Part 2 : MIXED UP!
Match the Solfege
Hand Signs to the
notes above!

Quiz #6:

Part 1 : WHICH NOTE?
Write the notes on
the blank lines!

Part 2 : MIXED UP!
Match the Solfege
Hand Signs to the
notes above!

Year 1, Week 28

Chapter 4 - Beet & Pineapple

LEQ: How is a triplet note different from an eighth note or quarter note?

Week 28 Checklist

	Watched Video	Sang/Played Along	Played Sheet Music 1-3 times	Completed Workbook Activities	Repeat video 2-5 tiunes or as needed for mastery
Activator: Beet & Cherry	*		N/A	N/A	
Core Lesson: Beet & Pineapple	*	*	*	*	
Performance: Gently Sleep & Au Claire De La Lune	*	*		N/A	
Extension: Row Your Boat)				N/A	

* Suggested Priority Activity

I. Overview: In this lesson, students will learn about triplets and their relationship to other beats.

II. Objective: By the end of this lesson, students should be able to clap, tap or stomp a triplet note.

III. Activator: Students begin by reviewing Chapter Three's Sweet Beets Rhythm Lesson, "Beet & Cherry". This review of quarter and eighth notes will help prime students to learn about the triplet!

IV. Core Lesson: The teacher should explain to students that today's lesson is a rhythm lesson. They won't need their bells for the core lesson today and instead should clap, tap or stomp along with "Beet & Pineapple".

After the video, the class should clap, tap or stomp through the sheet music for "Beet & Pineapple" as a group (or in smaller stations if that works better for the group). The teacher should lead the students by conducting a slow and steady tempo, or using a metronome at 60-90 BPM to help keep the beat.

Year 1, Week 28

Chapter 4 - Beet & Pineapple

LEQ: How is a triplet note different from an eighth note or quarter note?

After playing through the sheet music, students should complete the "Beet & Pineapple" worksheet activities that review triplets, quarter notes, and patterns.

  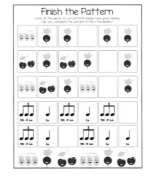 

V. Performance: As a group (or as assigned homework), students play along with either "Gently Sleep" or "Au Claire De La Lune", or both, which feature scrolling sheet music in the treble clef, as well as a handful of parts for other instruments (percussion, lyrics, hand-signs, chord arrangements, etc.).

VI. Summarizer: If students played the performance together, the teacher should instruct students to share one thing they liked about the performance with the person next to them (or with the whole group).

Before moving onto the review lesson, the teacher should review today's lesson by asking students some or all of the following questions: *How many beats are in a triplet?; Give an example of a word with the same number of syllables as a triplet; How is a triplet different from an eighth note or quarter note?*

VII. Extension: As a final activity (or as homework), students play along with "Row Your Boat". This song gives students a chance to practice triplet notes. Students can play along with this more challenging rendition of "Row Your Boat", or clap and sing along to emphasize the triplet rhythm.

Beet & Pineapple

☆☆☆☆☆

Clap, tap or stomp along while you sing with the sheet music below after you've watched the Beet & Pineapple video. The Pineapple rhythm is called a Triplet, which is a bit more difficult. If you have a hard time, move on and come back later!

CHORUS 1

Sweet Beets, we've got some!
If you want some Sweet Beets, we've got 'em.
If you want Sweet Beets, we've got some,
If you want some Sweet Beets, we've got 'em.

VERSE 1

REPEAT   REPEAT

BEET   **BEET**   PINEAPPLE   **BEET**   PINEAPPLE   PINEAPPLE   **BEET**   **BEET**

REPEAT   REPEAT

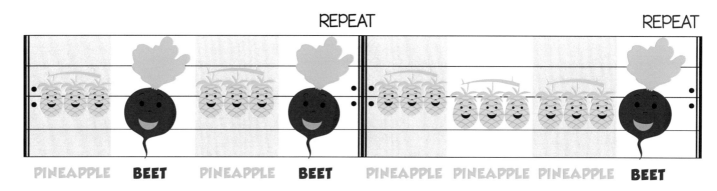

PINEAPPLE   **BEET**   PINEAPPLE   **BEET**   PINEAPPLE   PINEAPPLE   PINEAPPLE   **BEET**

CHORUS 2

Sweet Beets, we've got some!
If you want some Sweet Beets, we've got 'em.
If you want Sweet Beets, we've got some,
If you want some Sweet Beets, we've got 'em.

VERSE 2

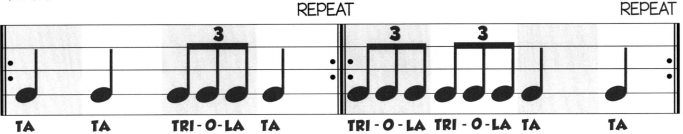

CHORUS 3

Sweet Beets, we've got some!
If you want some Sweet Beets, we've got 'em.
If you want Sweet Beets, we've got some,
If you want some Sweet Beets, we've got 'em.

VERSE 3

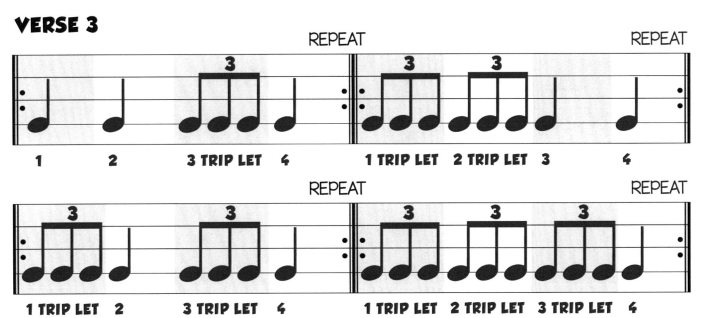

CHORUS 4: REPEAT CHORUS I

VERSE 5: REPEAT VERSE I

CHORUS 5: REPEAT CHORUS I

Triplets & Quarter Notes

Trace each word below, then circle the note above each picture
that represents the number of syllables in each word. Cross out the other note,
and then play, clap or sing along.

crocodile   skunk   porcupine   deer

elephant   owl   polar bear   horse

flamingo   pig   butterfly   wolf

rose

gorilla

octopus

moon

sea lion

leaf

basketball

bear

radio

fox

banana

cow

Finish the Pattern

Some of the pieces to our patterns below have gone missing.
Can you complete the pattern to fill in the blanks?

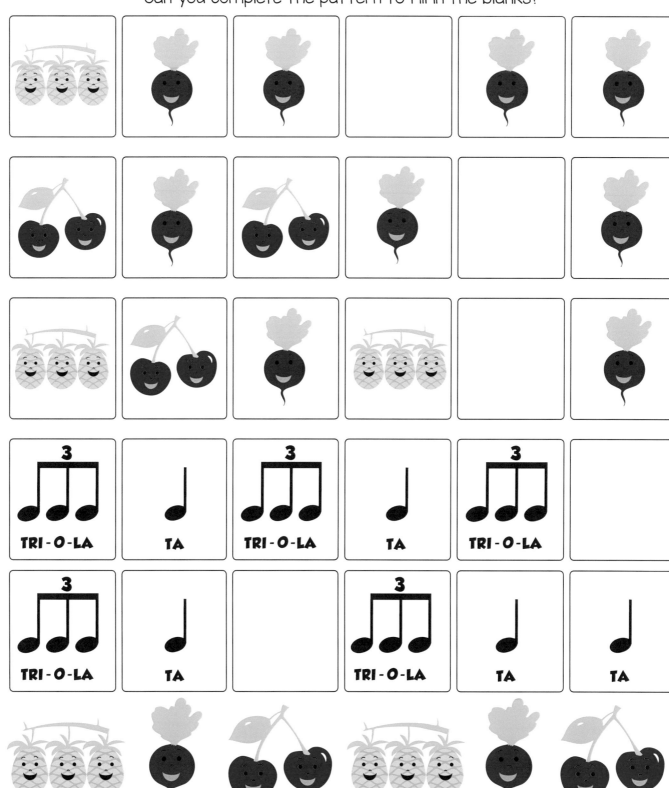

Finish the Pattern

Some of the pieces to our patterns below have gone missing.
Can you complete the pattern to fill in the blanks?

371

Circle the Notes

Circle the note that represnts the fraction in each row.

Gently Sleep
C Major

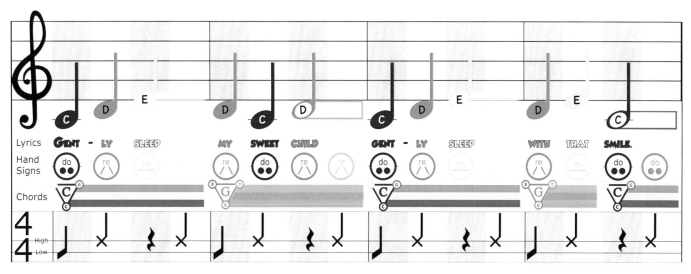

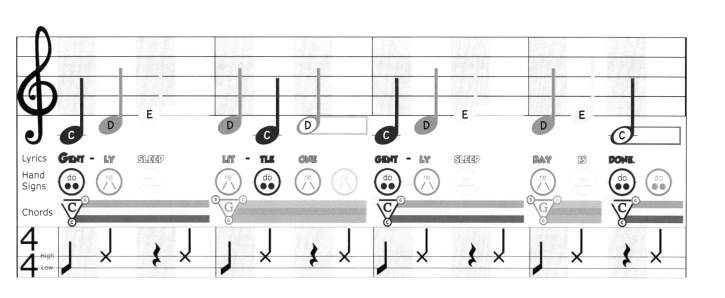

Notes Used:

Au Claire De La Lune
C Major

Year 1, Week 29

Chapter 4 - Merrily We Roll Along

LEQ: Which numbers and colors can help us memorize the notes C, D & E?

Week 29 Checklist

	Watched Video	Sang/Played Along	Played Sheet Music 1-3 times	Completed Workbook Activities	Repeat video 2-5 tiunes or as needed for mastery
Activator: Melodies #6	*			N/A	
Core Lesson: Merrily We Roll Along	*	*	*	*	
Performance: Merrily We Roll Along & Dinosaur	*	*		N/A	
Review: Mary Had a Little Lamb			N/A	N/A	

* Suggested Priority Activity

I. Overview: In this lesson, students modify chords to play "Merrily we Roll Along" using the notes C, D & E.

II. Objective: By the end of this lesson, students should be able to play "Merrily We Roll Along" using C, D & E and identify the colors and numbers associated wtih each note.

III. Activator: Students begin this lesson with "Melodies #6". The teacher should explain to students that in their main lesson today, they will continue to study C, D & E, but first, they will sing and review the hand-signs for these notes (and a few others) in a Melodies lesson.

IV. Core Lesson: Students should take out their C, D & E bells to play "Merrily We Roll Along".

In this lesson, Mr. Rob hand-signs and sings along with both the Solfege names and the lyrics to "Merrily We Roll Along". Students can begin by hand-signing one verse, and then play along on their bells. Alternatively, the teacher can instruct students to only hand-sign along and focus on the Solfege names for this lesson.

After the video, students should play along with the "Merrily We Roll Along" sheet music as a group (or in smaller stations if that works better for the group). The teacher should lead the students by conducting a slow and steady tempo, or using a metronome at 60-90 BPM to help keep the beat.

Year 1, Week 29

Chapter 4 - Merrily We Roll Along

LEQ: Which numbers and colors can help us memorize the notes C, D & E?

After playing through the sheet music, students should complete the "Merrily We Roll Along" worksheet activities that review C, D and E.

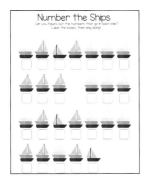

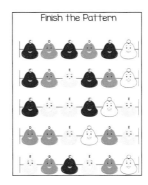

V. Performance: As a group (or as assigned homework), students play along with either "Merrily We Roll Along" or "Dinosaur", which feature scrolling sheet music in the treble clef, as well as a handful of parts for other instruments (percussion, lyrics, hand-signs, chord arrangements, etc.).

VI. Summarizer: If students played the performance together, the teacher should instruct students to share one thing they liked about the performance with the person next to them (or with the whole group).

Before moving onto the Review lesson, the teacher should review today's lesson by asking students some or all of the following questions: *Which number is associated with the note C?; Which number is associated with the note D?; which number is associated with the note E?; Which color is associated with the note C?; Which color is associated with the note D?; Which color is associated with the note E?*

VII. Review: As a final activity (or as homework), students play, sing and hand-sign along with Mary Had a Little Lamb. Students played this song a few weeks ago, so the teacher can vary the way students play it. For instance, the teacher can divide the class into three groups--a C group, D group and E group--where students only play their assigned note as they follow along with the video. In this case, it's best if students only have the bell they are assigned.

Merrily We Roll Along

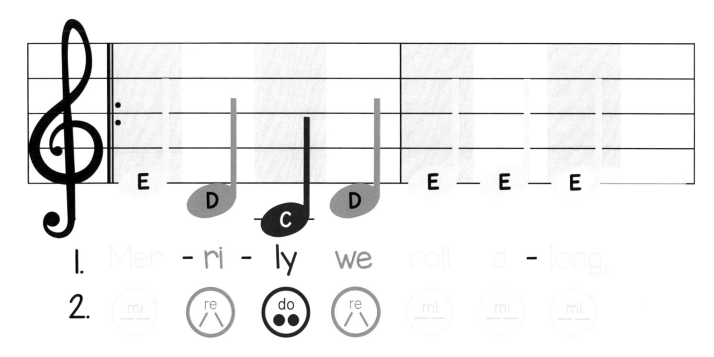

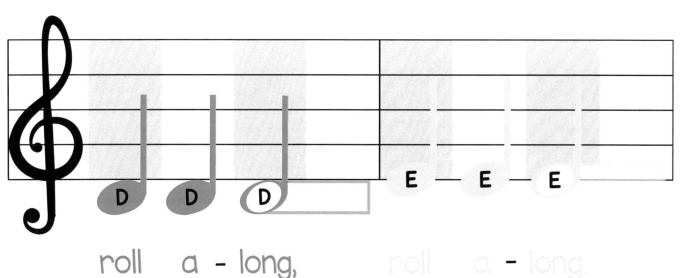

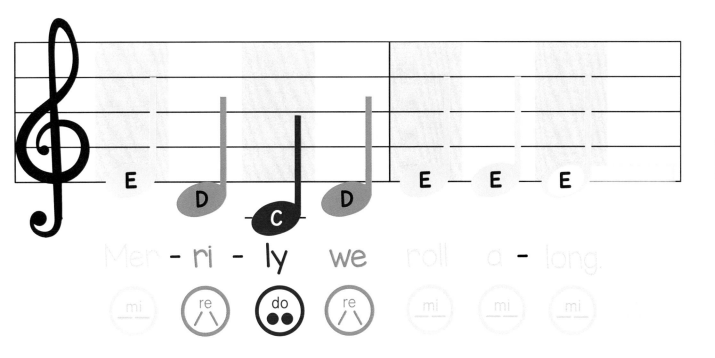

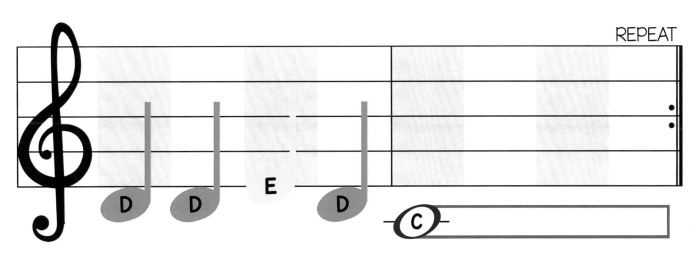

Number the Ships

Can you figure out the numbers that go in each ship?
Label the boxes, then sing along!

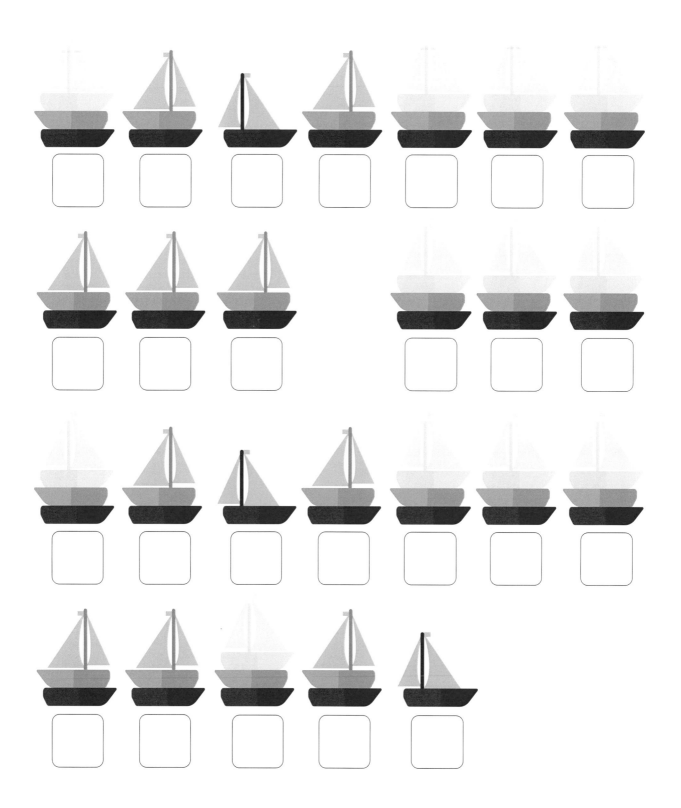

Coloring Page

Finish the Pattern

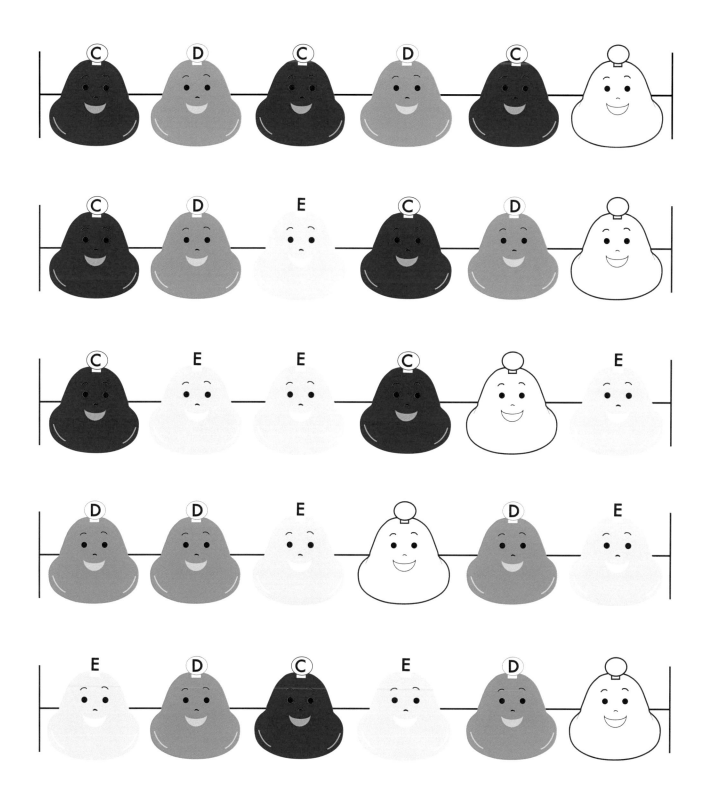

C, D & E Coloring

Play the pattern of notes below with your C, D & E bells. Then sing it with the Do, Re & Mi hand-signs. After that, color in C boxes red, D boxes orange & E boxes yellow.

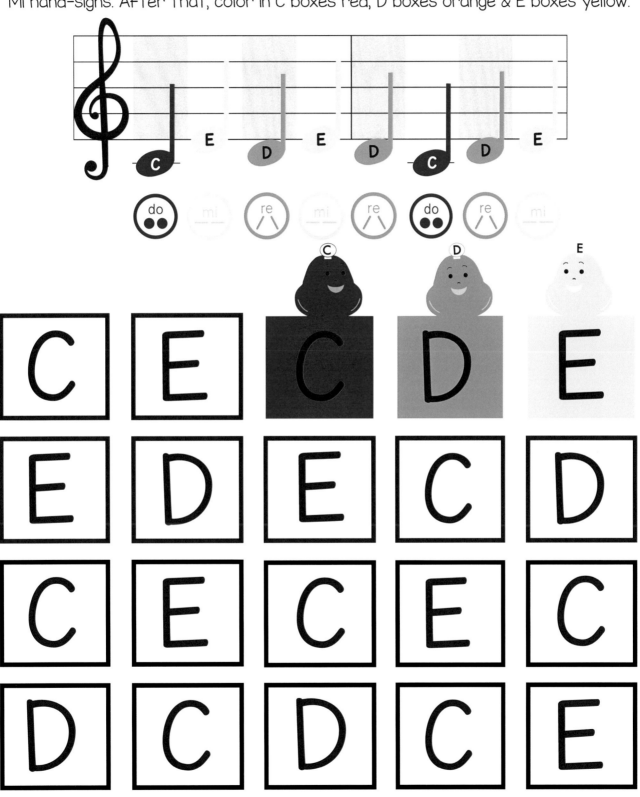

Notes Used:

Merrily We Roll Along
C Major

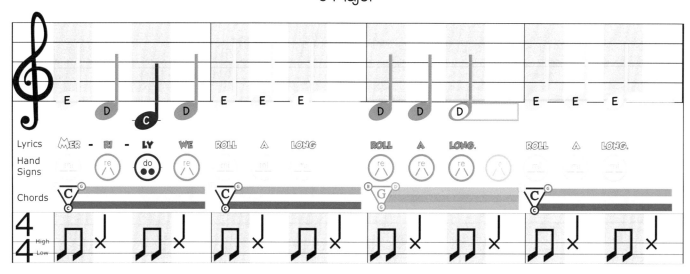

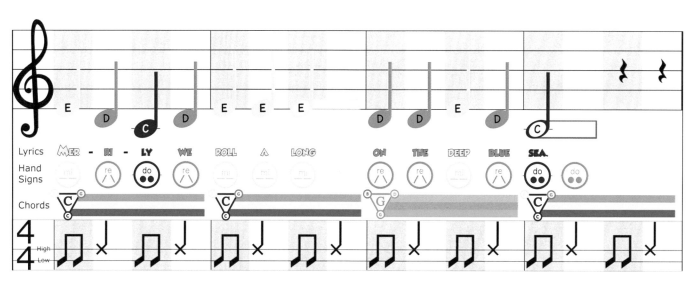

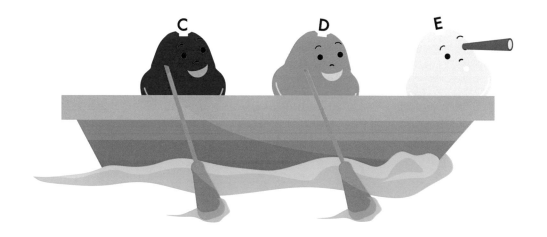

384

Dinosaur
C Major

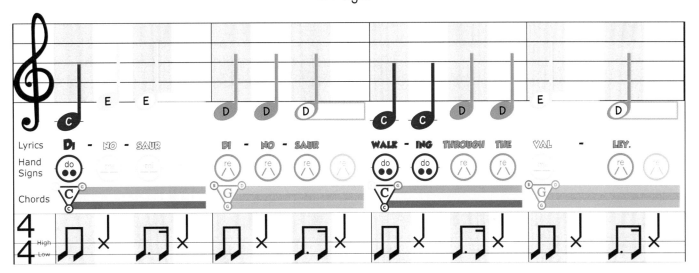

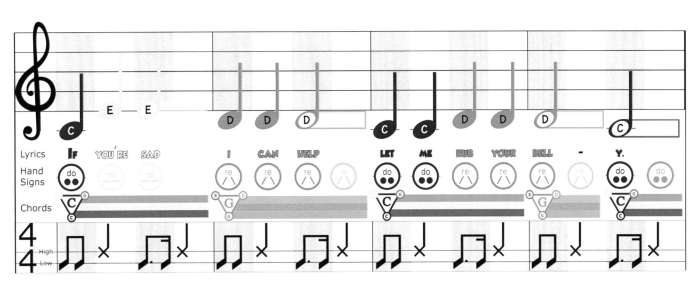

MELODY #5:
Do Re Mi Fa Do Ti Do

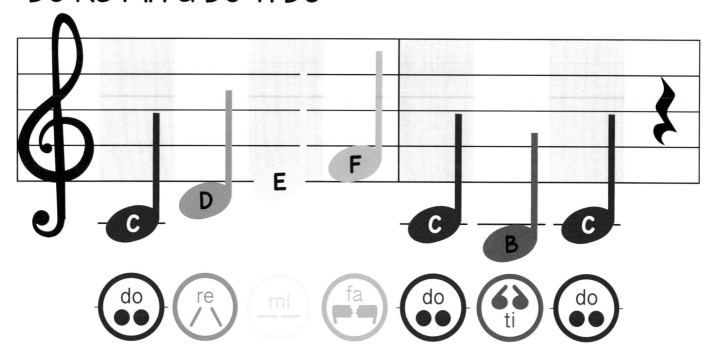

MELODY #6:
Sol Fa Mi Re Do Ti Do

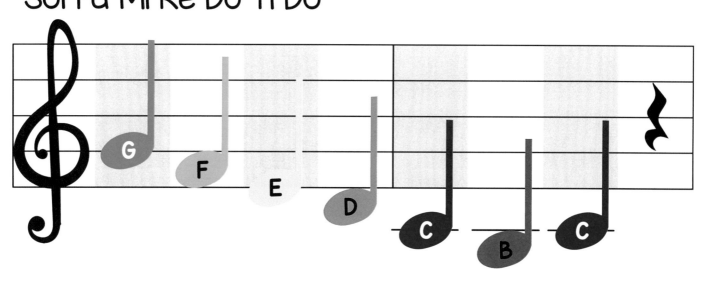

QUIZ #5:

Part 1 : WHICH NOTE?
Write the notes on the blank lines!

 _____ _____ _____ _____ _____ _____ _____

Part 2 : MIXED UP!
Match the Solfege Hand Signs to the notes above!

QUIZ #6:

Part 1 : WHICH NOTE?
Write the notes on the blank lines!

 _____ _____ _____ _____ _____ _____ _____

Part 2 : MIXED UP!
Match the Solfege Hand Signs to the notes above!

Year 1, Week 30

Chapter 4 - Sally the Camel

LEQ: How can a student use C, D & E to play "Sally the Camel"?

Week 30 Checklist

	Watched Video	Sang/Played Along	Played Sheet Music 1-3 times	Completed Workbook Activities	Repeat video 2-5 tiunes or as needed for mastery
Activator: Campfire Song	*		N/A	N/A	
Core Lesson: Sally the Camel	*	*	*	*	
Performance: Sally the Camel or Spaceship	*			N/A	
Review: Campfire Song	*		N/A	N/A	

★ Suggested Priority Activity

I. Overview: In this lesson, students continue to practice playing C, D & E using eighth notes and identifying them on the staff.

II. Objective: By the end of this lesson, students should be able to play C, D & E using eighth notes and quarter notes to play "Sally the Camel".

III. Activator: Students begin today's lesson by reviewing "Campfire Song" from Playtime Prodigies. This fun sing along is a great way to warm up with C, D & E. The teacher can choose to have the students perform the hand-signs, sing the solfege names or play along with the song on the bells.

Students should sing along with Mr. Rob, but only play or hand-sign along with the bells as the come across the screen.

IV. Core Lesson: Once students have warmed up with Do, Re & Mi, the class watches "Sally the Camel".

The teacher should explain that students will follow along with Mr. Rob, hand-signing first, then playing along on their C, D & E bells.

After the video, students should play along with the sheet music for "Sally the Camel" as a group (or in smaller stations if that works better for the group). The teacher should lead the students by conducting a slow and steady tempo, or using a metronome at 60-90 BPM to help keep the beat.

Year 1, Week 30

Chapter 4 - Sally the Camel

LEQ: How can a student use C, D & E to play "Sally the Camel"?

After playing through the sheet music, students should complete the "Sally the Camel" worksheet activities that review Roman Numerals, the C major chord and the G major chord.

V. Performance: As a group (or as assigned homework), students play along with either "Sally the Camel" or "Spaceship", which feature scrolling sheet music in the treble clef, as well as a handful of parts for other instruments (percussion, lyrics, hand-signs, chord arrangements, etc.).

VI. Summarizer: If students played the performance together, the teacher should instruct students to share one thing they liked about the performance with the person next to them (or with the whole group).

Before moving onto the review lesson, the teacher should review today's lesson by asking students some or all of the following questions: *Which three notes are used to play Sally the Camel?; Which note lengths are used to play Sally the Camel?; What is the hand-sign for Do?; What is the hand-sign for Re?; What is the hand-sign for Mi?*

VII. Review: As a final activity (or as homework), students play along with "Campfire Song". Since students played this song as an activator, it should be fresh in their minds. For a fun challenge, students can write a new first to "Campfire Song" using their own names and perform it for the class.

Alternatively, students could each be assigned Do, Re or Mi, and when that note comes across the screen, the stand up and quickly perform the hand-sign and quickly sit back

Sally the Camel

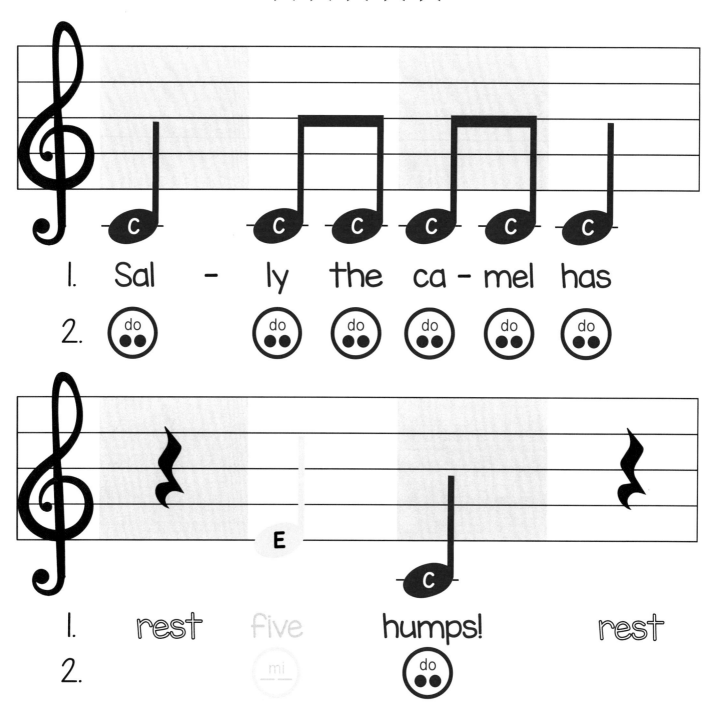

Solfège Camels

Write a song using the camels below! Color each camel's blanket to match the note you want in that place.

Circle the Ds

Trace the word below every picture, then
circle the picture in each row that begins with a D orange.

drums

robot

kite

dragon

leaf

heart

donut

rose

moon

Wrong Note

There are two incorrect notes in each measure below. Draw an X through the notes that are in the wrong place. Then write the note name on the two that are in the correct place.

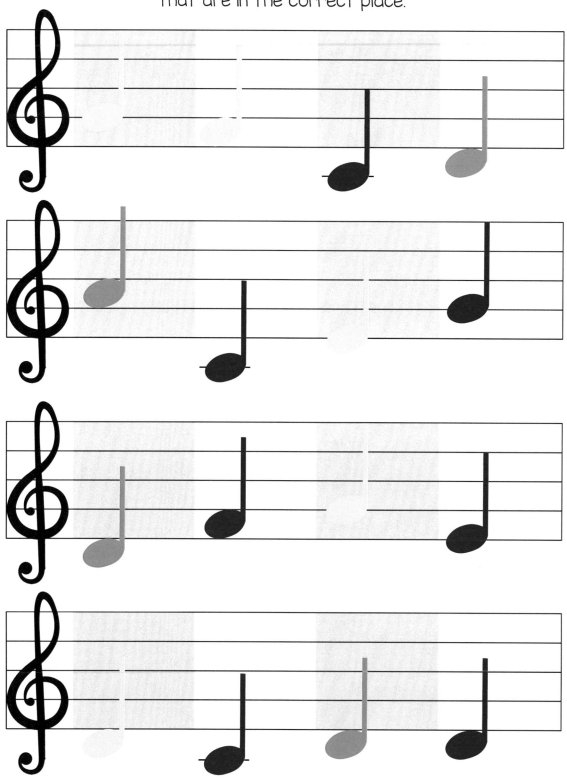

Label the Notes
Label the correct notes for Sally the Camel!

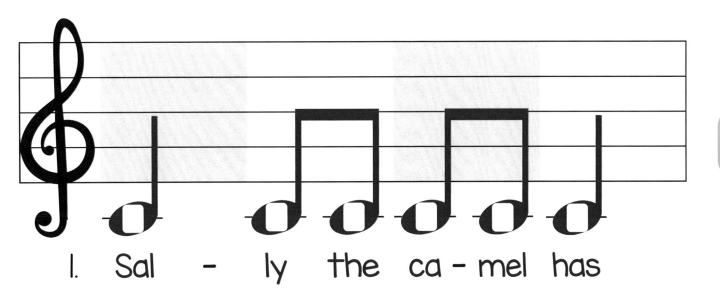

1. Sal – ly the ca – mel has

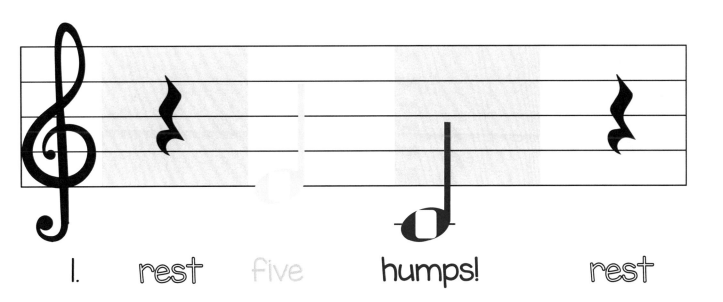

1. rest five humps! rest

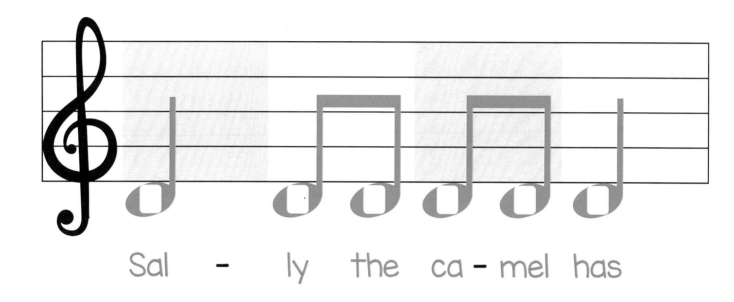

Sal - ly the ca - mel has

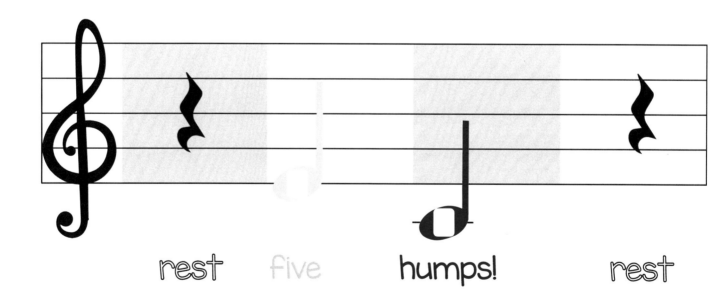

rest   five   humps!   rest

ride,   Sal - ly,

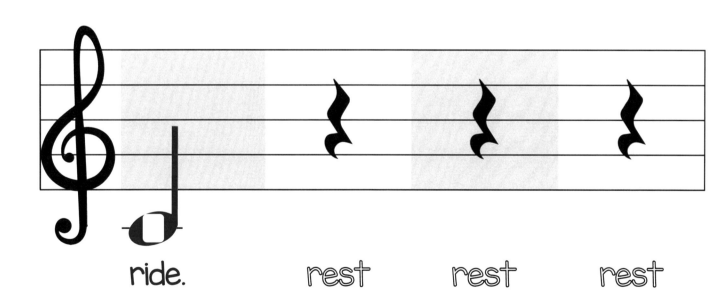

ride.   rest   rest   rest

Sally The Camel
C Major

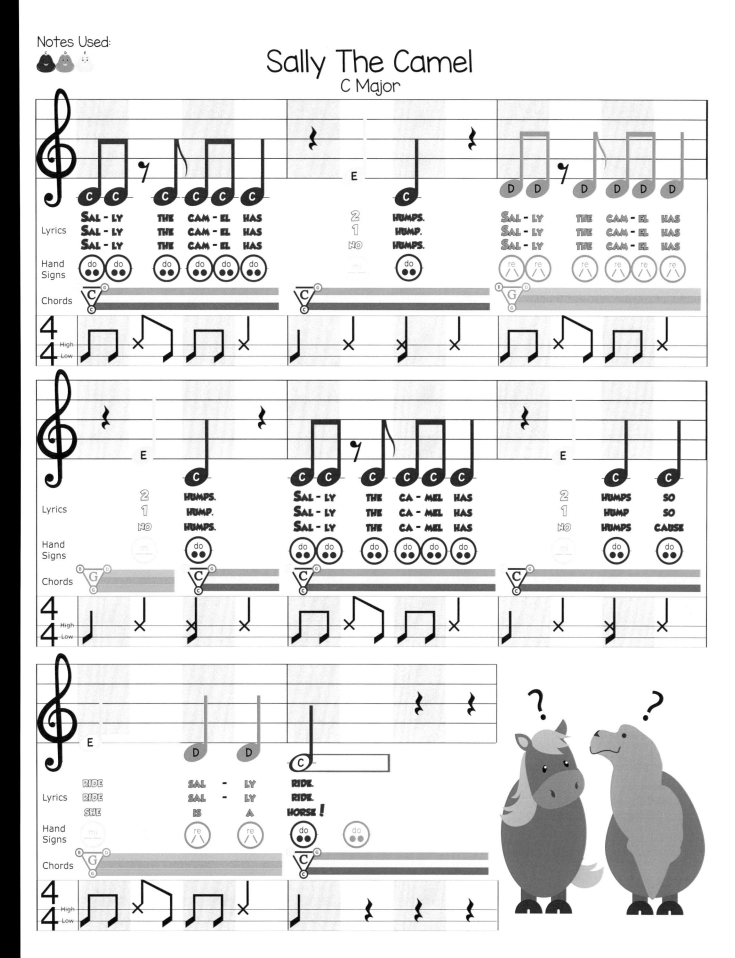

Spaceship
C Major

Notes Used:

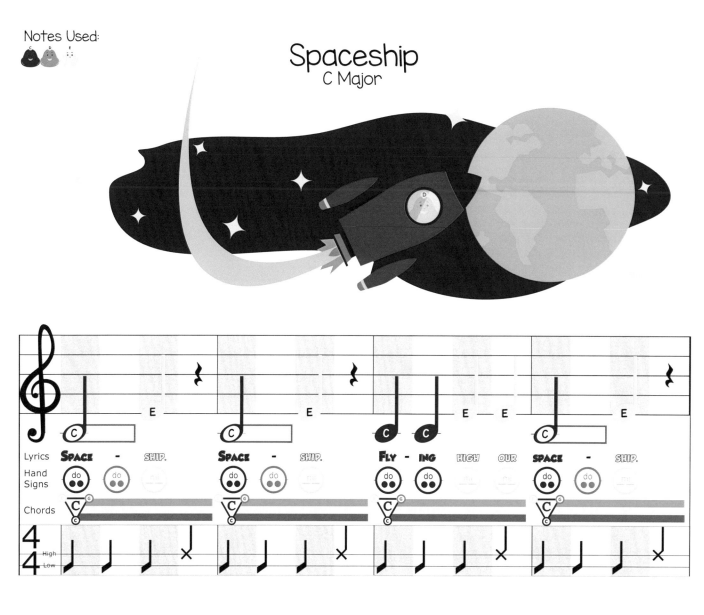

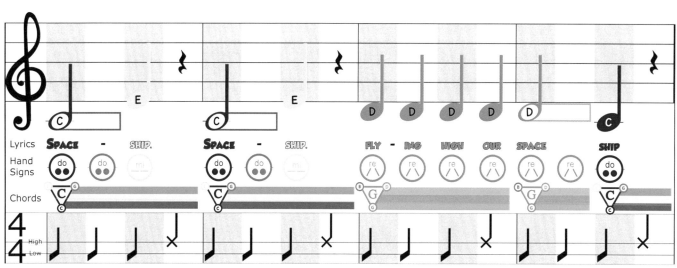

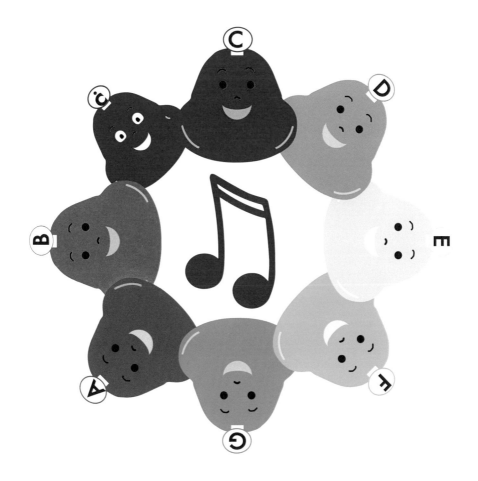

Year 1, Week 31

Chapter 4 - London Bridge

LEQ: How can a student play "London Bridge" using chords or individual notes?

Week 31 Checklist

	Watched Video	Sang/Played Along	Played Sheet Music 1-3 times	Completed Workbook Activities	Repeat video 2-5 tiunes or as needed for mastery
Activator: C & G Chords	*		N/A	N/A	
Core Lesson: London Bridge	*	*	*	*	
Performance: The Rainbows Shine	*	*		N/A	
Review: Merrily We Roll Along			N/A	N/A	

* Suggested Priority Activity

I. Overview: In this lesson, students use both a simplified chord structure and a more complicated melody to play "London Bridge".

II. Objective: By the end of this lesson, students should be able to play "London Bridge" with simplified versions of the G chord and C chord.

III. Activator: Students begin this lesson by reviewing the C and G Chords lesson from Chapter 3. The teacher should instruct students to take out their C, D, E, G, & B bells to play along with the video.

Once students have warmed up with the chords, they can put away all bells except for C, D & G to prepare for the core lesson.

IV. Core Lesson: The teacher should explain to students that they will play with Do, Re & Sol today instead of Do, Re, Mi.

The teacher should explain to students that by using Do, Re, & Sol, they can play a simplified version of a C chord and a G chord. Students should play along with Mr. Rob as he plays 2 note chords to play "London Bridge".

After, the class should play through the sheet music for "London Bridge" as a group (or in smaller stations if that works better for the group). The teacher should lead the students by conducting a slow and steady tempo, or use a metronome at 60-90 BPM to help keep the beat.

Year 1, Week 31

Chapter 4 - London Bridge

LEQ: How can a student play "London Bridge" using chords or individual notes?

After playing through the sheet music, students should complete the "London Bridge" workbook activities that review all 8 notes.

V. Performance: As a group (or as assigned homework), students play along with the Performance "The Rainbows Shine" which features scrolling sheet music in the treble clef, as well as a handful of parts for other instruments (percussion, lyrics, hand-signs, chord arrangements, etc.).

VI. Summarizer: If students played the performance together, the teacher should instruct students to share one thing they liked about the performance with the person next to them (or with the whole group).

Before moving onto the extension lesson, the teacher should review today's lesson by asking students some or all of the following questions: *Which colors are associated with all 8 notes in the C Major Scale?; Which two notes can make a simplified C chord?; Which two notes can make a simplified G chord?*

VII. Review: To connect this lesson to the rest of the chapter, students play along with "Merrily We Roll Along". In the next lesson, students will have the opportunity to perform a Do Re Mi performance from Chapter 4.

London Bridge

☆★★★☆

This song is written like a chord chart. Read from left to right, and then down to the next line. Sing the lyrics as you play each chord using a slow and steady half-note.

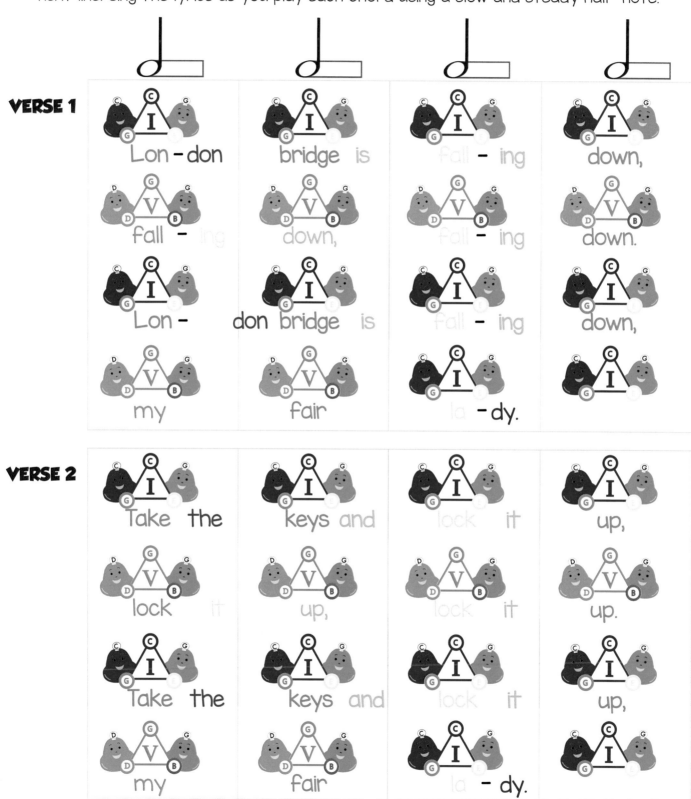

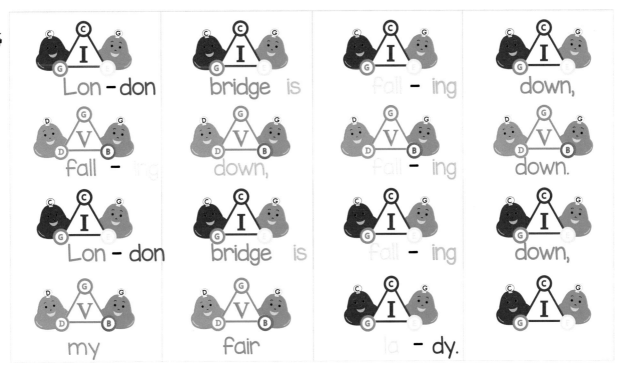

VERSE 3

VERSE 4

London Bridge

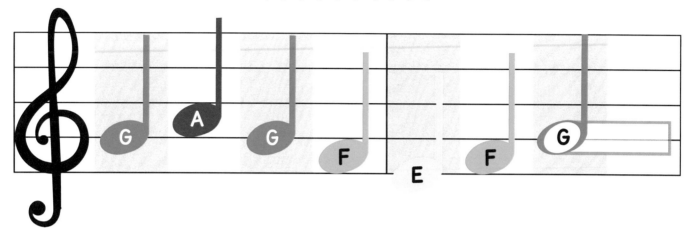

1. Lon - don bridge is fall - ing down,
2. Take the keys and lock her up,
3. Build it up with silver and gold,
4.

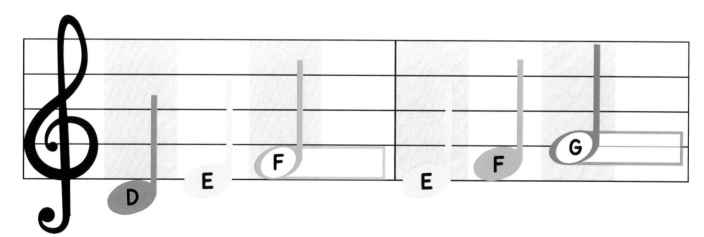

fall - ing down,   fall - ing down.
lock her up,   lock her up.
silver and gold,   silver and gold.

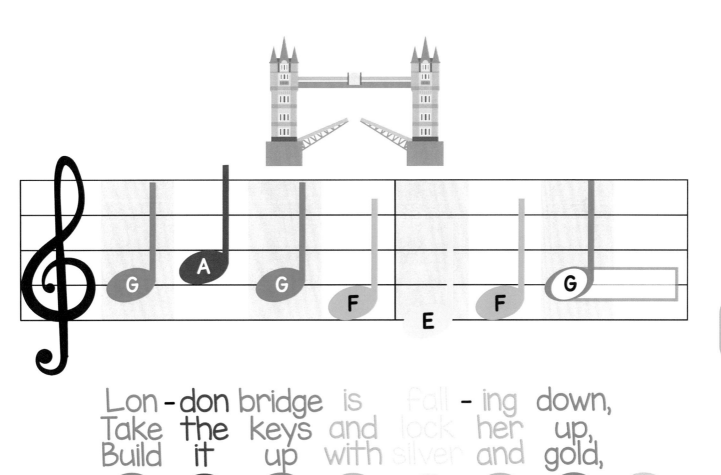

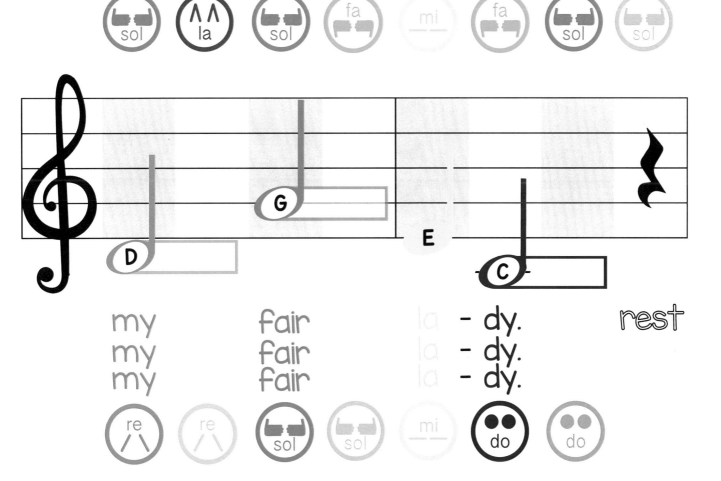

C Major Scale Song

Write a song that uses any of eight bells! Use the right color crayon
to draw each note for your song,

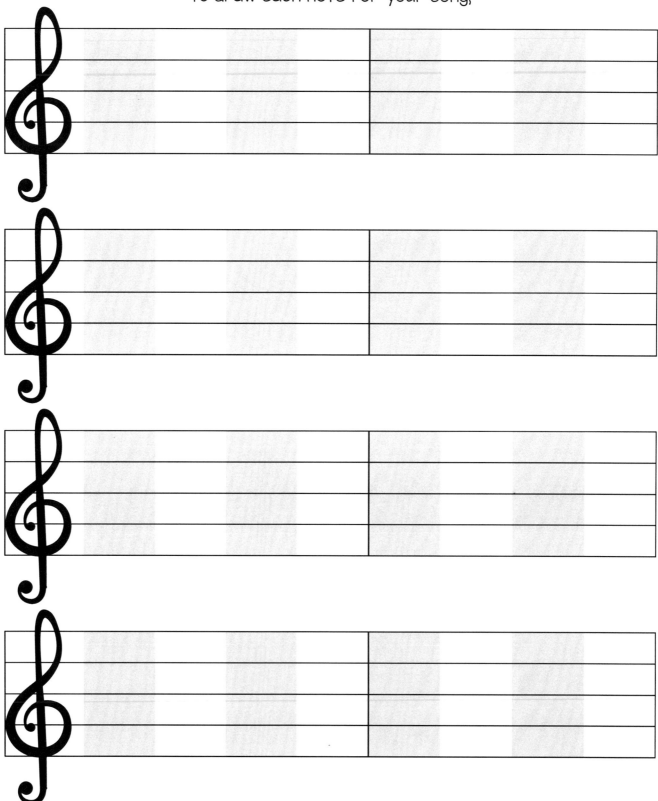

Vocabulary Word Search

Trace each vocabulary word from Chapters 1-4 below, then find
each word hidden in the word search. Words may appear up, down and across.

beat

measure

eighth

quarter

half

whole

solfège

rest

w	h	o	l	e
e	m	e	c	g
r	e	s	t	e
e	a	o	e	i
t	s	l	h	g
r	u	f	a	h
a	r	e	l	t
u	e	g	f	h
q	b	e	a	t

Missing Pieces

Write in the missing note name, draw the missing hand-sign, color the blank bell and write in the missing scale degree.

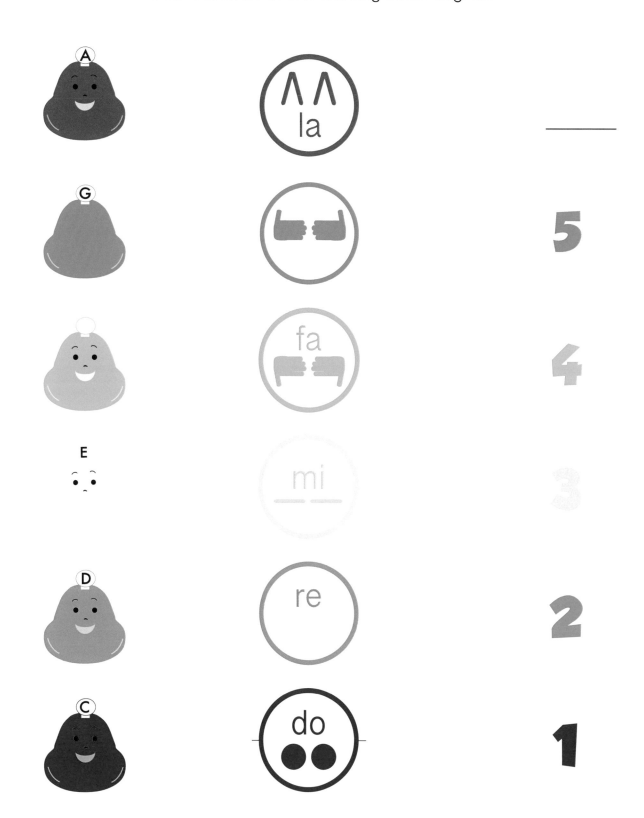

Notes Used:

The Rainbows Shine
C Major

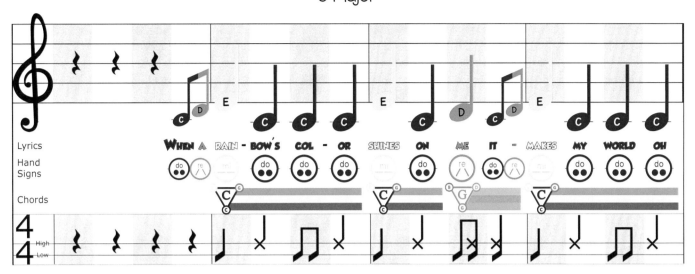

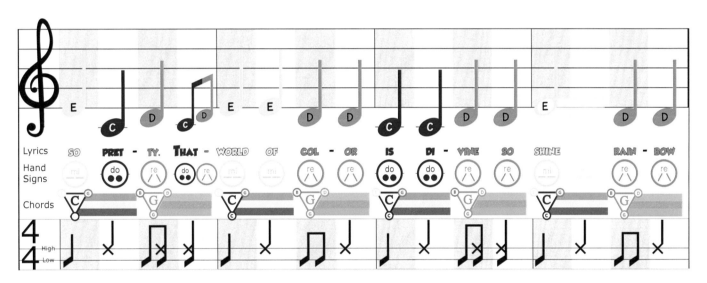

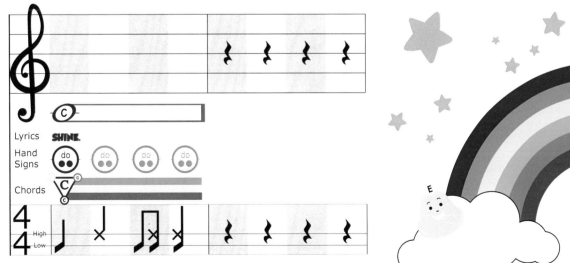

Year 1, Week 32

Chapter 4 - Perform and Assess
LEQ: How can a student differentiate between the notes C, D & E?

Week 32 Checklist

	Watched Video	Sang/Played Along	Played Sheet Music 1-3 times	Completed Workbook Activities	Repeat video 2-5 tiunes or as needed for mastery
Activator: Sally the Camel	*	*		N/A	N/A
Performance: Do, Re, Mi Performance Playlist	*	*			N/A
Review/Assess: Name that Note #3 & What Note Is It? #4	*	*		N/A	
Review/Assess: Interactive Quiz #4				N/A	N/A

* Suggested Priority Activity

I. Overview: In this lesson, students take turns performing various performance tracks for the class. Then, students attempt to identify the notes C, D & E just by listening.

II. Objective: By the end of this lesson, students should be able to play a C, D & E performance track alone or in a small group.

III. Activator: To begin today's lesson, students will follow along with "Sally the Camel". This lesson from two weeks ago will give students a chance to review the C, D & E before jumping into their performances.

IV. Performance: The teacher should explain to students that they will each play a different performance today in front of the class. Students can play individually, or if it makes more sense, in small groups. Students can play the same part or different parts (hand-signing, percussion, etc.).

There is a playlist of all the performances on this week's lesson page, so the teacher can scroll through and assign students a performance track, or (if it's possible with this group of students), students can choose the performance track they'd like to perform.

As each student performs, the teacher should play a metronome at 60-90 BPM to keep the beat. The performers can play along with either the video or just the sheet music if they prefer.

Year 1, Week 32

Chapter 4 - Perform and Assess

LEQ: How can a student differentiate between the notes C, D & E?

V. Review/Assess: After student performances, the class will play two listening games: "What Note Is It?" number 4--Do, Re, Mi and "Name that Note" with all 8 notes.

The teacher should give each student a copy of the "What Note Is It" handouts and explain that as students listen, they should not call out their guess, but circle the matching bell on their paper.

The teacher may decide to model the first guess for students if they are unclear about what to do. The host of the listening game will reveal the answer after each question, so students should mark each of their answers right or wrong.

At the end of each video, the teacher should debrief with students: *Which note was easiest to identify?; Which note was most difficult to identify?; Were there any notes that students consistently got wrong?; Were there any notes that students consistently got right?*

If students become frustrated, the teacher should explain that they have 4 more chapters of content to learn before they will really develop their ears, and that they should keep

VI. Summarizer: The teacher should begin by summarizing the performance part of this week's lesson. The teacher should ask: *What was students' favorite part of the performance?; What were they most impressed by?; What was one thing they were surprised by?; What is one thing that they could do better (personally) next time?*

Since this is the last lesson in Chapter Four, the teacher should ask students to reflect on the chapter. Which lesson was their favorite and if there's time, review the essential questions from each lesson: *how can a student perform the hand-signs for C, D and E?; how can a student identify C, D and E?; how can a student refer to neighboring notes?; how is a triplet note different from an eighth note or quarter note?; which numbers and colors can help us memorize the notes C, D & E?; how can a student use C, D & E to play "Sally the Camel"?; how can a student play "London Bridge" using chords or individual notes?; how can a student differentiate between the notes C, D & E?*

VII. Review/Assess: As a final activity (or as homework), students complete an interactive quiz.

What Note Is It?

Draw a circle around the bell you hear in each box!

1	C	D	E		8	C	D	E
2	C	D	E		9	C	D	E
3	C	D	E		10	C	D	E
4	C	D	E		11	C	D	E
5	C	D	E		12	C	D	E
6	C	D	E		13	C	D	E
7	C	D	E		14	C	D	E

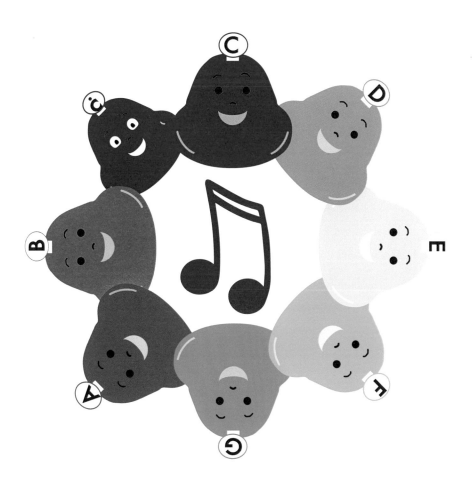

417

Warm Up #1
C Major

419

Notes Used:

Warm Up #2
C Major

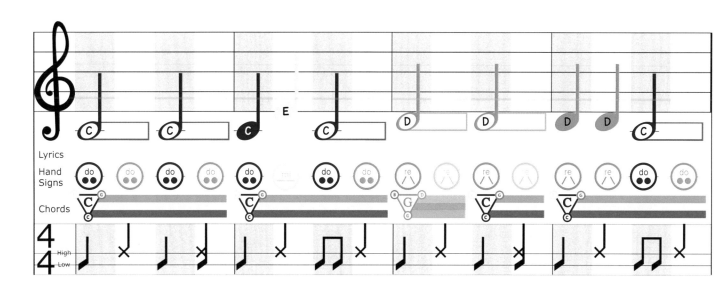

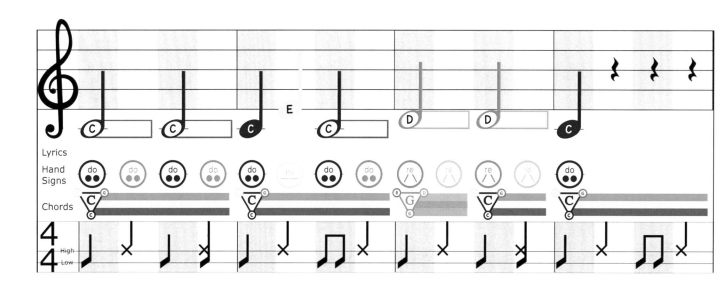

Hot Cross Buns (easy)
C Major

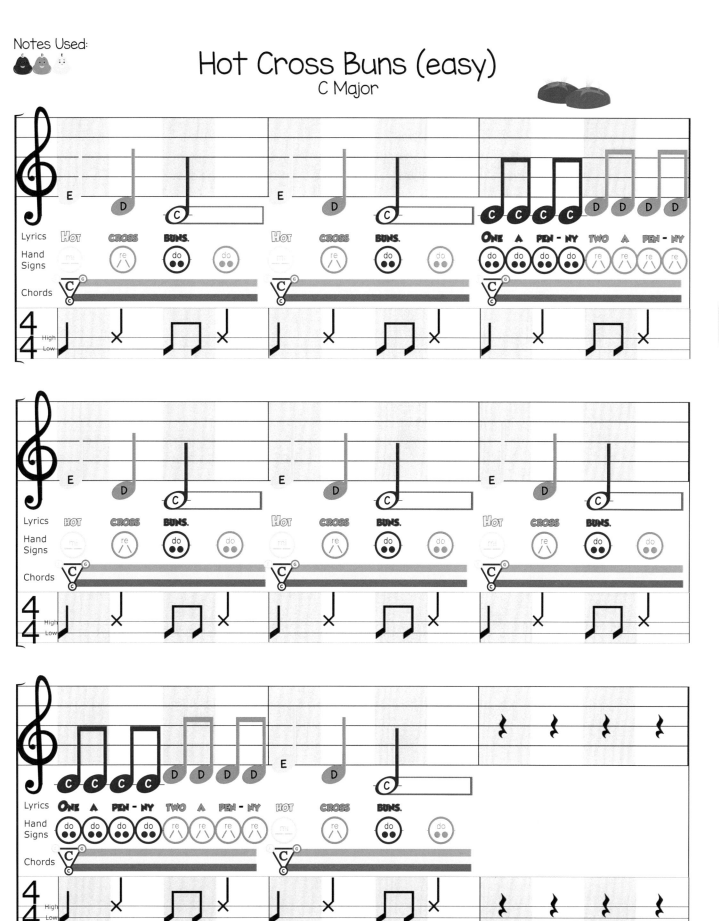

Merrily We Roll Along
C Major

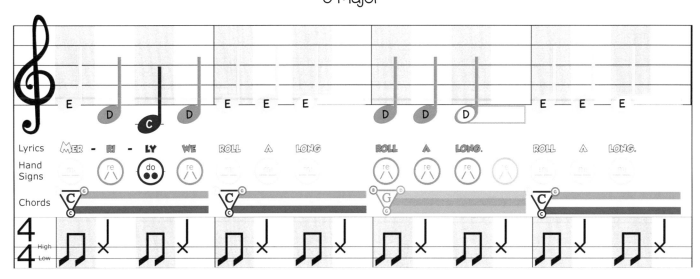

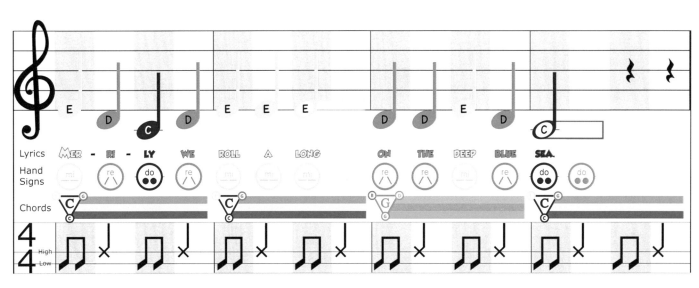

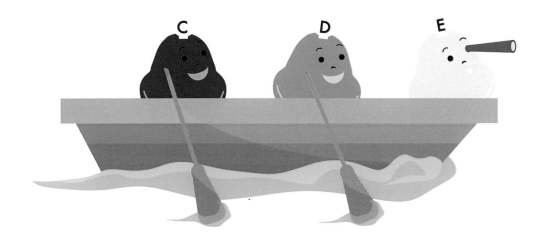

Spaceship
C Major

Notes Used:

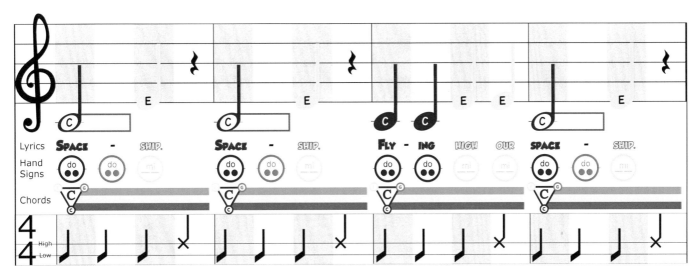

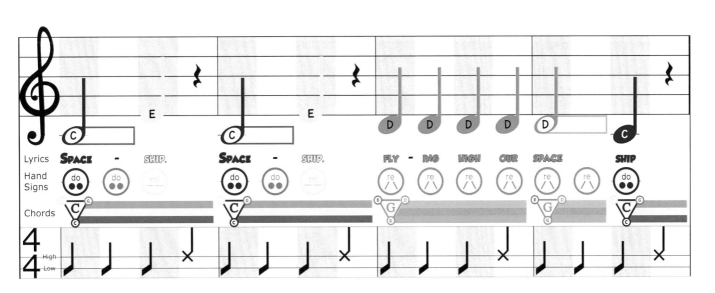

Notes Used:

Gently Sleep
C Major

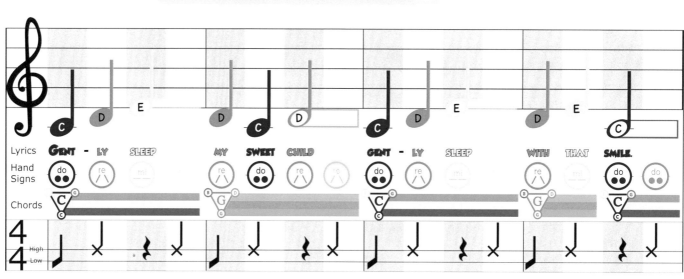

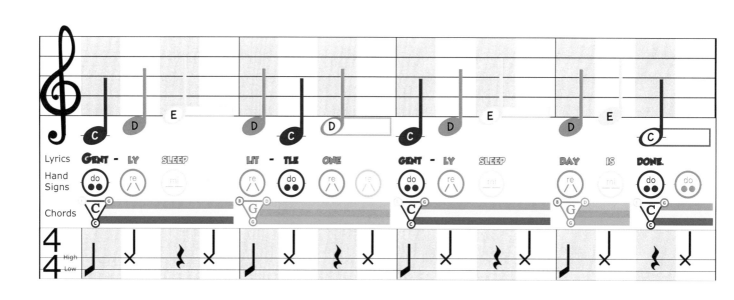

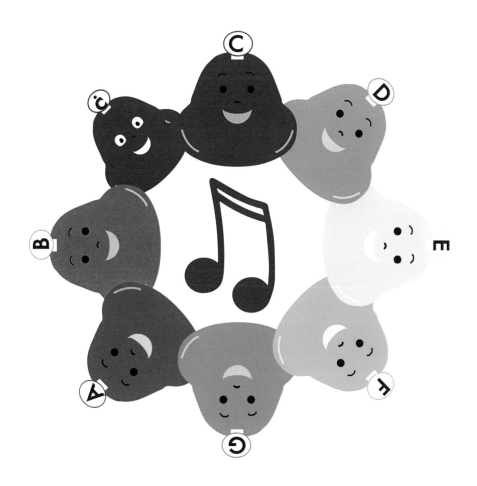

Notes Used:

Mary Had a Little Lamb
C Major

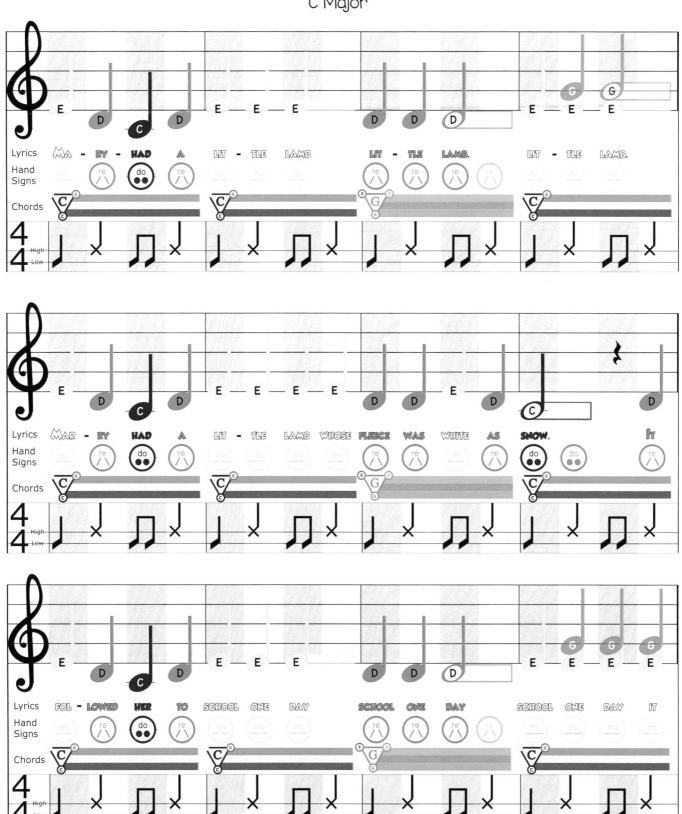

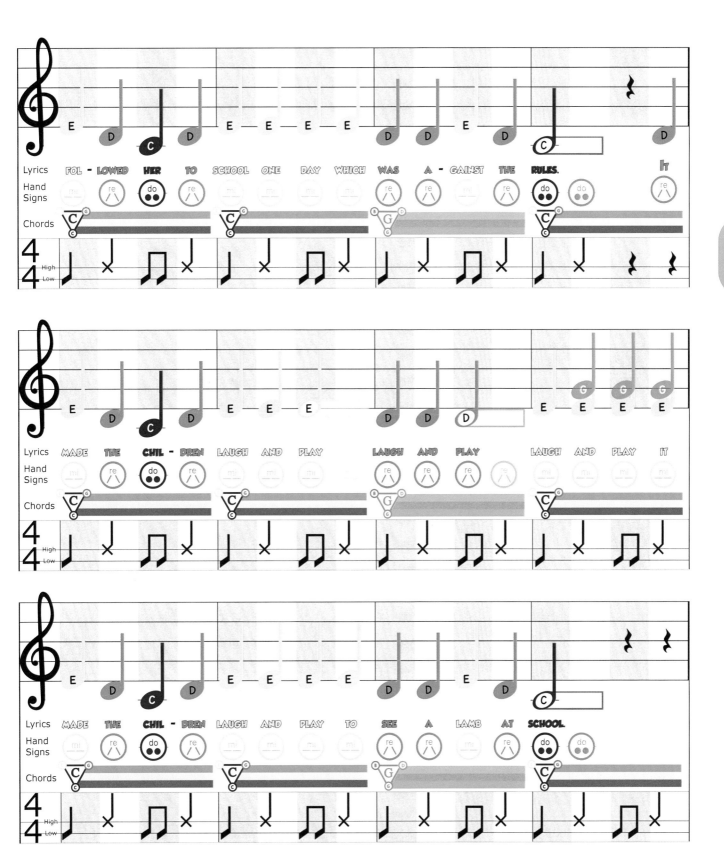

427

Au Claire De La Lune
C Major

Notes Used:

Hot Cross Buns (hard)
C Major

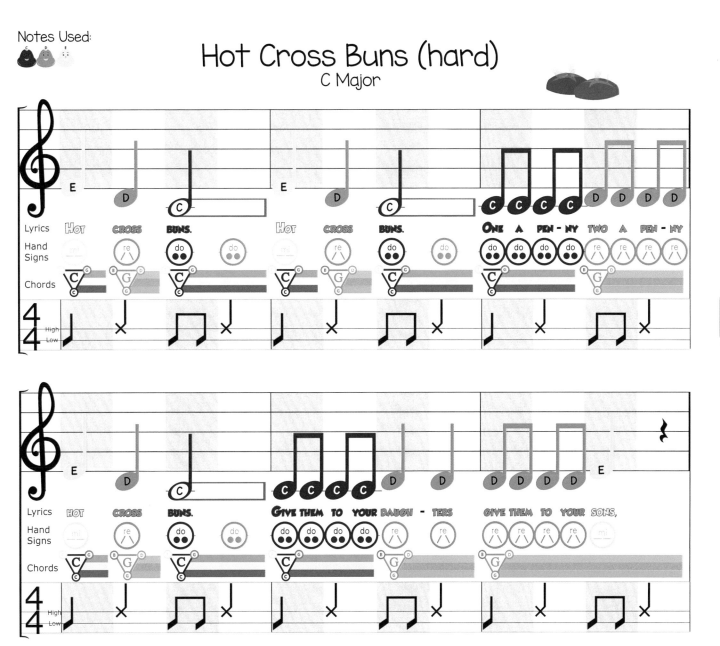

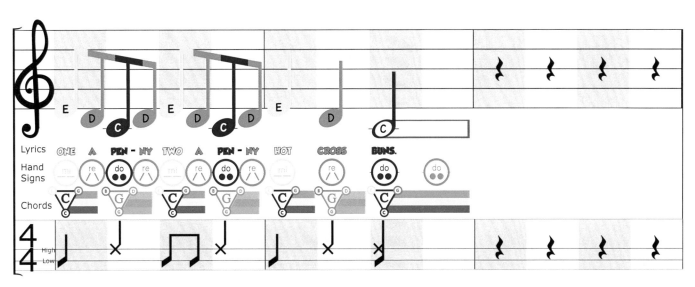

Notes Used:

Dinosaur
C Major

Sally The Camel

C Major

Notes Used:

The Rainbows Shine
C Major

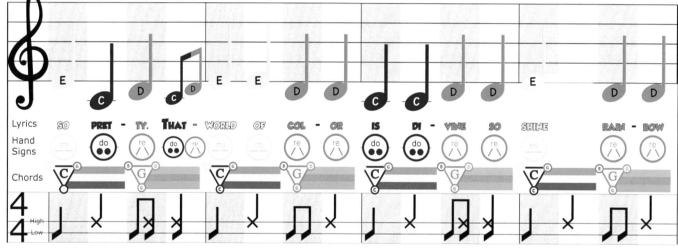